IMAGES
of America

MOUNT CALVARY CEMETERY

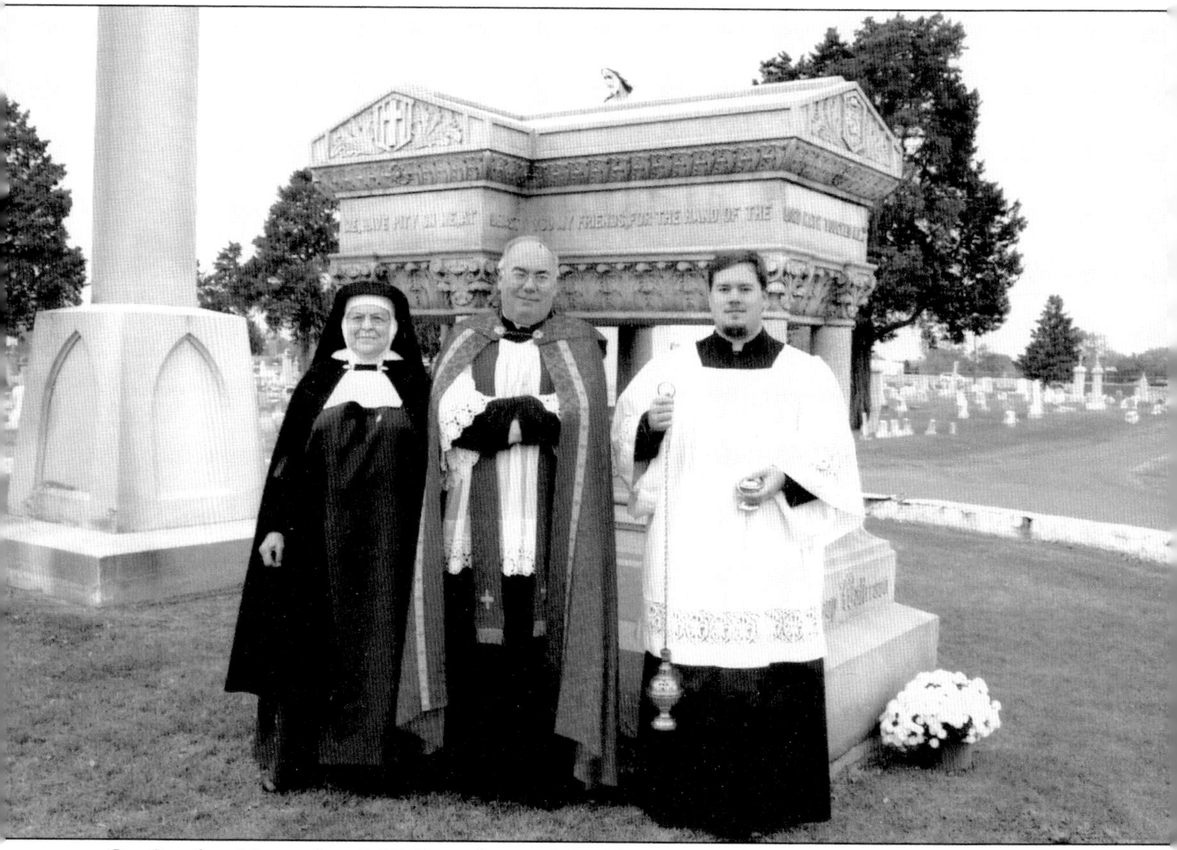

On Sunday, November 4, 2007, in front of the "Priests' Circle," a service for all those that had died was held in Mount Calvary Cemetery in front of Rev. John Ambrose Watterson's stately monument. In the church, All Saints Day, November 1, is a holy day of obligation. Fr. Kevin Lutz (center), pastor of the Holy Family Parish, was the celebrant with Sister Mary Francis, O.S.F., and Zach Kelley. (Author's collection.)

On the cover: Within the 40 acres of Mount Calvary Cemetery, this sacred place has assembled some of the most magnificent monuments found in any cemetery. Throughout this burial ground of approximately 40,000 souls can be seen a collection of beautiful monuments carved from marble, sandstone, and granite. Statuesque beauty forms angelic angels and saintly figurines which grace the final resting place of many Columbus citizens. Throughout the cemetery are visible monuments crowned with overwhelming crosses of great height and those of meager proportion—each monument with a story to tell. (Photograph by Carol Evans.)

IMAGES
of America

MOUNT CALVARY CEMETERY

C. L. Miller

ARCADIA
PUBLISHING

ISBN 978-0-7385-5205-7

Published by Arcadia Publishing
Charleston, South Carolina

Printed in the United States of America

Library of Congress Catalog Card Number: 2008920510

For all general information contact Arcadia Publishing at:
Telephone 843-853-2070
Fax 843-853-0044
E-mail sales@arcadiapublishing.com
For customer service and orders:
Toll-Free 1-888-313-2665

Visit us on the Internet at www.arcadiapublishing.com

For You Tobey Anna
"Of the wonderful days that were."
"There Is No Death, What Seems So Is Transition."

CONTENTS

Acknowledgments

The development and research for any projects could never have been completed without the assistance and full support of family members and the many friends. If I have overlooked anyone, I apologize at this time.

Thanks go to the Columbus Metropolitan Library, Biography, History and Travel departments; Mount Calvary Catholic Cemetery Staff; Richard Finn, director Catholic Cemeteries of Columbus; Cindy McLaughlin, archivist the Columbus Jewish Historical Society; and Don Schlegel, Catholic Records Society, Diocese of Columbus.

Without those who offered me their encouragement, contribution and friendship, I could never have undertaken this project: Martha Allman, Jim Brochowski, Julie Callahan, Teresa Carstensen, Scott Caputo, Bonnie Chandler, Louanne Conner, and Geoff Dean. Special thanks also to translator Michela DiTommaso, Cliff and Barb Dowden, Carol Evans, Maxine Fitzpatrick, Brenda Fleming, Dave Masters, Andy Miller, Jane Miller-Matson, Russ Pollitt, Kara Prem, Tom Reitz, Deborah Rittenhouse, Diane Selby, Virginia Smith, Rev. Father Michael Sweeney, Nick Taggart, and Michael and Kia Winbush.

A special thanks to Jan Gerst for her friendship, support, and her invaluable assistance in acquiring information and documents for this publication.

Unless otherwise noted, the images in this book come from the author's collection.

INTRODUCTION

When it comes to a historical cemetery, people aren't concerned with the architectural styles; they want to know about the people interred. They all have a story to tell, and this is the story of a cemetery and those interred. In 1858, "It is on the death-bed that the rich and the poor are equalized."

The first Columbus Catholic cemetery was located on the corner of Washington and Mount Vernon Avenues, where the present Columbus State Community College is now located. The cemetery may have been referred to as "St. Patrick's Cemetery" because of its location close to St. Patrick's Catholic Church. On October 6, 1846, Peter and Johanatta Ury sold the tract of land for $600. It is believed that the cemetery was never consecrated. Within 10 years, the cemetery was encircled by the growing city, and citizens petitioned city council to forbid any interments to continue to take place in the cemetery. The council passed the ordinance in July 21, 1856, but by August 18, it was repealed, and the Catholic cemetery remained in use for another two decades.

The cemetery was divided into ethnic sections; an Irish section that was overseen by Fr. Edward M. Fitzgerald of St. Patrick's Church, and a German section that was overseen by a board of trustees.

By December 29, 1868, the cemetery had become almost full, and at Mount Calvary Cemetery, the first burials had already been made. Consecration of Mount Calvary Cemetery took place in 1874, and Bishop Sylvester Harden Rosecrans directed no further burials were to take place in the old St. Patrick's Cemetery.

In 1871, Bishop John Ambrose Watterson purchased three adjoining tracts of land at each of the southern corners of Mount Calvary.

In 1887, Columbus Catholics were encouraged to remove any remains of any family member to Mount Calvary Cemetery. Johanatta Ury, the widow of Peter Ury, objected to the request claiming "that as Catholic citizens of Columbus they had the right upon their decease to be buried in the old cemetery with Peter, whose remains they refused to move." Johanatta demanded that the land be returned to them or be maintained as a cemetery. In 1888, Bishop John Ambrose Watterson filed the first petition, and the case went to the supreme court of Ohio declaring the cemetery as no longer practicable.

Located near the old Harrisburg turnpike and just beyond the original city limits of the city of Columbus is located one of the most historical cemeteries, Mount Calvary. Founded in 1812 on the site of the Scioto and Olentangy Rivers, Columbus, the state capital, is rich in history. The largest city in Ohio, named for the famed explorer Christopher Columbus, it assumed the functions of the state capital in 1816.

Throughout history people have been fascinated with old graveyards, from the majestic to a forgotten tract off a lonely country road. Those interred in either burial site are a representation of personal history and deserve to be remembered for what they achieved and who they were. Either rich or poor, washerwoman or day laborer to socially prominent citizen, each interment has offered something to society and has something to tell.

Columbus has numerous cemeteries and memorial parks. Many of those remain to be written about, and many are lost in time to the new century. The historical Mount Calvary Cemetery, on the west side of Columbus, was established in 1865 and opened for burial purposes in April 1867. It is the oldest surviving Catholic cemetery in Franklin County and rich in Columbus history. The original plot was purchased in 1865 and covered 25 acres that were located west of the present cemetery. The land was purchased from Jacob Gall and John F. Zimmer. Additional land was added to the original tract in 1866 and 1869.

The Catholics of Columbus purchased 27 acres in 1865 for $3,000. This cemetery is intended for the interment of Catholics who are entitled to Christian burial according to the rules of the Roman Catholic Church. Approximately 40,000 are interred in this 40-acre cemetery. Many of Columbus' first immigrants are interred in Mount Calvary Cemetery. The cemetery is divided into sections. It is hearsay that the sections were created for ethnic backgrounds.

In 1865, more land was purchased from Phil N. White and his wife. In 1866, two more acres were purchased from Jacob Gall and then Zimmer sold these two plots of land to the Diocese in 1868. From the time burials began on the land that was to be Mount Calvary Cemetery up to the time of its consecration, more than 1,400 internments were made. Lot sizes were 16 by 20 feet. Anton Witzigman was the cemetery sexton and resided on the premises.

In 1866, the Germans of the Holy Cross Church paid the English Catholics $300 for the choice between the two halves of the tract, and took the north half. The secretary was Cornelius Lang, and Henry Theado was treasurer of the German cemetery organization. Patrick Egan was secretary and treasurer of the English Catholics.

The cemetery was created in part to replace the earlier Catholic Cemetery, and St. Jacob Cemetery (also known as Frey Cemetery that was located near East Broad Street and Stanwood Road) later became known as the German Catholic Cemetery. Later the remains from that cemetery were eventually moved to Mount Calvary Cemetery during the period of 1906–1908. One of those moved was Margaretha Klaus, who died November 1853. She is often referred to as the "mystery tombstone lady," as her stone was not moved with her remains and was later found in a yard on the east side of Columbus. Since then, Mount Calvary Cemetery has her monument, but her burial site cannot be located.

The Catholic Diocese of Columbus cares for the cemetery, and it was consecrated November 2, 1874, by Bishop Rosecrans, a convert, who was the first Bishop of Columbus, born at Homer, Ohio, on February 5, 1827, and died October 21, 1878. He is entombed in the undercroft of St. Joseph's Cathedral.

Adjacent to the southeast corner of Mount Calvary Cemetery is a small tract of land purchased in 1874 by the Jewish community for $1,000. The Jewish community had been refused use of a tract of land in Greenlawn Cemetery after a long period of negotiations. The earliest Jewish cemetery was located in the East Graveyard at Meadow Lane and Livingston Avenue. In 1881, the city passed an ordinance prohibiting interment within the city, and the Jewish community was forced to remove 100 graves from East Graveyard to Mount Calvary Cemetery. During the flood of 1913, records of this cemetery were destroyed. Many of the stone monuments were washed away; some are in their original place. This small tract of land is now closed to burials. Today St. Joseph's Cemetery maintains this burial site.

Mount Calvary Cemetery lacks the environment of a dense setting of vegetation; overhead a hawk circles the few trees, warning those intruding on this consecrated site. A few trees lend a somewhat bleak atmosphere to this cemetery. The atmosphere is alleviated by the personalities of the monuments; many of which display porcelain portraits, relief sculpture, historically significant statues, and obelisks crowned by capitals and finials adorn this cemetery.

Monuments have an inscribed base some with an epitaph, often in verse that memorialized the deceased.

The cemetery is divided into two different sections, the north section referred to as "Holycross" (German), and the south section is the "Cathedral" (Irish) section. The Irish and the German parishes paid for their sections of land, and those parishes separately administered each section. The dividing line is at the Priests' Circle in the center of the cemetery; this section of ground was set apart as a burial place for the Catholic clergy. Rev. John W. Brumer was the first Catholic priest whose remains are interred in that section of ground. There is a cloister of nuns interned that belonged to various orders. Bishop Watterson's grave is located in the center of the cemetery under a very large crucifix. Bishop Watterson was one of the most loved bishops in the Columbus Diocese. He not only spoke in Catholic churches and facilities, but he also spoke on the statehouse lawn regularly. A Columbus Catholic high school is named after him.

On March 25, 1913, a catastrophic flood devastated the neighborhood of Franklinton, leaving over 90 people dead and thousands of west-side residents homeless. The water covered the western portion of Mount Calvary Cemetery.

This publication provides a brief insight to those who are interred in this peaceful cemetery. It is impossible to photograph and/or describe every interment in this historical cemetery. Either through a name, country of origin, dates of birth and death, porcelain portrait, or an epitaph, each simple headstone or grand monument has stories to tell. For 142 years, this cemetery has received the dead. Only those holding deeds are interred today, otherwise this cemetery is closed to burials.

History remains to be written on many of Columbus' cemeteries that are rich in history.

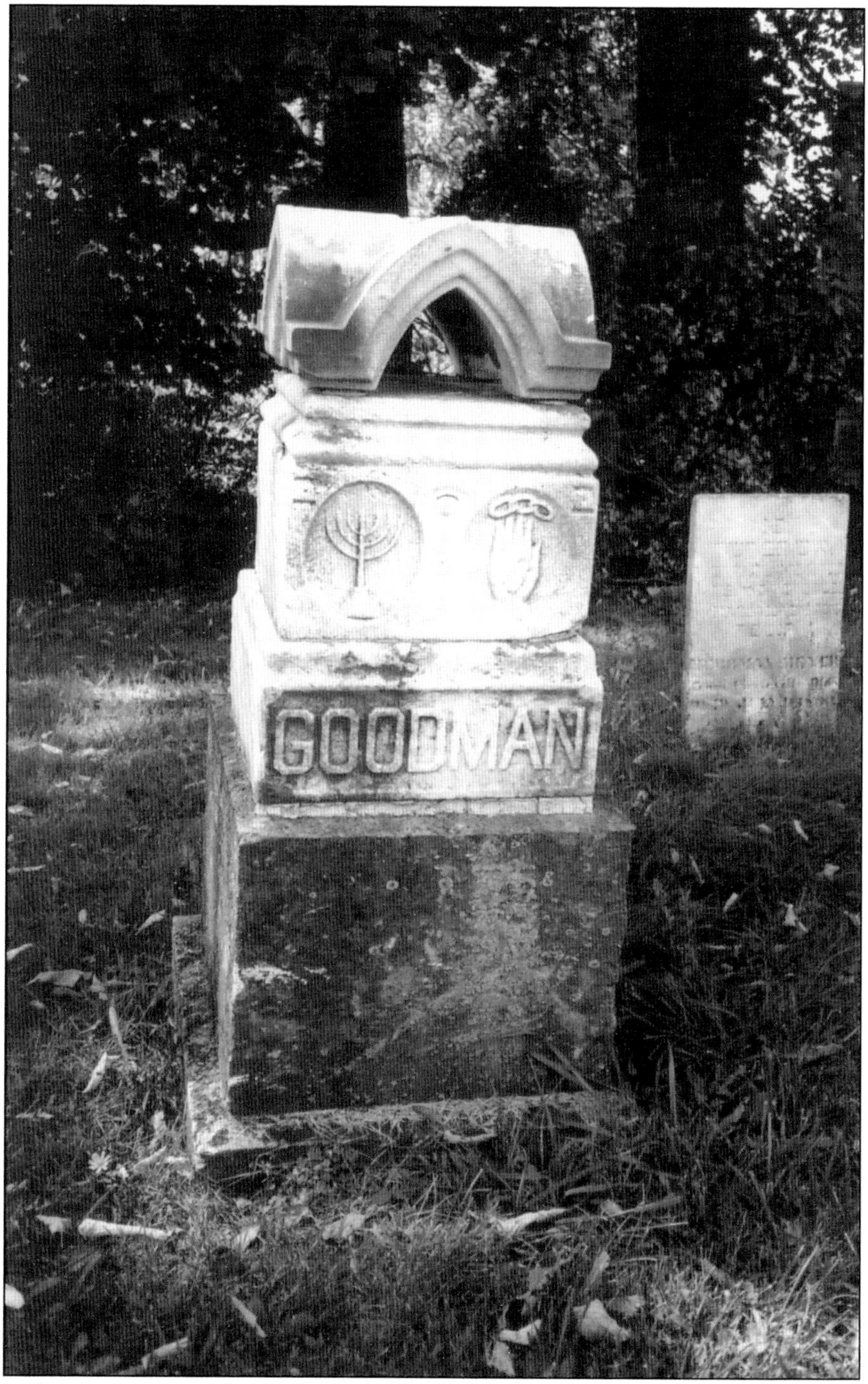

The Jewish community used a small tract of land adjacent to Mount Calvary as their cemetery. Plots were offered for sale at a congregational meeting on January 3, 1875. Twenty-three members of the congregational paid $5 each to reserve grave plots. This is the monument of J. A. Goodman who died October 22, 1876, at age 59 years, erected by his children. Erosion and vandalism has impacted this section.

One

Priests' Circle

Mount Calvary Cemetery is divided into two separate ethnic sections. The north section is referred to as the German section and marked "Holycross," and the southern section is referred to as the Irish section and marked "Cathedral." Separating these two sections and located in the center on a small knoll is the Priests' Circle, often referred to as the Bishops' Circle. This circle is surrounded by a ring of concrete and within this section are interred well-known and beloved clergy.

The first interment occurred in 1871, when Fr. Thomas O'Dea was the first occupant of the circle. Following Father O'Dea was Rev. J. W. Brummer in 1872. In 1878, Fr. John Meara was interred, followed by Fr. J. B. Hemsteger in October. During 1891, the Reverend T. J. Lane was laid to rest. In 1894, Rev. J. Mahoney was buried within the circle. Rev. D. A. Thompson followed in 1898, and then in 1899, Rev. W. I. Glauter was interred, followed by the most beloved Bishop John Ambrose Watterson later in the year. Watterson is interred under a magnificent sculptured tomb that is located directly in the center of the circle, located beneath a large crucifix.

Following his tragic death, Rev. B. P. Horny was interred in 1903. In 1906, Rev. F. Moitrier was interred. Msgr. F. X. Specht was buried in 1913, and in 1918, Rev. C. Wirtz was buried there. In 1925, Fr. M. M. Meara was interred.

A descendant of Thomas J. Bergin (1829–1897), interred in Mount Calvary Cemetery, tells an interesting story. When the cemetery was opened, Catholics were encouraged to purchase plots in the new cemetery. A coin was tossed between John Joyce and Bergin for the prime plot close to the circle. Bergin lost, and Joyce purchased his plots in Cathedral section B across from the circle and is interred there today. Just south of Joyce, slightly further from the circle, is interred four generations of the Bergin family also in Cathedral section B. Both the Joyce and the Bergin families are still close to the circle and their beloved clergy.

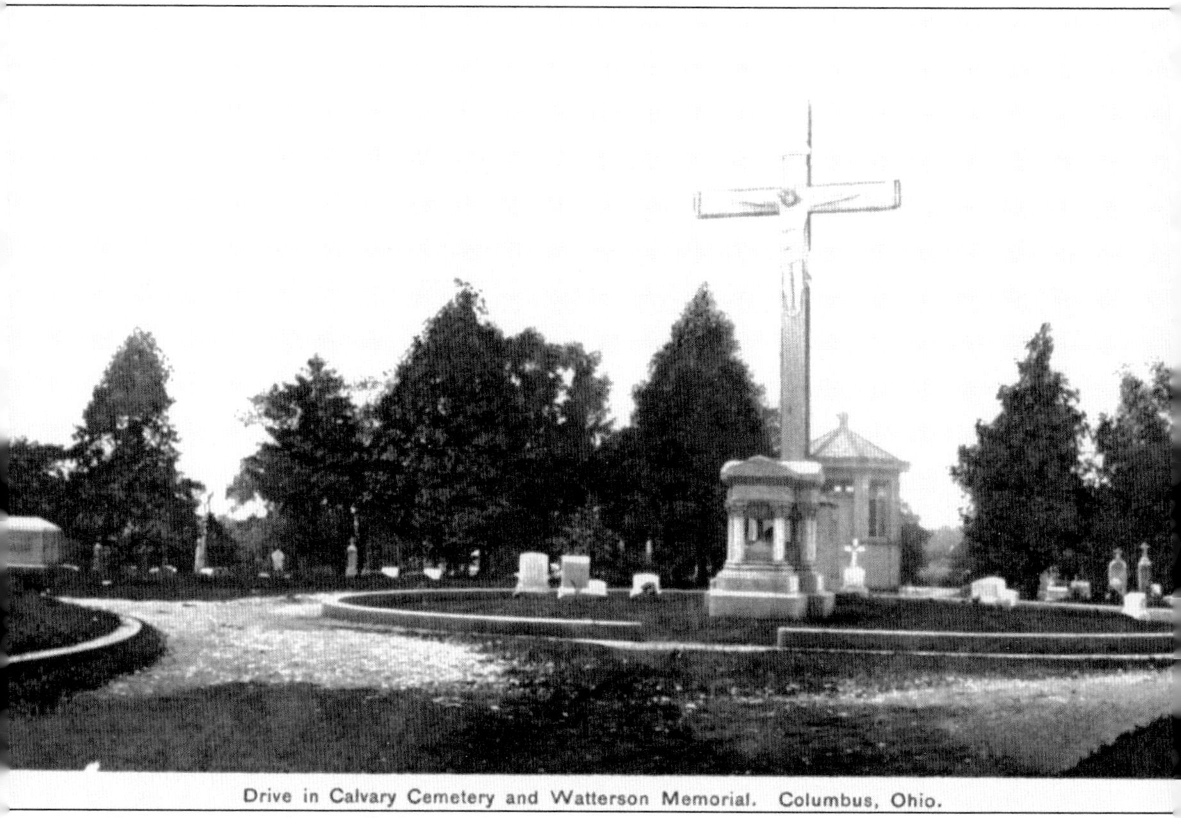

Prior to 1913 and centrally located behind the Priests' Circle was a receiving vault. Such vaults were used for temporary storage of remains during cold weather when graves were dug by hand. The vault is no longer present. (Dean Collection.)

The Right Reverend John Ambrose Watterson, D.D., was born May 27, 1844, in Blairsville, Pennsylvania, the son of John S. and Sarah McAfee Watterson. He died April 17, 1899. The Watterson family came to America from the Isle of Mann in 1762. John Ambrose was bishop during the period from 1889 until his unexpected death in 1899. (Columbus Metropolitan Library.)

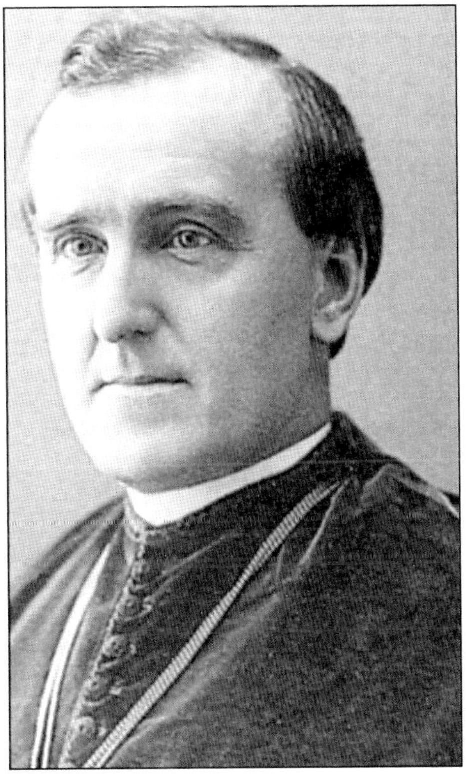

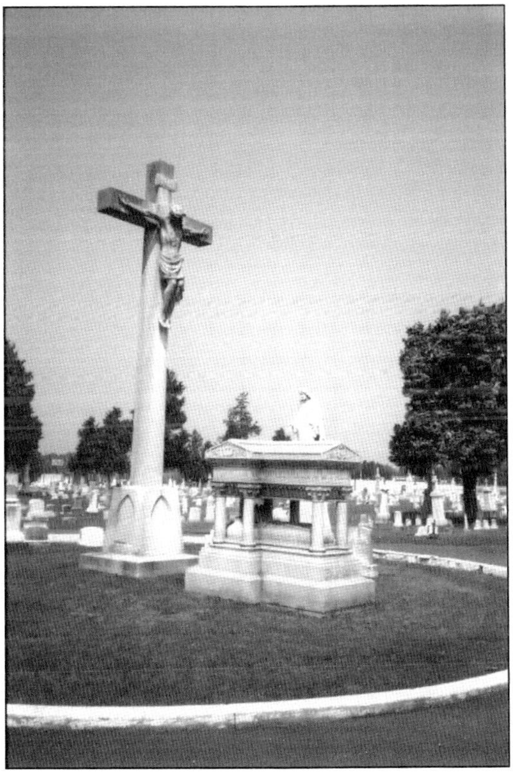

In March 1880, Watterson was appointed second bishop of Columbus. He was consecrated August 8, 1880, at St. Joseph's Cathedral. During his episcopate, St. Anthony and Mount Carmel hospitals were founded. Watterson was a strong believer in temperance. No saloon owner was allowed to be an officer in any Catholic organization in the diocese, and he made all those he confirmed promise not to drink until they were 21.

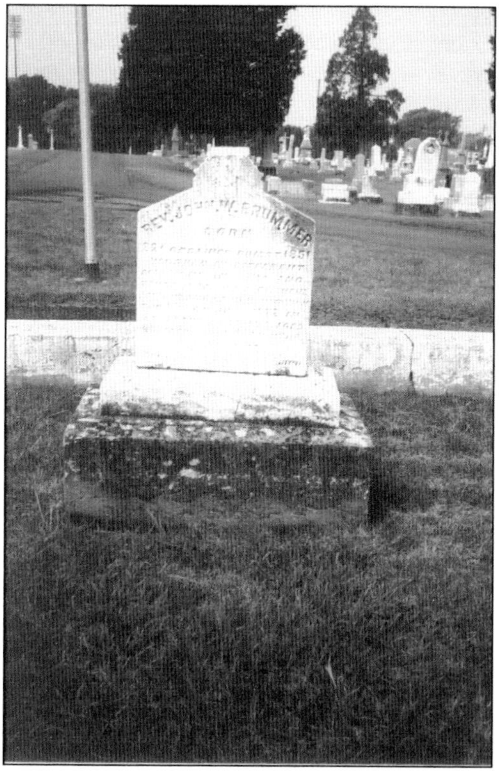

Rev. John W. Brummer was born in 1824 and died June 19, 1872. He was ordained in 1851. Brummer was educated at St. Xavier's College in Cincinnati and St. Surplice, Paris. He had been ill for two years prior to his death at St. Francis Hospital. His funeral was held at Holy Cross Church.

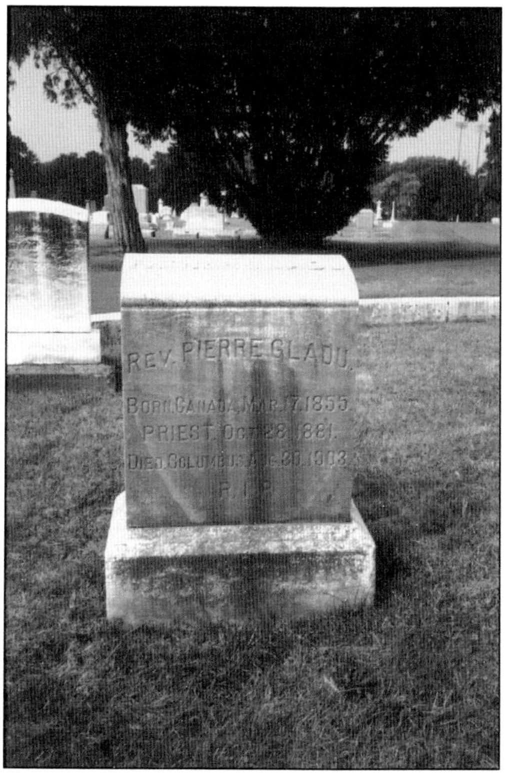

Rev. Pierre Gladu was born March 17, 1855, in Canada and died August 30, 1903. He was ordained October 28, 1891, in Canada. Gladu was forced to resign because of his health and go to New Mexico for the purpose of recuperating. He returned to Ohio. His funeral took place in St. Joseph's Cathedral. Rev. A. M. Leyden, a personal friend of Gladu, delivered the funeral sermon.

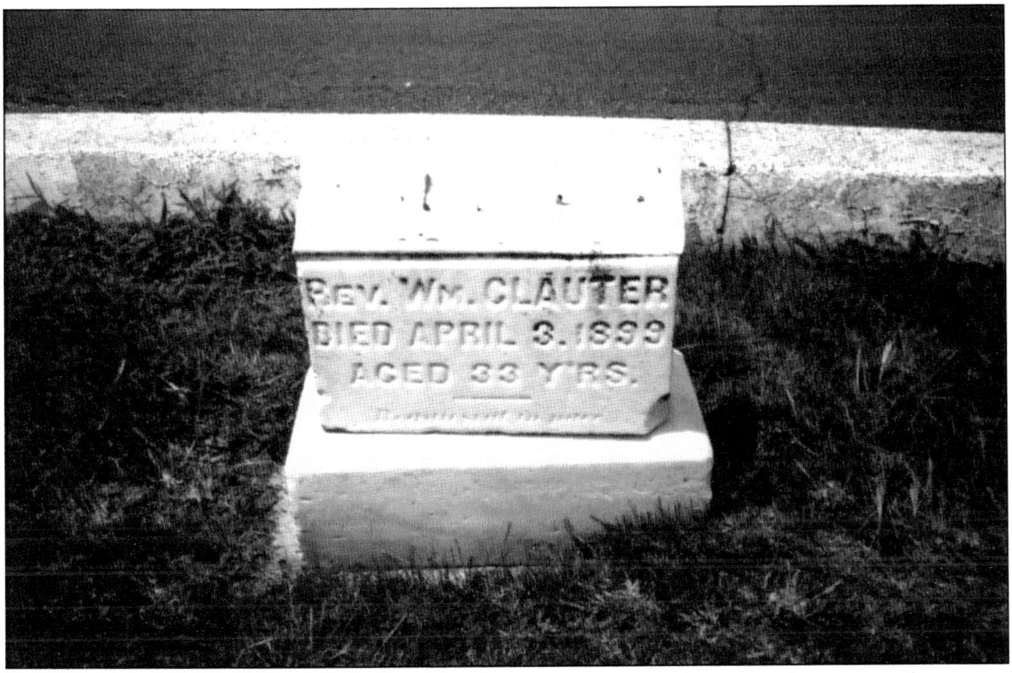

Rev. William Ignatius Glauter was born in 1866 in Pomeroy, Ohio, and died April 3, 1899. Glauter attended the Jesuit College at Buffalo and made his philosophical course in Mount St. Mary's Seminary in Cincinnati. He was ordained in 1896 by the Bishop of Saltzburg for the Diocese of Columbus. He was a professor at Pontifical College Josephinum up to his death.

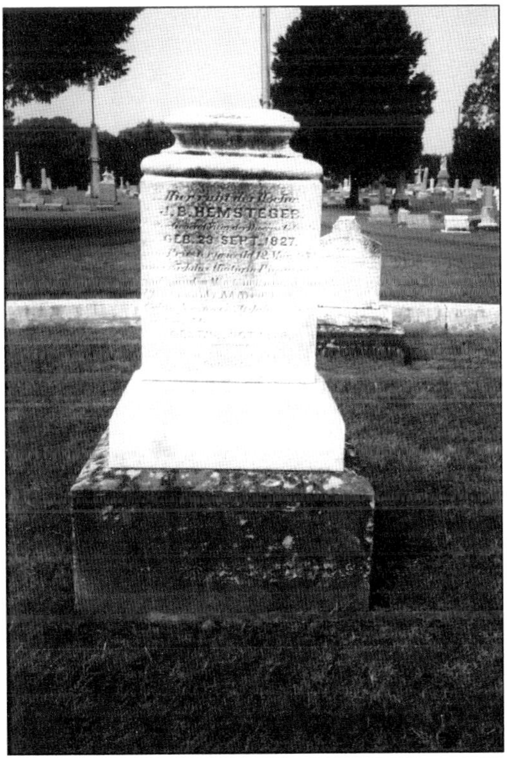

Rev. J. B. Hemsteger was born September 23, 1827, and died October 18, 1878. Hemsteger was ordained March 12, 1851, by Archbishop Purcell in Cincinnati. Father Hemsteger was vicar general of the Cincinnati Diocese. Later he was a citizen of Columbus and pastor of Holy Cross Church for about 20 years. Prior to coming to Columbus, Father Hemsteger was stationed at Piqua.

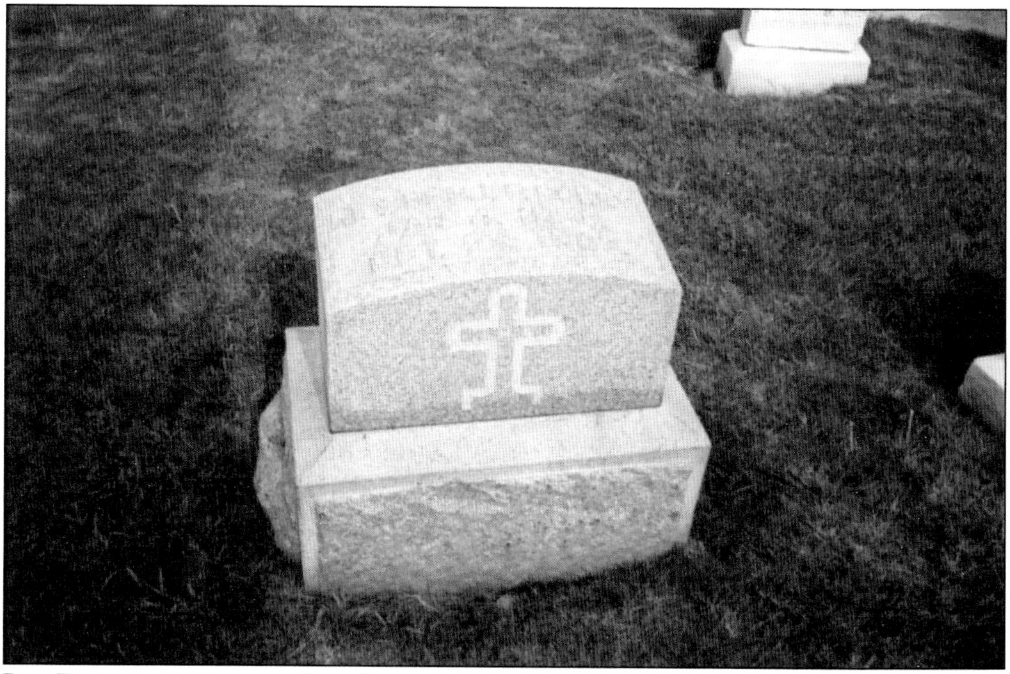

Rev. Benjamin P. Horny was born January 4, 1856, and died October 29, 1903. He was struck by a streetcar and dragged, causing many injuries. Horny spent 17 years as assistant to the rector of St. Mary's Church. He studied in Detroit for the priesthood, and later at Berlin, Canada, where he was ordained at the age of 20.

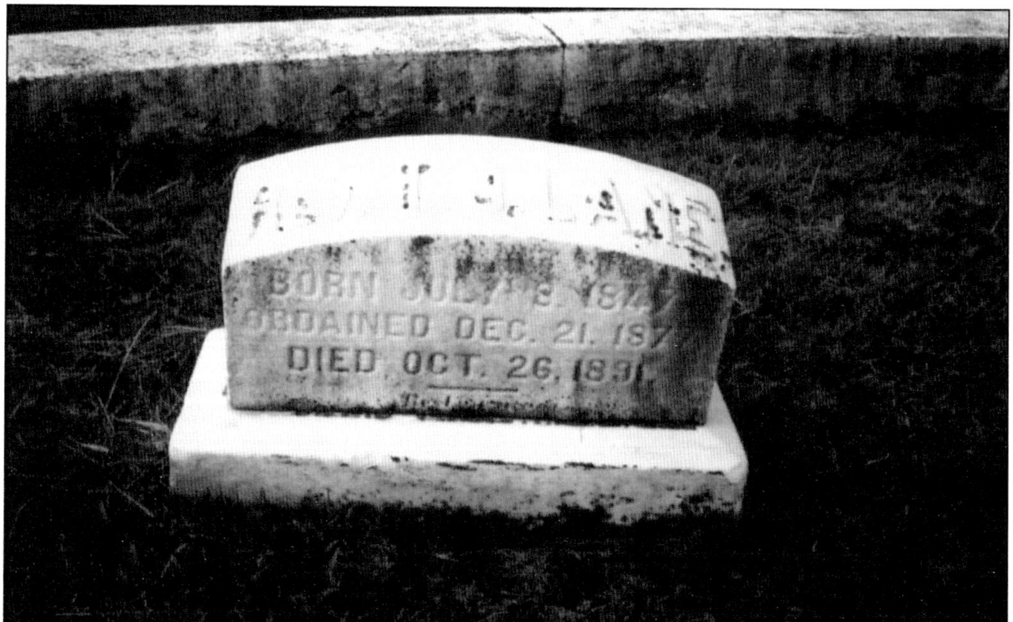

Rev. Thomas J. Lane was born July 8, 1847, and died October 26, 1891. Lane was ordained December 21, 1877. Lane's funeral took place from St. Joseph's Cathedral. The clergy of the diocese chanted the solemn office of the dead.

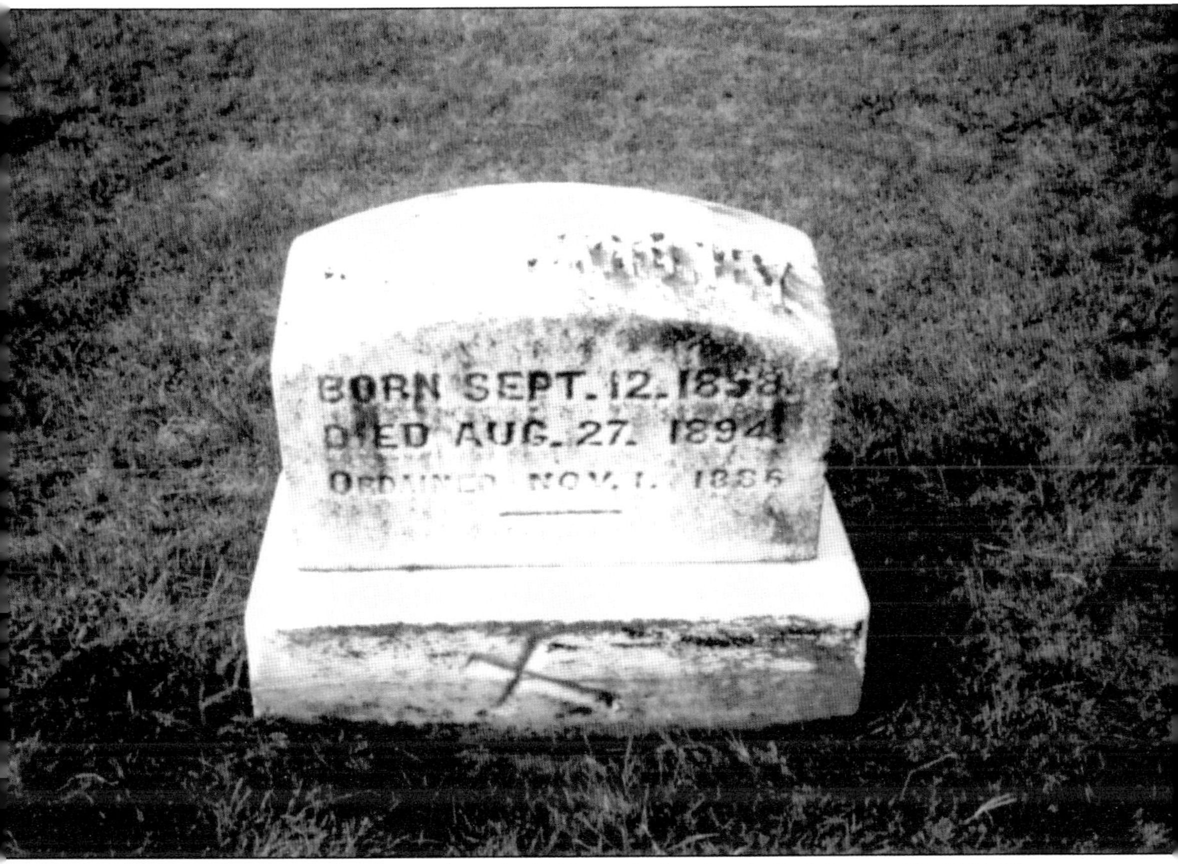

Rev. J. Mahoney was born September 12, 1868, in England and died August 27, 1894. He was ordained November 1, 1886, in England. He took his first lessons for the priesthood under Fr. John B. Eis at Holy Cross Church in Columbus and completed his studies in England. Fr. James Mahoney was a private secretary to Bishop John Ambrose Watterson for several years. Mahoney was a fine musician and choir director at the cathedral.

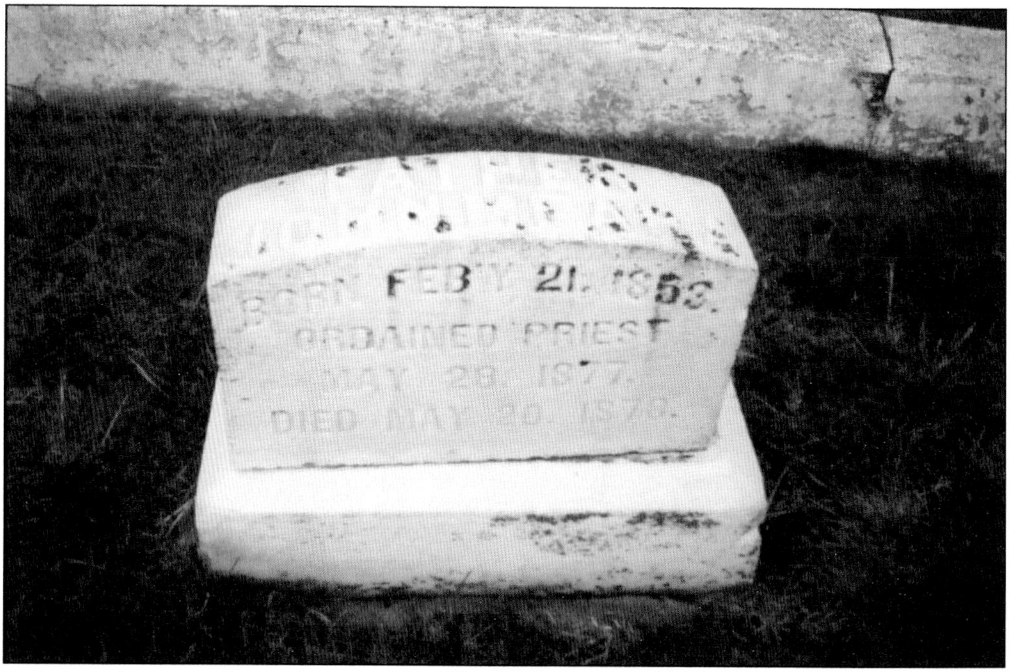

Fr. John Meara was born February 21, 1853, in Cincinnati and died May 30, 1878. He was ordained May 28, 1877, and a year later, he died. He was the son of Stephen and Ellen Maher Meara and the brother of Rev. Fr. Michael M. Meara.

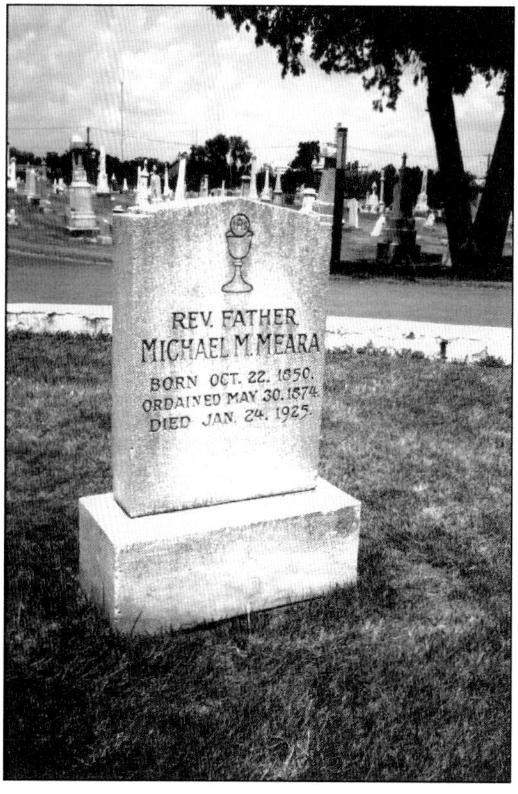

Rev. Michael Meara was born October 22, 1850, and died January 24, 1925. He was pastor in Circleville, Ohio, and realized the need for a school. In 1886, the school was completed, paid for, and opened. In 1874, he went to Santa Fe to fortify himself against a threatened disease. He returned to his duties in Columbus and celebrated his golden jubilee of his ordination May 20, 1924.

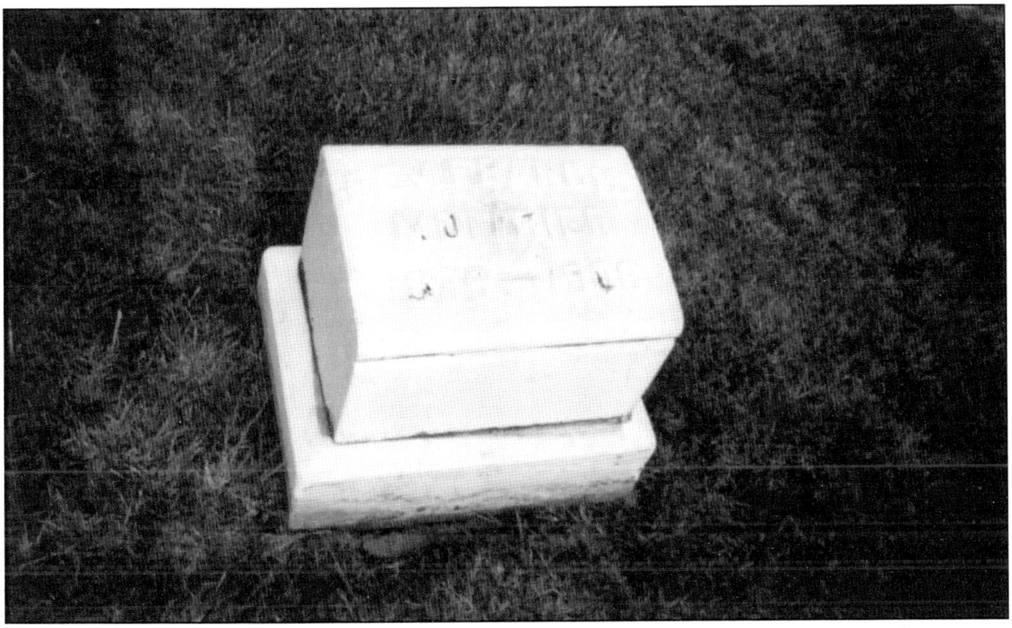

Rev. Francis Moitrier was born in 1839 and died September 24, 1906. In 1876, he was at St. Luke's Church and was pastor of St. Rose Church in New Lexington, Ohio. In 1876, he was the pastor of St. Dominic Church in Perry County, Ohio. Moitrier showed what were the first movies in the history of the county. He made his own slides and proceeds were used for the benefit of the congregation.

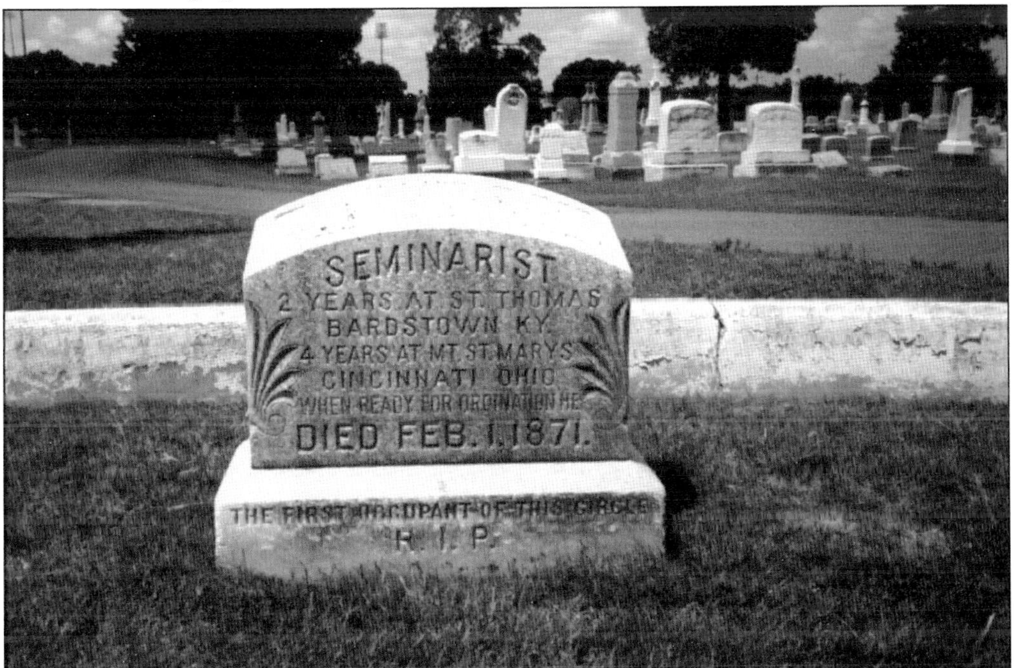

Rev. Father Thomas O'Dea, who died February 1, 1871, was the first occupant of the circle, seminarist. He was at St. Thomas Church in Bardstown, Kentucky, and four years at Mount St. Mary's Church in Cincinnati.

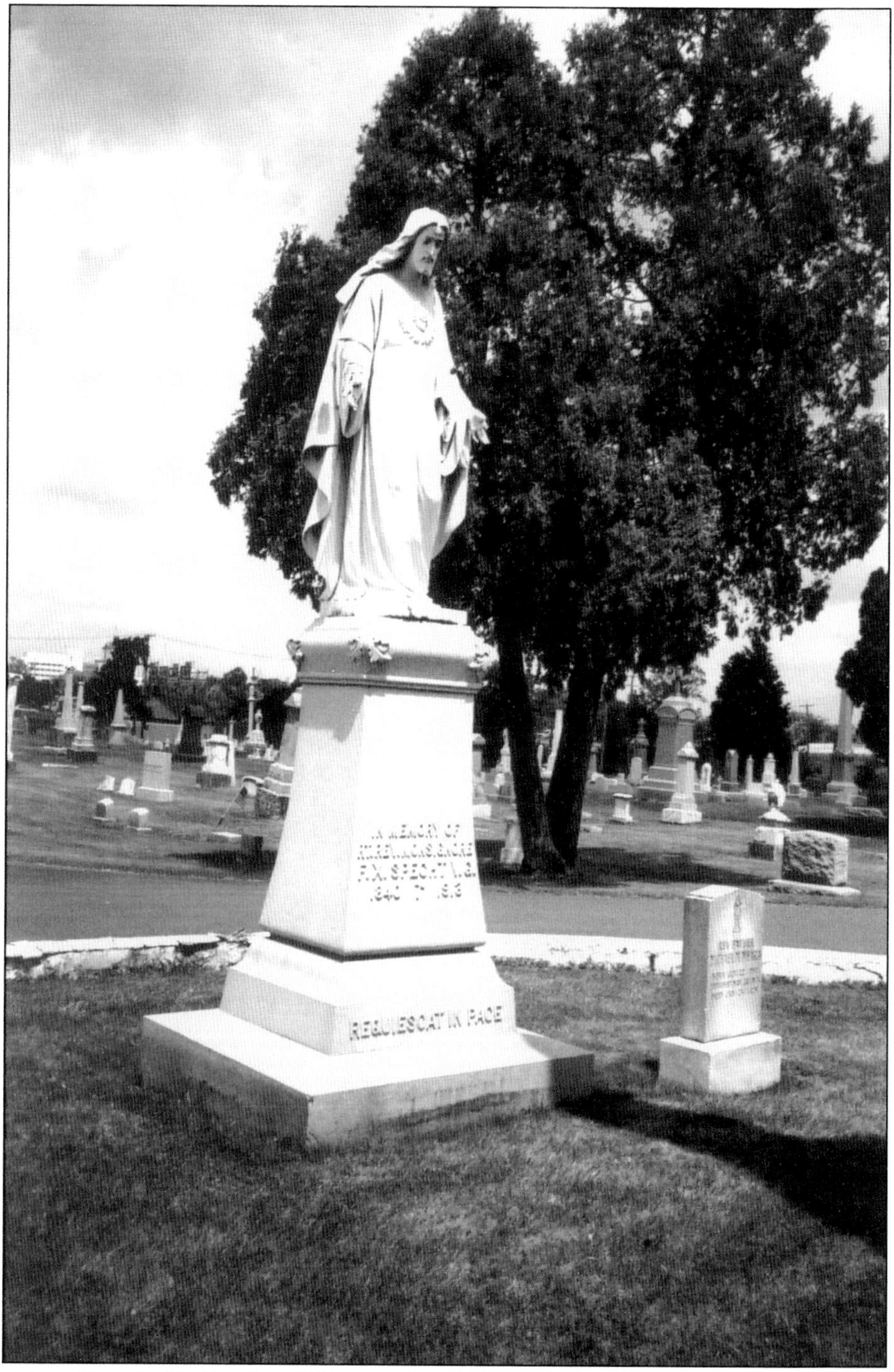

Rev. Msgr. Francis X. Specht, V.G., was born November 4, 1840, in Germany and died May 29, 1913. He entered Mount St. Mary's Seminary in Cincinnati and was ordained March 12, 1864. Pope Leo XIII made him domestic prelate, which gave him the title of monsignor and the right to wear the purple collar. He was known for his generous charity and was a patron of St. Vincent's Orphan Asylum.

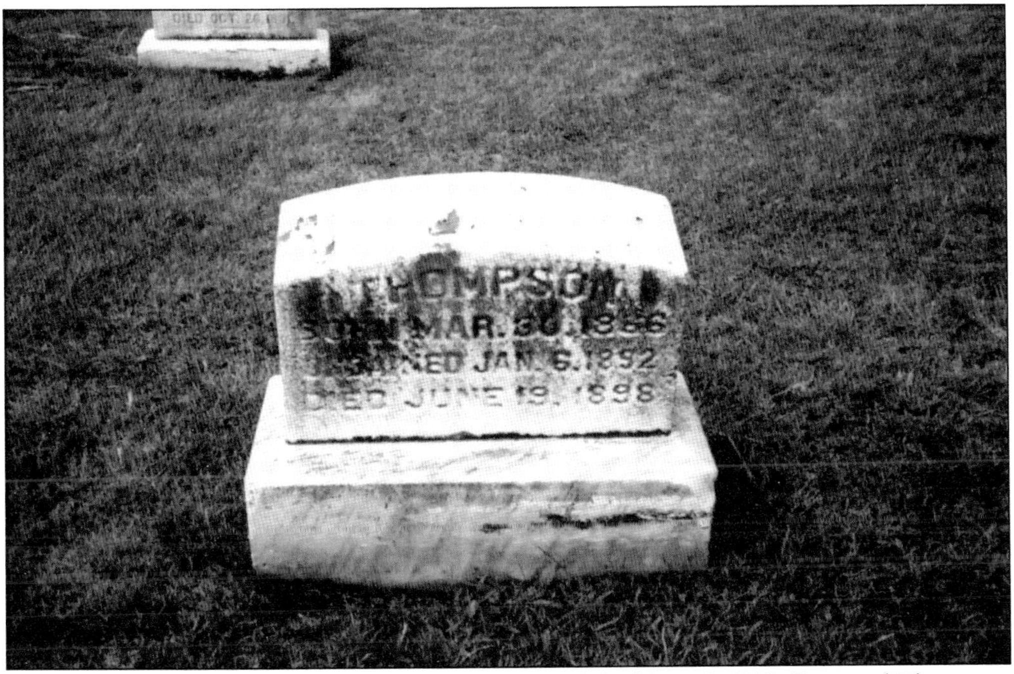

Rev. David A. Thompson was born May 30, 1866, and died June 9, 1898. Reverend Thompson was ordained January 6, 1892.

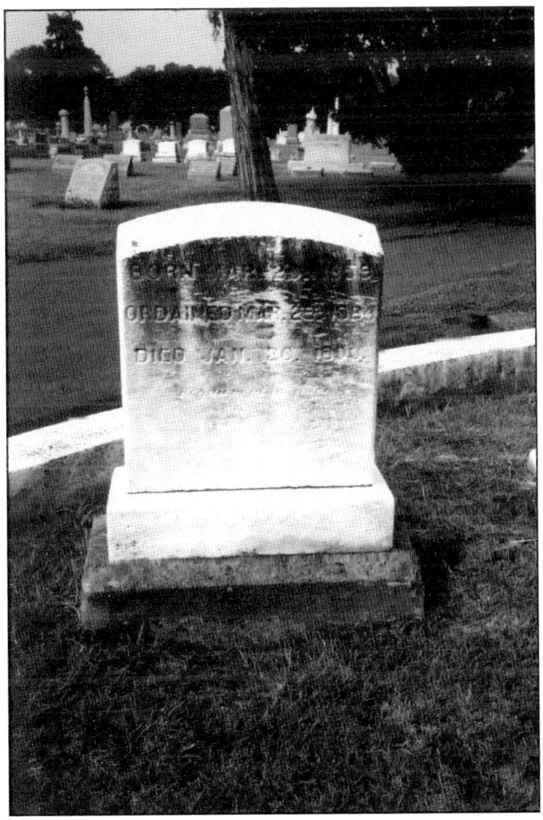

Rev. J. P. White was born March 29, 1859, in Boston, and he died January 26, 1893. He was ordained March 29, 1884. Reverend White, after his ordination, came to the cathedral in Columbus and later was appointed chaplain of St. Anthony's Hospital. Reverend White was one of the promising clergymen of the church, and he was loved and esteemed by his parishioners.

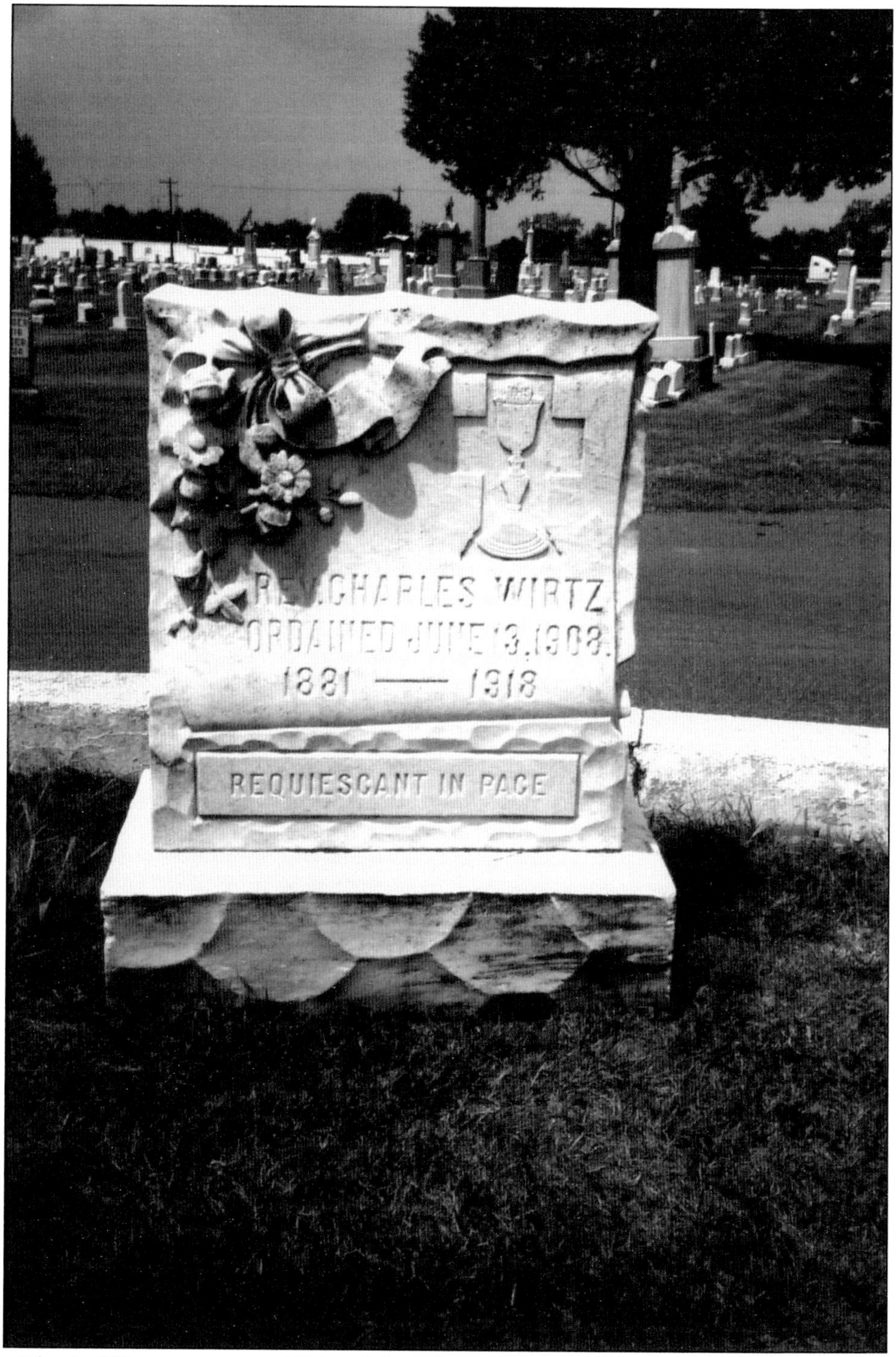

Rev. Charles Wirtz was born in 1881 and died November 5, 1918. He was a member of St. Mary's Parish and attended St. Mary's School. He entered the Josephinum College and was ordained June 13, 1908. His mother and St. John's Parish of Dry Ridge, Ohio, erected his monument. His first charge was in Springfield, and later, he was assigned to Dry Ridge Parish.

Two

Cloistered Women and Religious Figures

In the Catholic Church a religious order is referred to as an "Institute of Consecrated Life." These people vow to serve God all their life and form a communion of daily prayer, work, and sometimes also silence. In the church, members of such orders termed religious are not members of the clergy, which make up hierarchy, but belong to the laity unless these individuals are ordained as priests.

Male members are termed monks, and females are referred to as nuns. Many of them hold positions of service to a community in the form of teachers, medical positions, or religious producers of artworks and texts. Many fabricate religious vestments or create religious books and still maintain distinctiveness in communal living.

Some religious orders have what is referred to as "Third Orders." This order is a group of lay members who have made promises to live in accordance with the values of the religious order with whom they are affiliated, yet still live in the world. They take vows of poverty or purity. Religious orders are also distinct from secular institutes and other lay ecclesial movements.

The traditional term "nun" is reserved for cloistered women. It is often used loosely to describe religious sisters who live in community but are active in broader society.

Few monastic religious orders practice literal isolation "cloistering." There are those orders living in the world rather than communally. Some of these may be distinguished by vows taken as poverty, chastity, obedience, stability, and sometimes loyalty. Others undertake self-denial, fasting, or silence as members of their religious order.

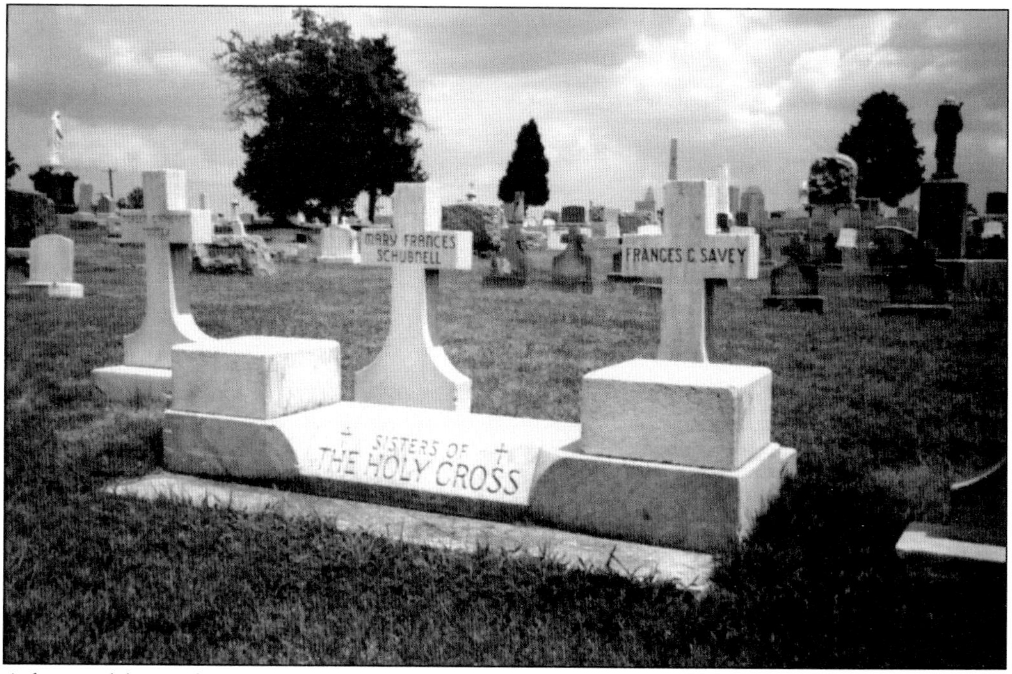

A hospital located at West Street and Davis Avenue was founded in 1885 by Dr. William B. Hawkes, and run by Sisters of the Holy Cross. While under the direction of Dr. J. W. Hamilton, this hospital later became Mount Carmel Hospital. Seen here is a marker of the Sisters of the Holy Cross.

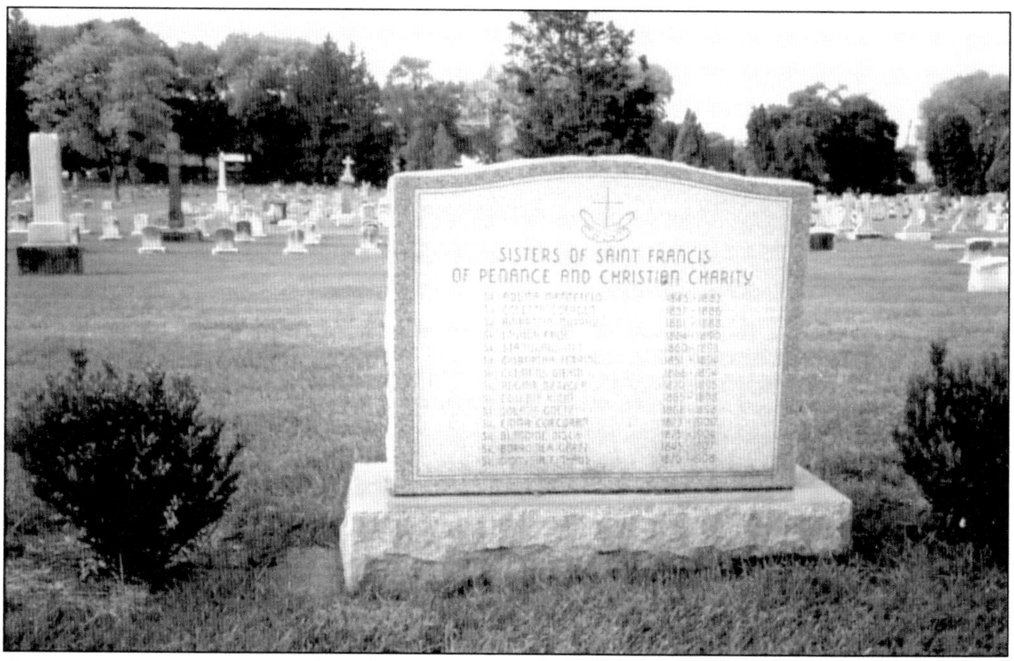

A series of names are engraved on this monument erected to the Sisters of St. Francis of Penance and Christian Charity.

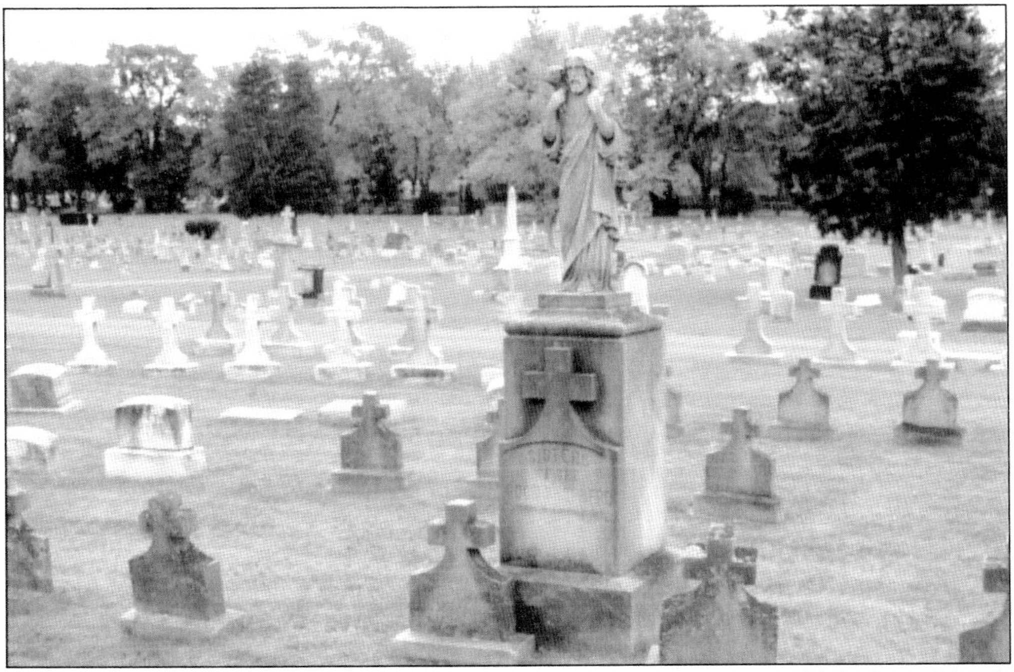

Founded by the Sisters of the Good Shepherd, the Rosemont Center was established in 1876 with support of Sarah Worthington King Peter, the daughter of the first Ohio governor. Originally, it provided care for neglected women during the Civil War who were prisoner of war at Camp Chase. In the first years of operation, the Sisters of the Good Shepherd also responded to the needs of the homeless and orphaned children.

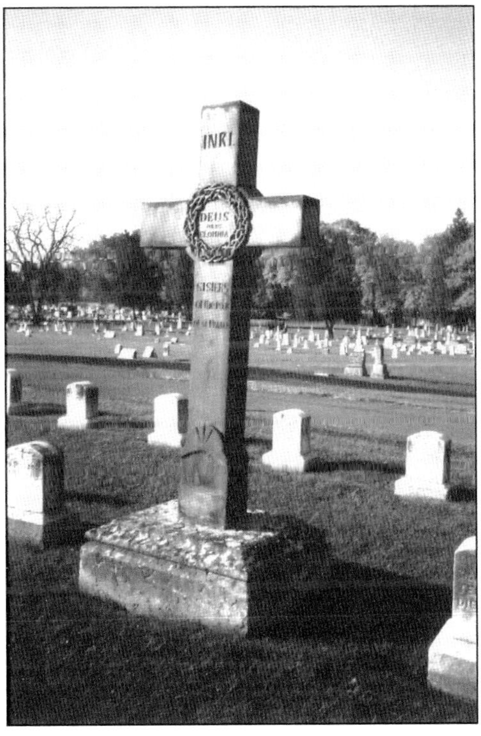

The first medical school and hospital in the United States was constructed in 1847 and opened as the Howard Infirmary. In 1862, local physicians were able to move a group of nuns to the community to serve as health care workers. In 1865, a lease was granted to the Sisters of the Poor of St. Francis to operate what became known as St. Francis Hospital. Starling Loving, a Columbus physician, assisted the sisters in organizing their hospital.

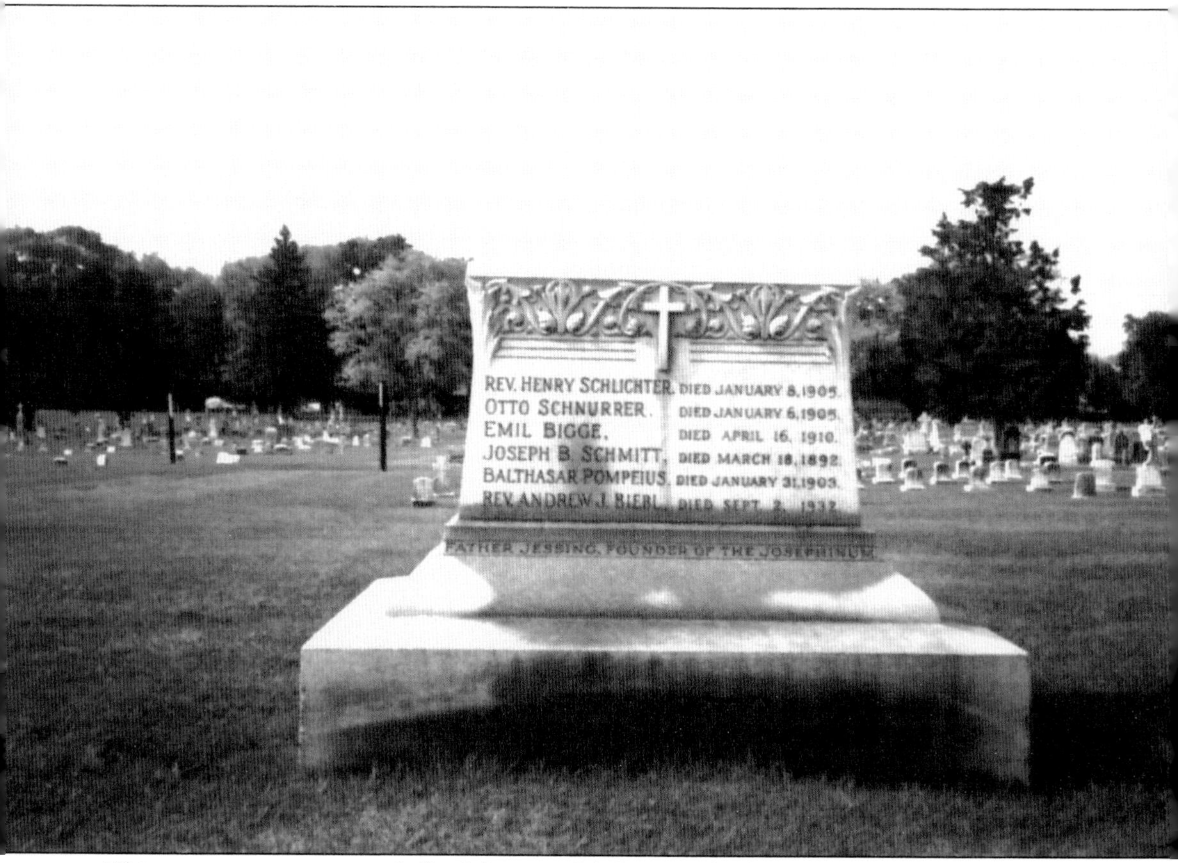

This monument is erected "In Memory Of Some Of The Faithful Helpers And Wards Of Father Jessing, Founder of the Josephinum." Engraved names included Rev. Dr. Otto Schnurrer, Rev. Henry J. Schlichter, Prof. Emil Bigge, Joseph Schmitt, Balthasar Pompeius, and Rev. Fr. Andrew Joseph Biebl. Also listed were names of orphans and students.

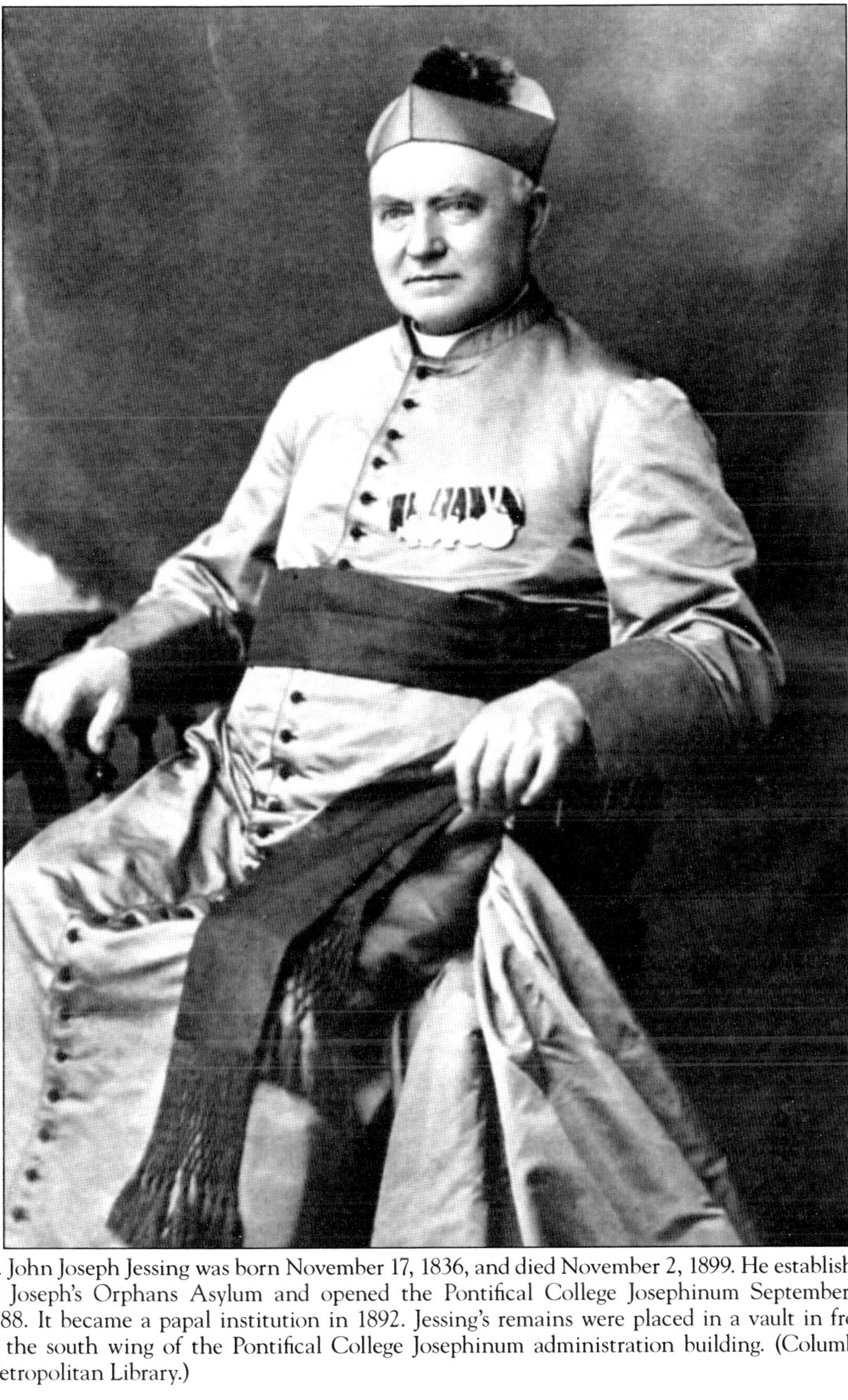

Fr. John Joseph Jessing was born November 17, 1836, and died November 2, 1899. He established St Joseph's Orphans Asylum and opened the Pontifical College Josephinum September 1, 1888. It became a papal institution in 1892. Jessing's remains were placed in a vault in front of the south wing of the Pontifical College Josephinum administration building. (Columbus Metropolitan Library.)

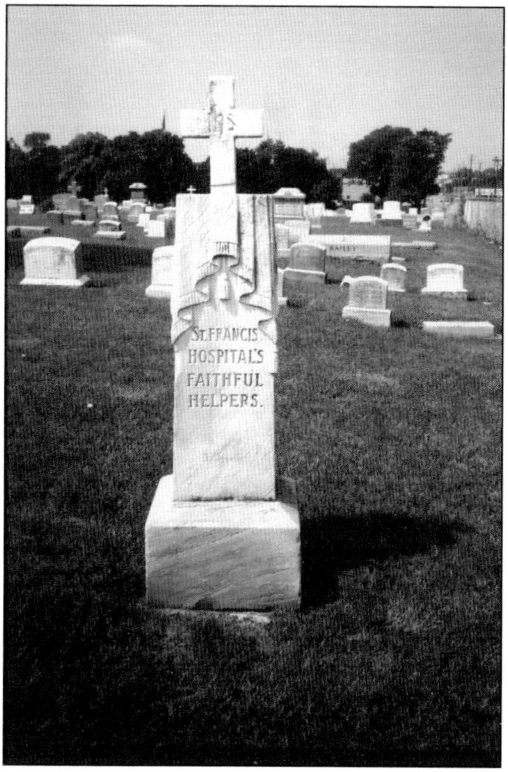

"St. Francis Hospitals' Faithful Helpers" is engraved on the front of this monument and on the side a listing of helpers shows Theresia Dehler 1847–1930; Josepha Riehle 1857–1931; John Buehler, died 1927; and Margaret Herbst 1860–1940.

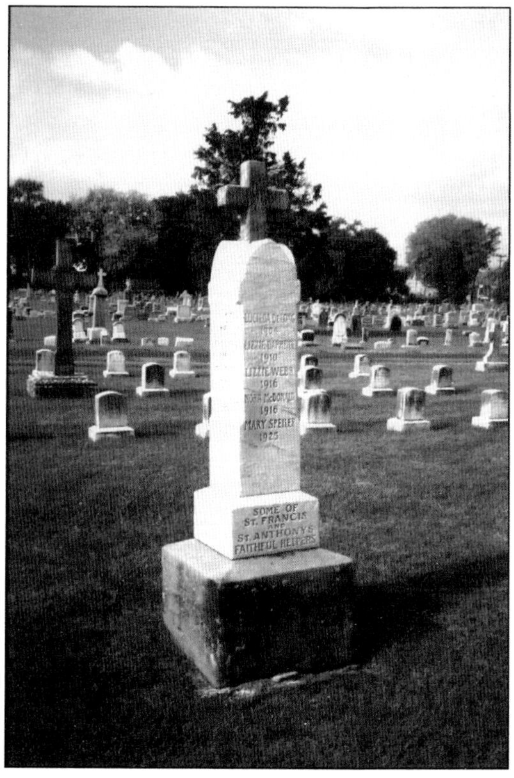

Here is another monument for "Some of St. Francis and St. Anthony's Faithful Helpers." The names of those interred within this section are engraved on this monument in memory of those helpers.

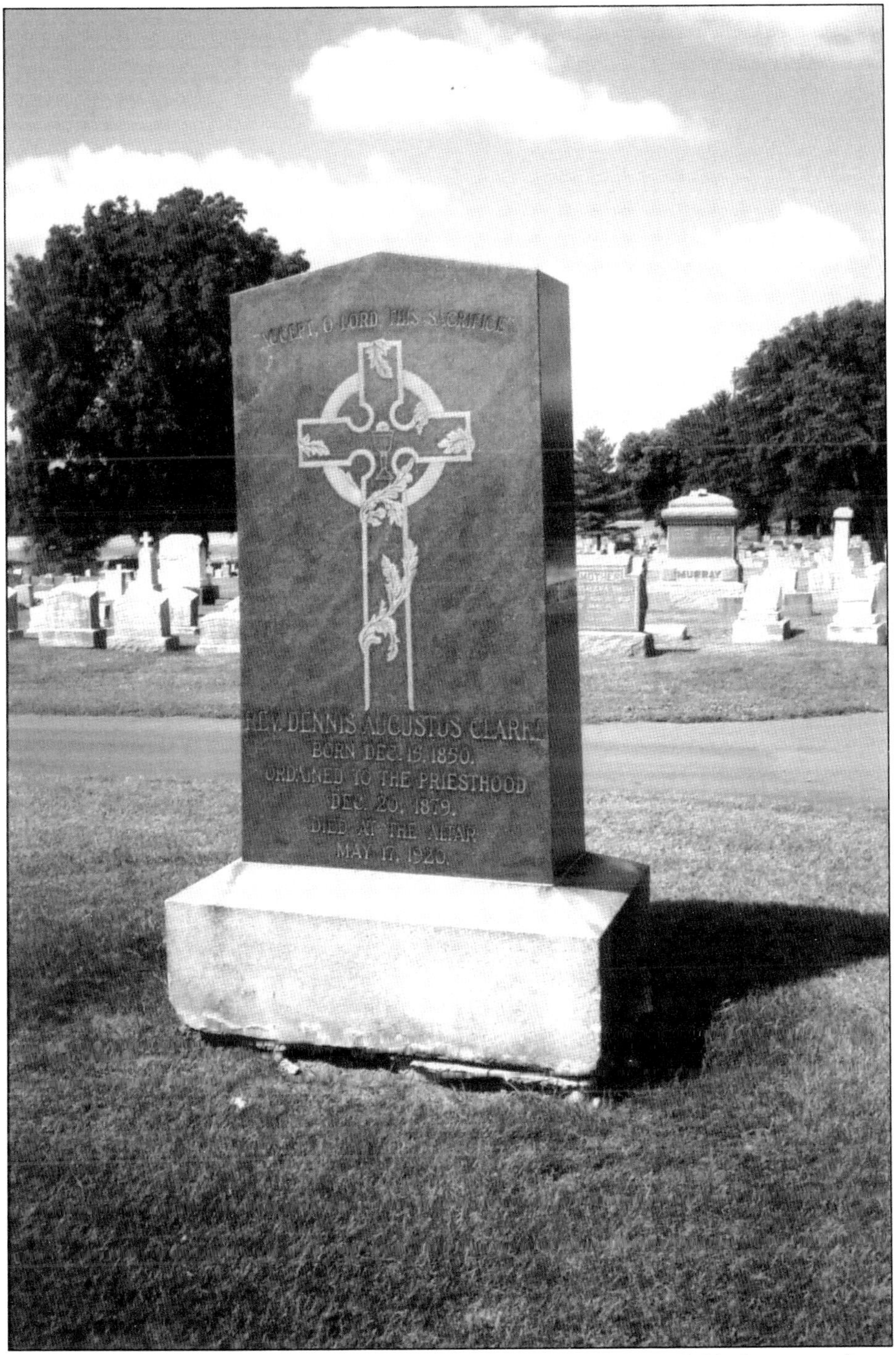

Rev. Dennis Augustus Clarke was born December 15, 1850. Reverend Clarke was ordained to the Priesthood December 20, 1879. Reverend Clarke died at the altar on May 17, 1920. He was instrumental in building up the congregation of Holy Family Church and supervised the construction of the parish's buildings, among which was a new $50,000 Holy Family School, dedicated in March 1914 at Sandusky and Shepherd Streets in Columbus.

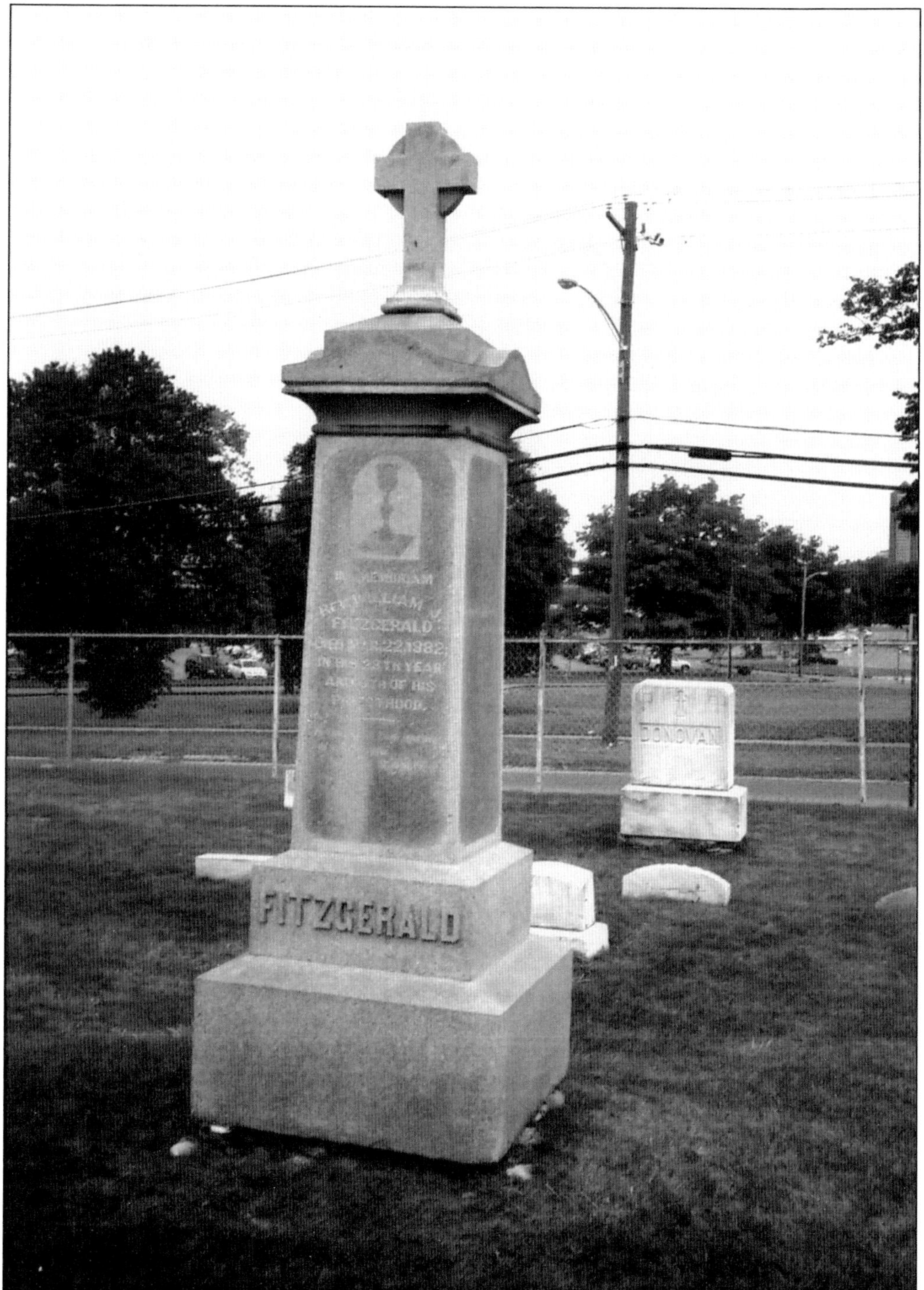

The west side of this monument is engraved, "In Memory Rev. William J. Fitzgerald Died March 22, 1882, In The 28th Year And 6th Of His Priesthood." The north side of the monument is engraved, "Rev. R. J. Fitzgerald Died July 15, 1897 in The 20th Year of His Priesthood."

Three

SLEEPING IN SILENCE

During the mid-1800s, sculptors began collaborating with monument designers and cemetery officials in bringing beautiful sculptured religious monuments in various forms from marble to majestic bronze into many of the cemeteries. The obelisk remains the most impressive of all memorials for its grandeur and elevation. Memorials of the tablet type are most prevalent of all monuments in most cemeteries. The cross and the cross tablet are the most significant of all for Christian cemeteries. The columnar monument has compelled mankind since the days of ancient Greeks. The pedestal and square monument, when families of three or more are interred on a plot, and the foursquare type of memorial affords each family an equally important side for the family name.

Funerary symbolism appears in many different forms and styles. It is impossible to provide readers with every form of funerary symbolism and epitaphs that can be found in any cemetery. The most popular was the anchor. Early Christians used the anchor as a disguised cross and/or a guide to a secret meeting places. It is also the symbol of hope, an occupational symbol of seaman and St. Nicholas, the patron saint of seamen. It symbolized hope and steadfastness. Under no circumstances should a sacred symbol be placed below the family name and never used as mere ornament.

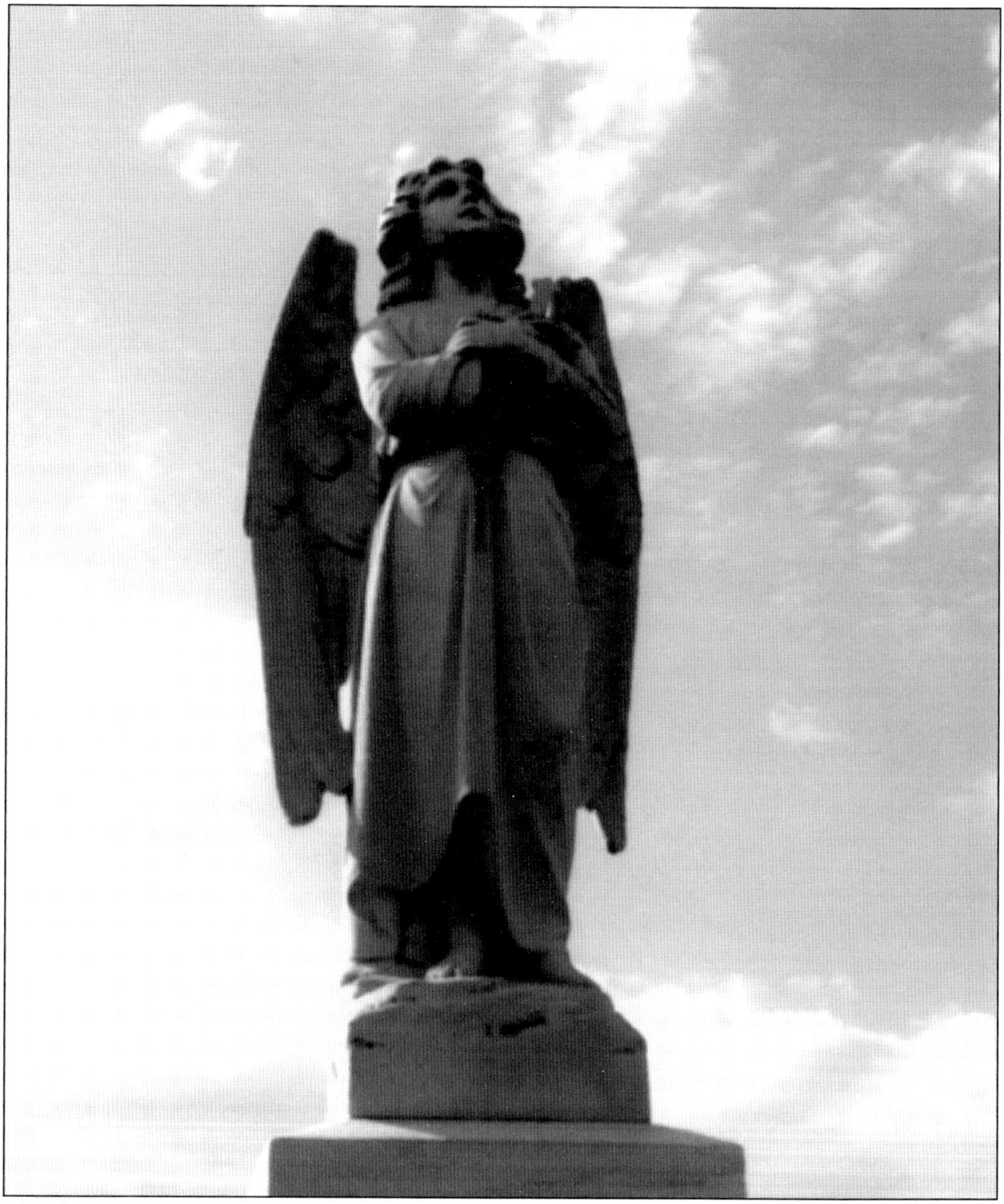

This historical cemetery does not lack the beauty of sculptured memorial monuments. This angelic heavenly spirit casts her gaze upward to heaven. (Carol Evans.)

Egan Undertaking Company interred the first person in Mount Calvary Cemetery. Mary Duffy died June 21, 1867, and was interred in the Cathedral section B, No. 126. Engraved on this monument is "Dennis Duffy, Grandfather." In 1923, John Duffy's son Thomas purchased 12 spaces in St. Joseph's Cemetery and had John and Mary moved. Children John and James Duffy and grandfather Dennis Duffy were not moved.

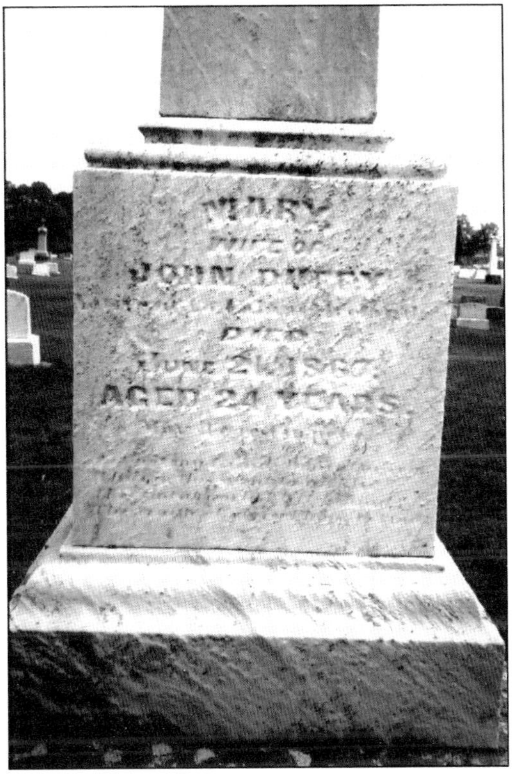

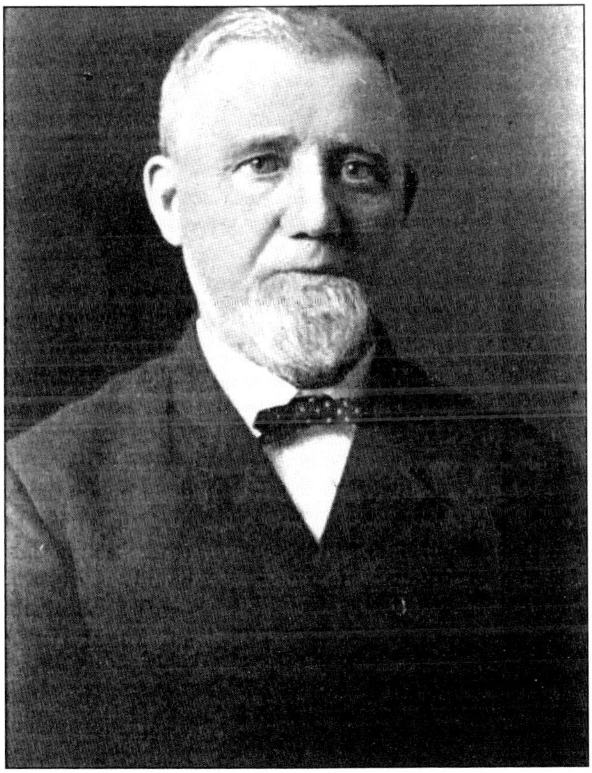

John was born June 1840 in Ireland, the son of Dennis and Margaret Powers Duffy, and died November 11, 1912. John operated a grocery store in 1861. In April 1872, John was selling "passenger tickets" by the Cunard, National, and Anchor lines of steamers. He also issued drafts for any amount, payable in gold, on any bank in Europe. Duffy was moved from Mount Calvary Cemetery to St. Joseph's Cemetery. (Columbus Metropolitan Library.)

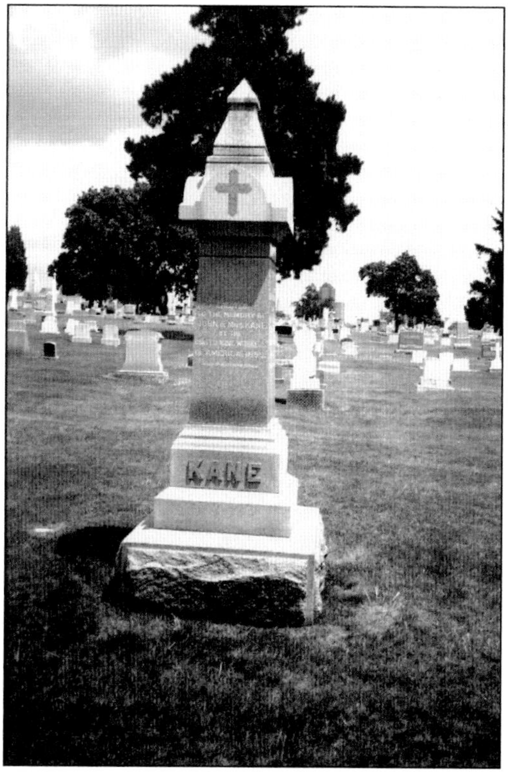

John Kane was born May 21, 1859, and died July 19, 1897. Kane was vice president of the United Mine Workers of America. Rebecca Kane was born in 1865 and died November 7, 1897, at the home of her brother-in-law Thomas Kane in Pennsylvania. The monument is engraved "Erected To The Memory Of John and Mrs. Kane By The United Mine Workers of America. 1898. May They Rest In Peace."

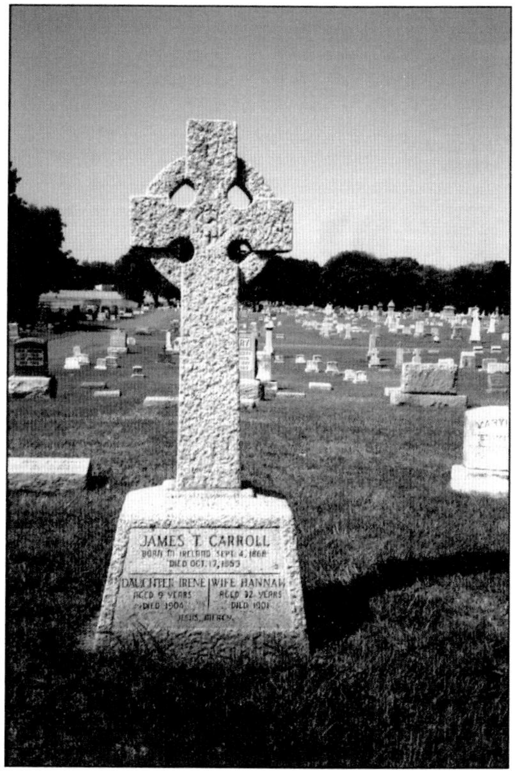

James T. Carroll was born in 1868 in Ireland and died October 27, 1953. He was former editor and publisher of the *Catholic Columbian* and a former editor and publisher of the *Catholic Forester*. He owned the Columbus Printing Company and was a member of the state legislature from 1912 to 1913. He was director of the Columbus Chamber of Commerce, the Ohio National Bank, and a former president and director of the Union Building and Loan Company.

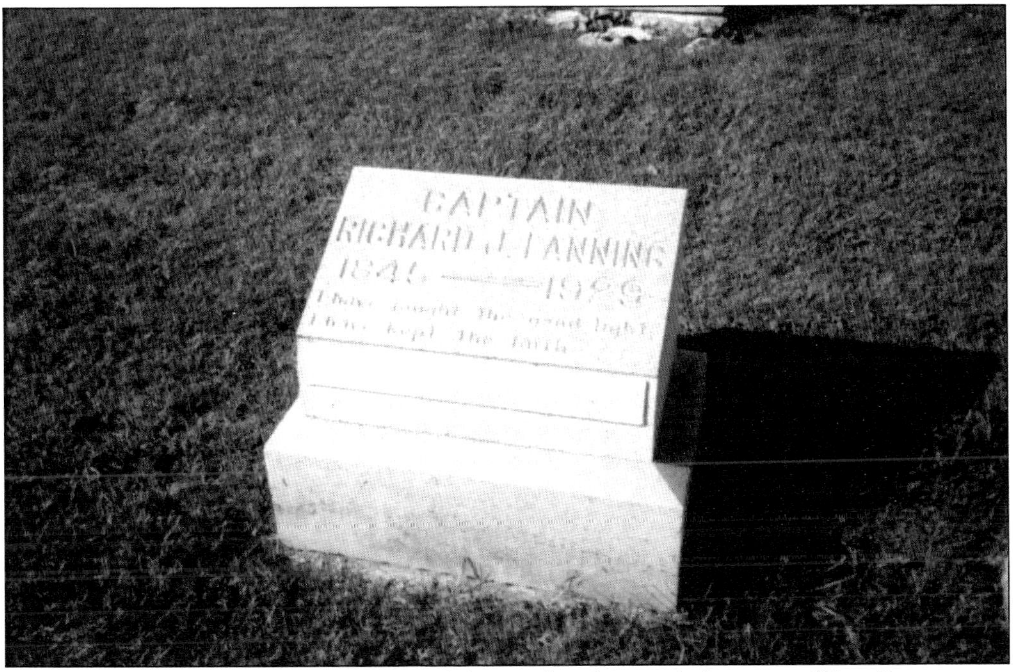

Capt. Richard J. Fanning was a veteran of the Civil and Spanish-American Wars. Fanning was born July 31, 1845, and died January 5, 1929.

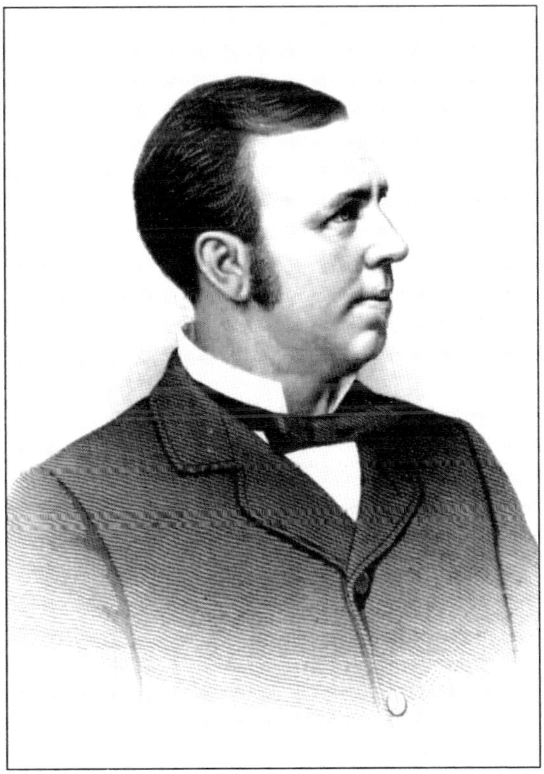

Captain Fanning served as clerk of the Supreme Court of Ohio and, in 1886, as railroad commissioner of Ohio. Fanning served with the Army of the Potomac and fought in the seven-day battles in front of Richmond. He was commissioned captain and assistant quartermaster at the outbreak of the Spanish-American War and was captain of the 41st U.S. Volunteer Infantry during the Philippine insurrection. (Columbus Metropolitan Library.)

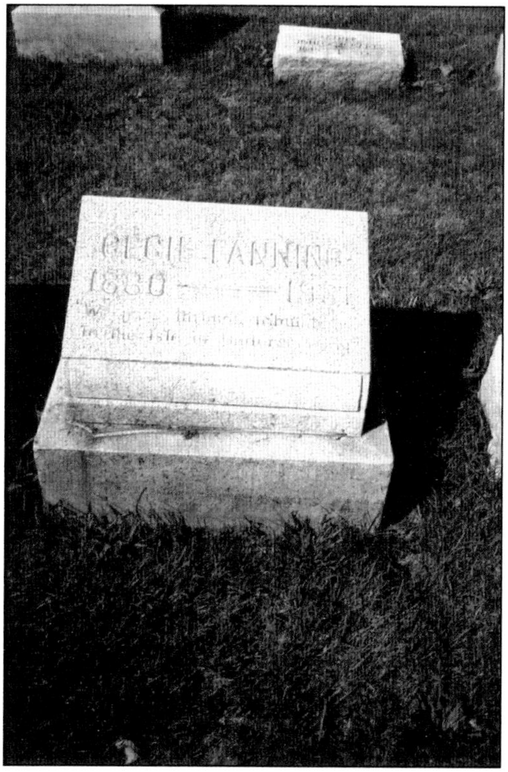

Dr. Cecil Fanning was born November 28, 1880, the son of Capt. Richard and Cecilia Miller Fanning, and he died December 7, 1931. Cecil was a boy soprano and was trained by H. B. Turpin. He made his music debut in England, in 1908; he sang the following year for King Edward VII and Queen Alexandra. In 1912, he made his debut in Berlin and his recital debut in New York City in 1916.

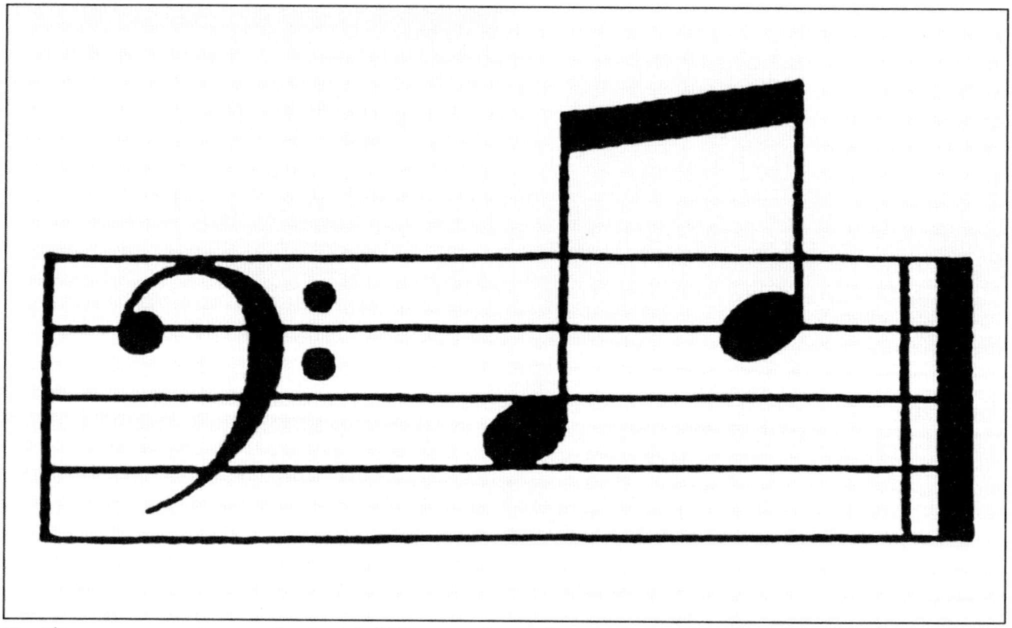

Cecil's monument is inscribed with "We pass through tribulation/To the Isle of Understanding" and engraved into the monument is a staff with a clef and two notes. He was head of the voice department of the Capital College of Oratory and Music, director of the choir of the Bryden Road Temple, and was, at one time, a soloist and choir director in the First Methodist Episcopal Church.

Theodore Leonard was born October 25, 1820, in Canada and died in Columbus on July 6, 1887. Leonard Avenue is named after him. He died a man of comparative wealth. (Columbus Metropolitan Library.)

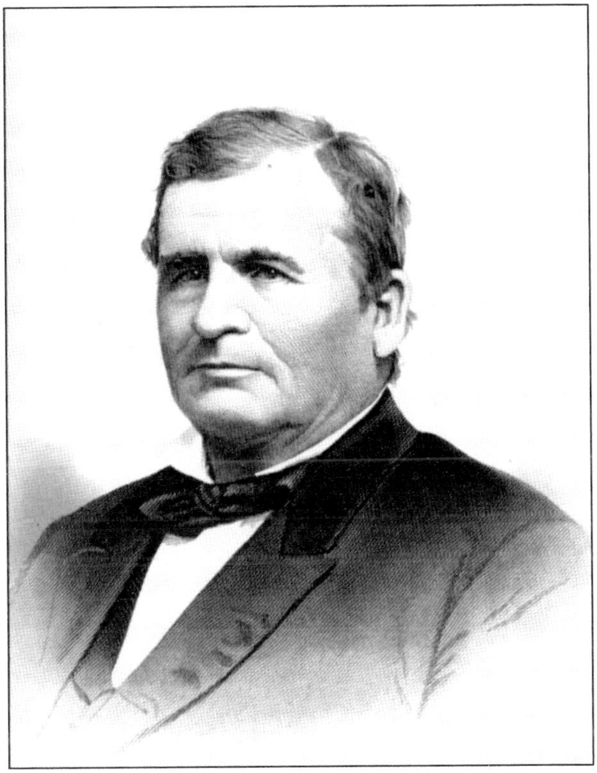

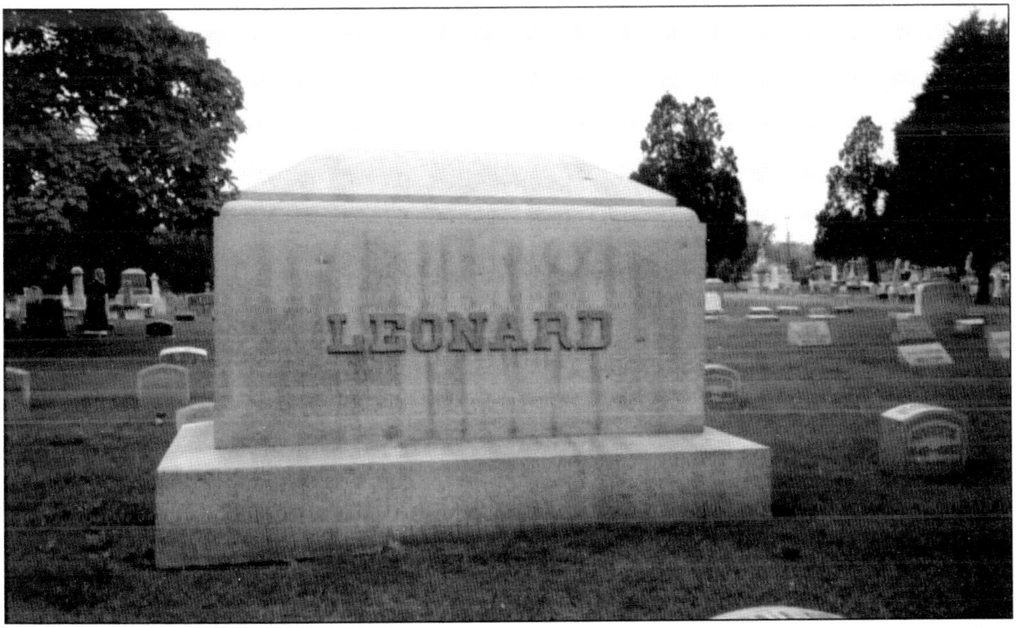

Leonard came to Franklin County in 1840, purchased 50 acres of land in Clinton Township, and later acquired 368 acres of land in Mifflin Township. He founded the brickyard of Leonard and Roberts, as well as a grocery store. A charitable man, he gave $5,000 to the building fund of St. Joseph's Cathedral and to St. Mary's of the Springs, he gave 33 acres of land and $10,000 in cash.

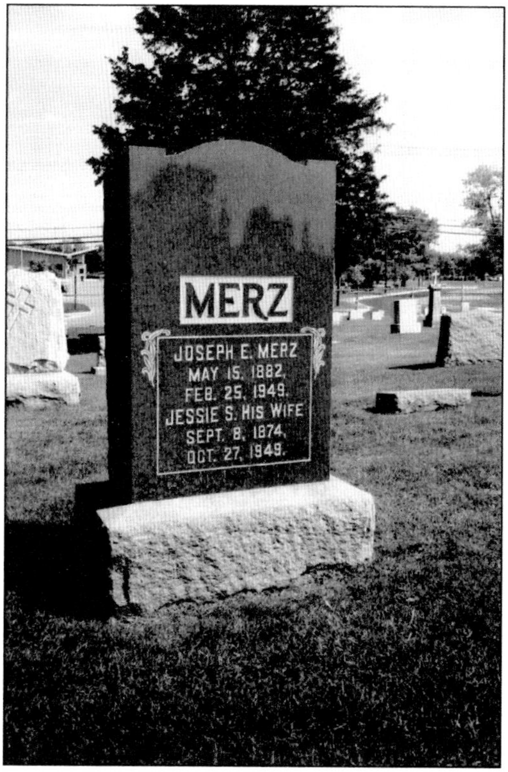

Joseph E. Merz was born May 15, 1882, and died February 25, 1949. Jessie S. Merz was born September 8, 1874, and died October 27, 1949. Joseph was associated with the Columbus Packing Company. The Columbus Packing Company operated during the period of 1901–1957 at 1981 South High Street. It was not uncommon for married couples to pass on shortly after the death of one of the spouses as is in this case.

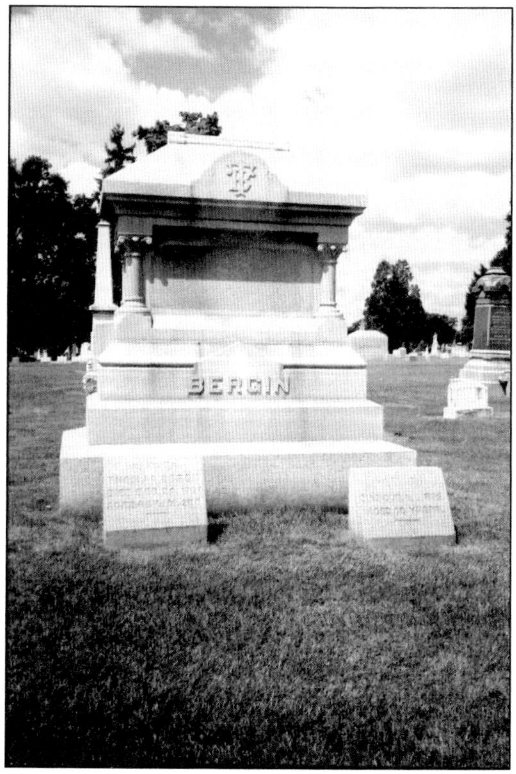

Thomas Bergin was born in Ireland in 1829 and came to the United States in 1847. He died December 24, 1897, at the age of 68 years. Bergin operated a grocery store on the corner of High and Broad Streets. He served on the city council and was a member of the first board of police commissioners. He was a trustee of the school for the blind.

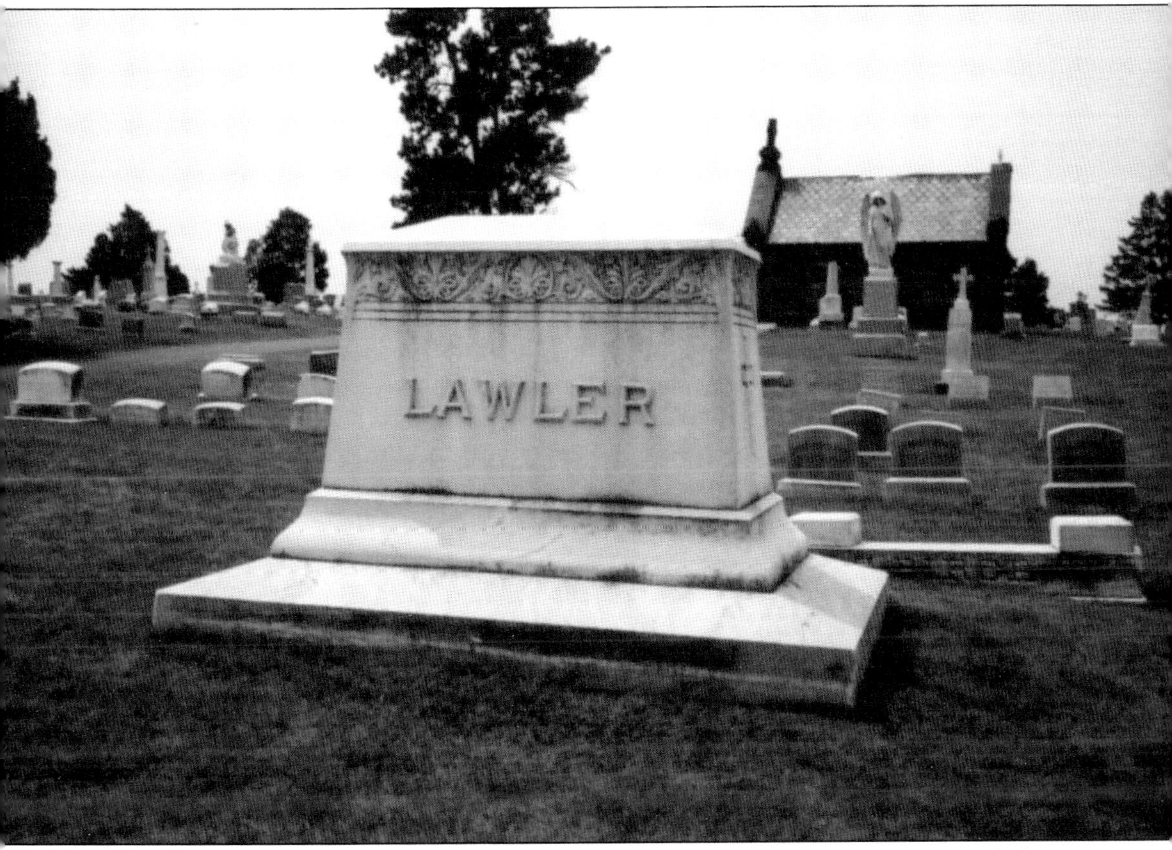

John L. Lawler was born August 5, 1846, and died July 2, 1916. Lawler was an extensive dealer in coal, ore, and limestone. He was the first vice president and director of the Union Building and Loan Savings Company, director of the Keever Starch Company, and director of the Lincoln Savings Bank. He married Catherine C. Doran from Pennsylvania. Catherine was born in 1855 and died in 1949.

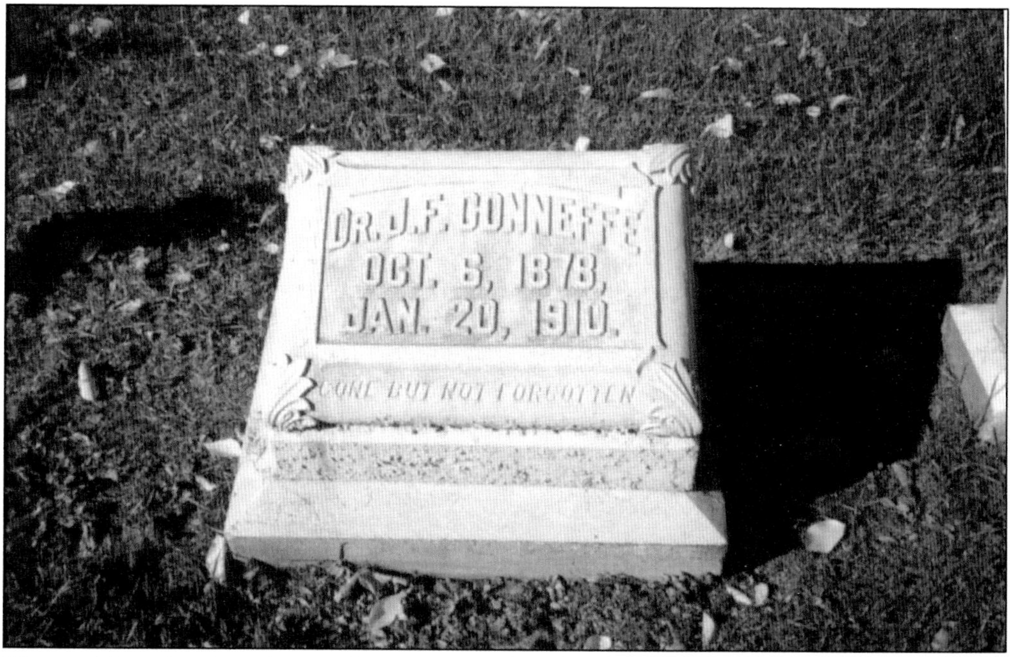

Wrapped from head to feet in sheets saturated with a strong solution of chloride and zinc, Dr. James F. Conneffe, a victim of the dreaded typhus fever, died January 20, 1910. He was born October 6, 1878, in Philadelphia. His death was the first record of typhus fever at the local health office. The only mourners were his brothers and his sister. Services were held in the chapel of the hospital without the presence of his body.

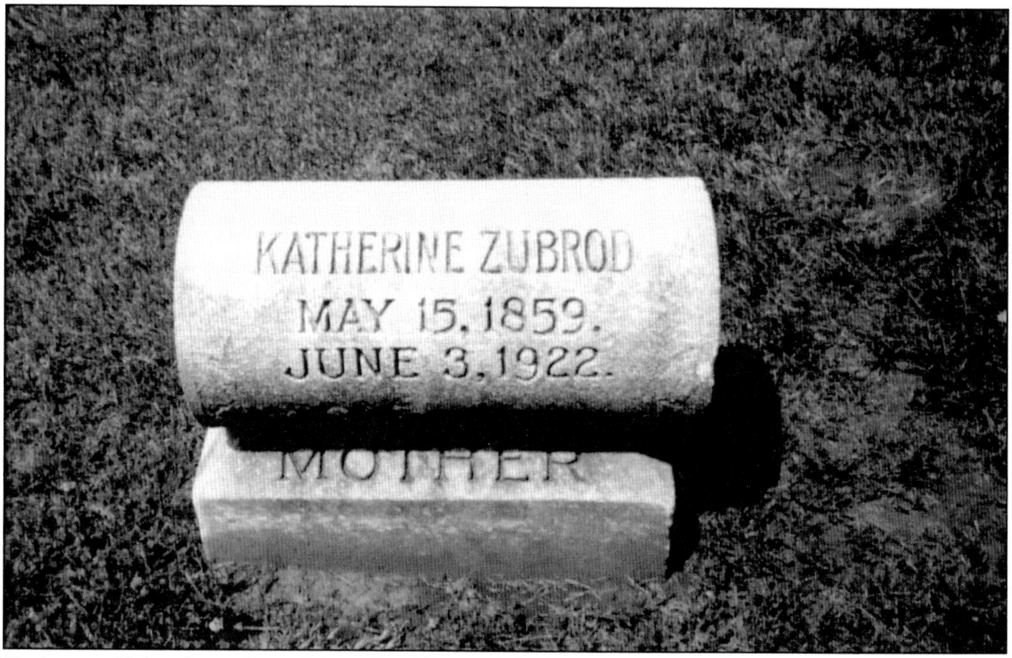

Katherine Zubrod was born May 15, 1859, and died June 3, 1922. She was the widow of John Zubrod. Her body was taken to the home of her daughter Mrs. Otto Nuber, 649 Jenkins Avenue. A daughter, a sister, and four brothers survived Katherine.

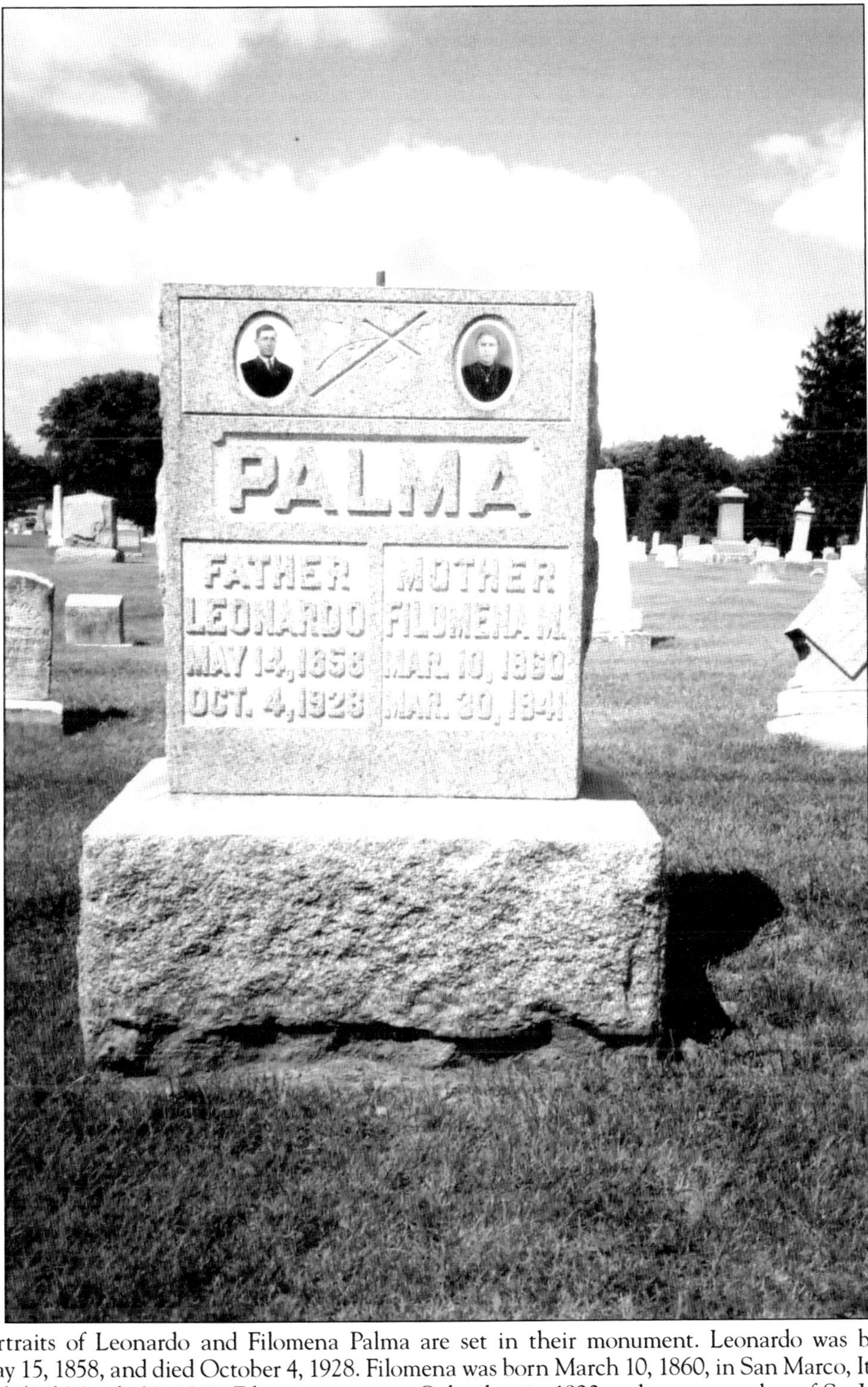

Portraits of Leonardo and Filomena Palma are set in their monument. Leonardo was born May 15, 1858, and died October 4, 1928. Filomena was born March 10, 1860, in San Marco, Italy, and died March 30, 1941. Filomena came to Columbus in 1920 and was a member of St. John the Baptist Church.

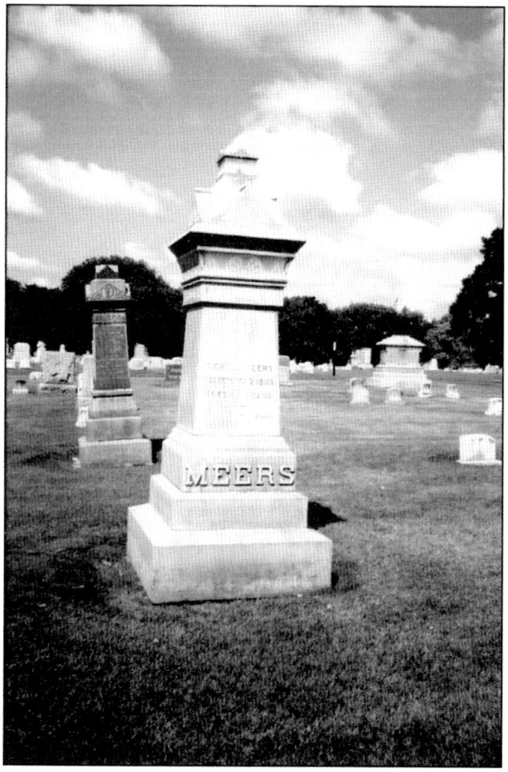

Michael Meers was born in 1813 and died October 7, 1889, at the age of 76 years in the Hawkes Hospital. Dr. W. B. Hawkes donated $10,000 and four lots on March 3, 1882, for the construction of a hospital that was to be named after its benefactor. An additional $10,000 was added before the completion of the hospital. The hospital was erected in 1886 and today is the Mount Carmel Medical Center.

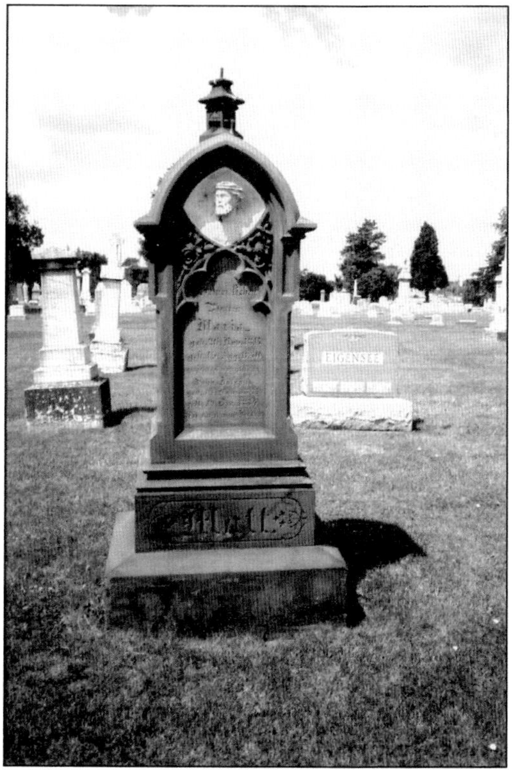

John Matt died December 19, 1874. He was a druggist and chemist. In 1873, he joined the American Pharmaceutical Association. His wife, Maria Matt, died August 13, 1870. In 1870, he was listed as a druggist at City Pharmacy, 254 South High Street, with his residence at the same address. In 1874, he was working as a druggist at the same address of 254 South High Street.

John Joyce was born July 14, 1840, in Ireland and died January 31, 1908. He was the founder of the Miller, Green and Joyce Dry Goods Company in 1866, which became the Green and Joyce Company in 1903. Green-Joyce Wholesale Dry Goods operated until 1928. He built a 21-room house for $90,000. Son Albert Green Joyce was president of the company for seven years prior to his death. (Columbus Metropolitan Library.)

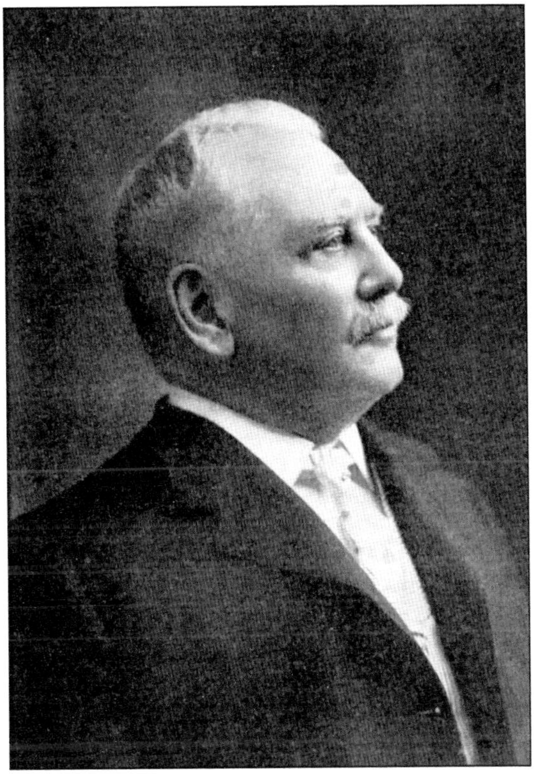

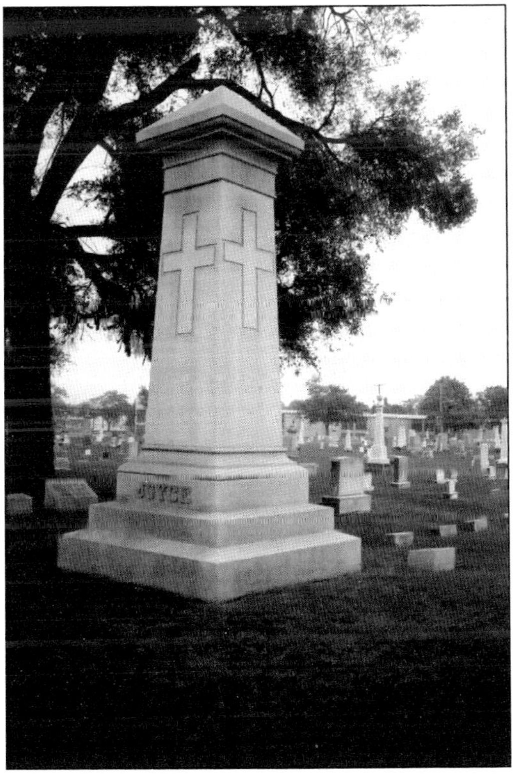

Joyce arrived in America in 1850. His wife, Eliza Joyce Needle Brun Miller Joyce, was born April 5, 1840, and died May 28, 1911. She was a descendant of John Horner, who donated the ground upon which Princeton University now stands. Her father, Thomas Miller, was one of the early Columbus bankers. She was involved with the children's hospital and was an officer in the Daughters of the American Revolution.

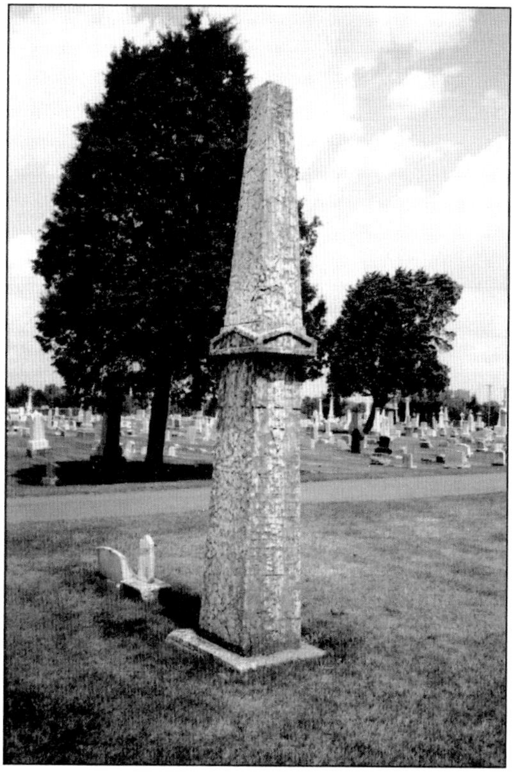

"This Monument Was Cut And Erected By Dennis Quill In memory Of His Son Simon Quill Who Was Born Near The Town of Odensburg State Of New York The 29th Day Of September 1840 And Died In Columbus The 20th Day Of July 1860," is engraved in this tombstone. The front states, "Sacred To The Memory Of Mary Quill July 8th, 1879 Aged 73 Years." An inscription on a grave marker usually includes biographical information and the epitaph.

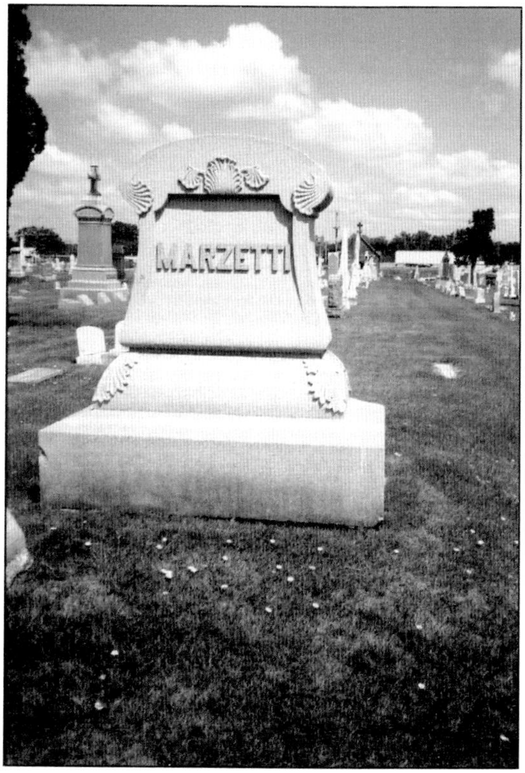

John Marzetti was born July 28, 1836, in Italy and died December 25, 1899. He had a trading boat on the Ohio River and settled in Columbus and began selling fruits and invested in real estate. Marzetti was the first Italian to settle in Columbus in June 1861. He gave the land for St. John the Baptist Church. He married Marie Simons, born in 1838 and died in 1907. Marzetti is known for manufacturing Marzetti salad dressing.

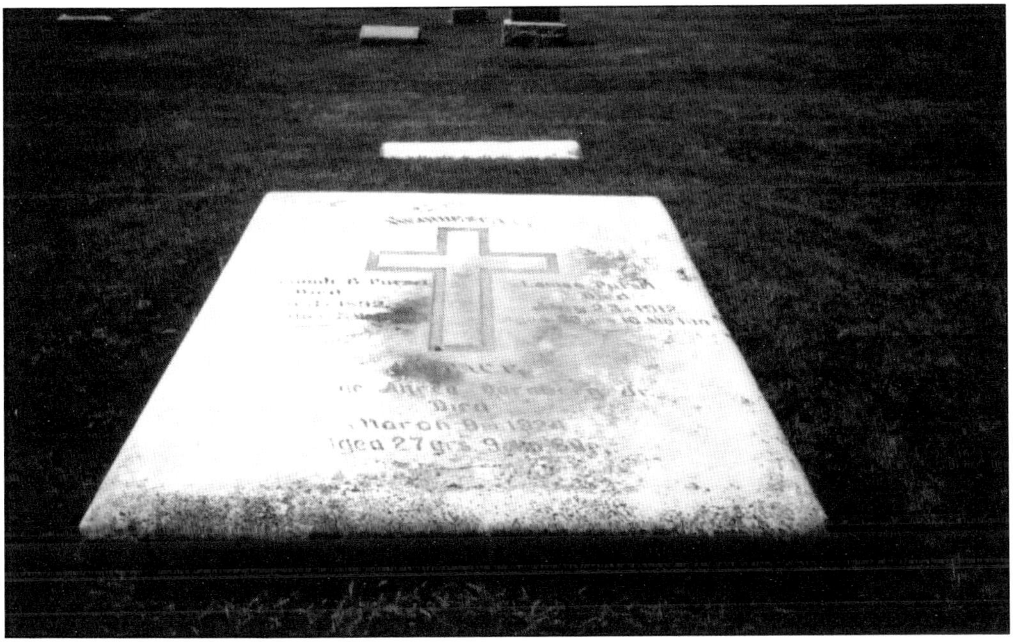

Here is the final resting place of Zephinniah Pursel, who died May 31, 1892, and Louise Pursel, who died May 23, 1912. Interred under this monument is a grandson, George Alfred Dornberg Jr., who died March 8, 1924. He was the 27-year-old son of Mr. and Mrs. G. A. Dornberg of Pittsburgh. A "ledger" stone grave marker is placed horizontally over the grave and flush with the surface of the earth.

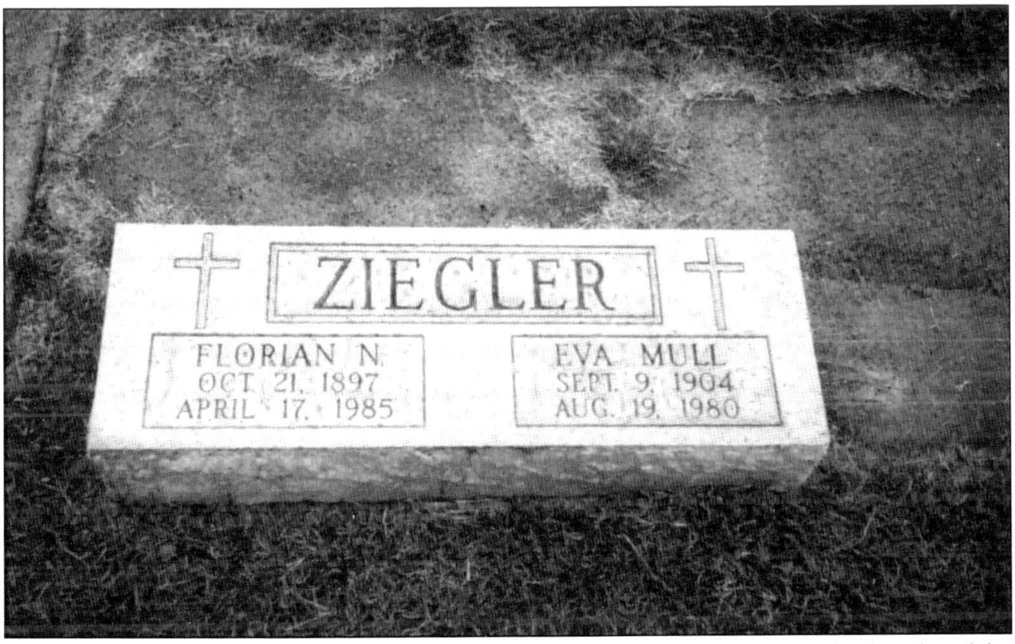

Florian N. Ziegler was born October 21, 1897, and died April 17, 1985. He was the founder of the Buckeye Letter Service in 1920 and active in the business for 65 years, serving as president and later chairman of the board. His wife, Eva Mull Ziegler, was born September 19, 1904, and died August 19, 1980.

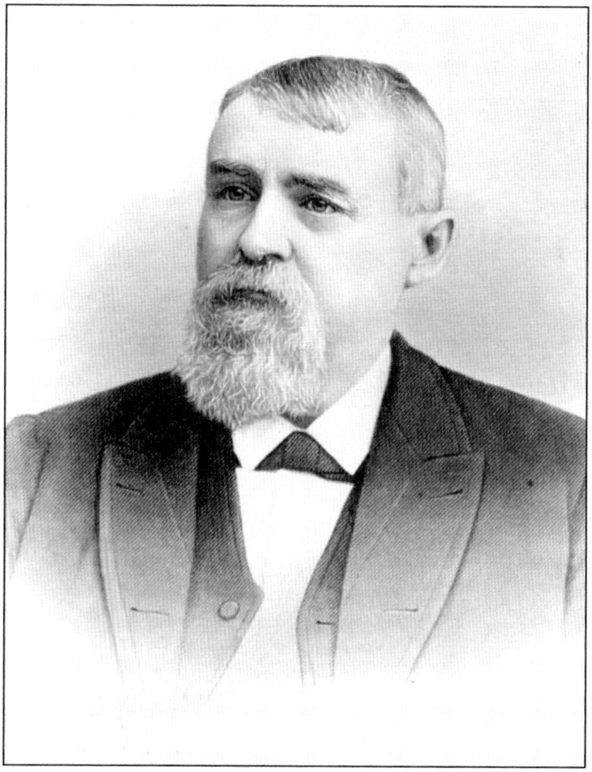

Louis Zettler was born February 1832 in Germany and died October 14, 1907. Louis was the son of Jacob Zettler, who was born in 1795 and died in 1858, and Maria Cornelia Spindler Zettler, born 1796 and died 1865. (Columbus Metropolitan Library.)

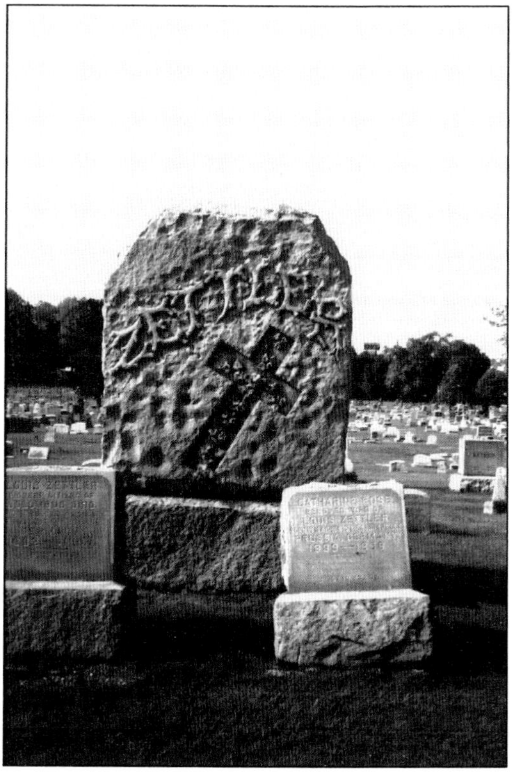

This monument reads, "Pioneer Citizen of Columbus, Ohio," and on the reverse side is chiseled, "1892." Zettler came to Columbus in 1837 and in May 1844, opened a grocery and a pork-packing business. He served as a Columbus city councilman (1871–1872) and the police commissioner (1875–1877). In 1886, with four of his sons, he established Zettler Hardware Company, the oldest hardware store still operating in Columbus.

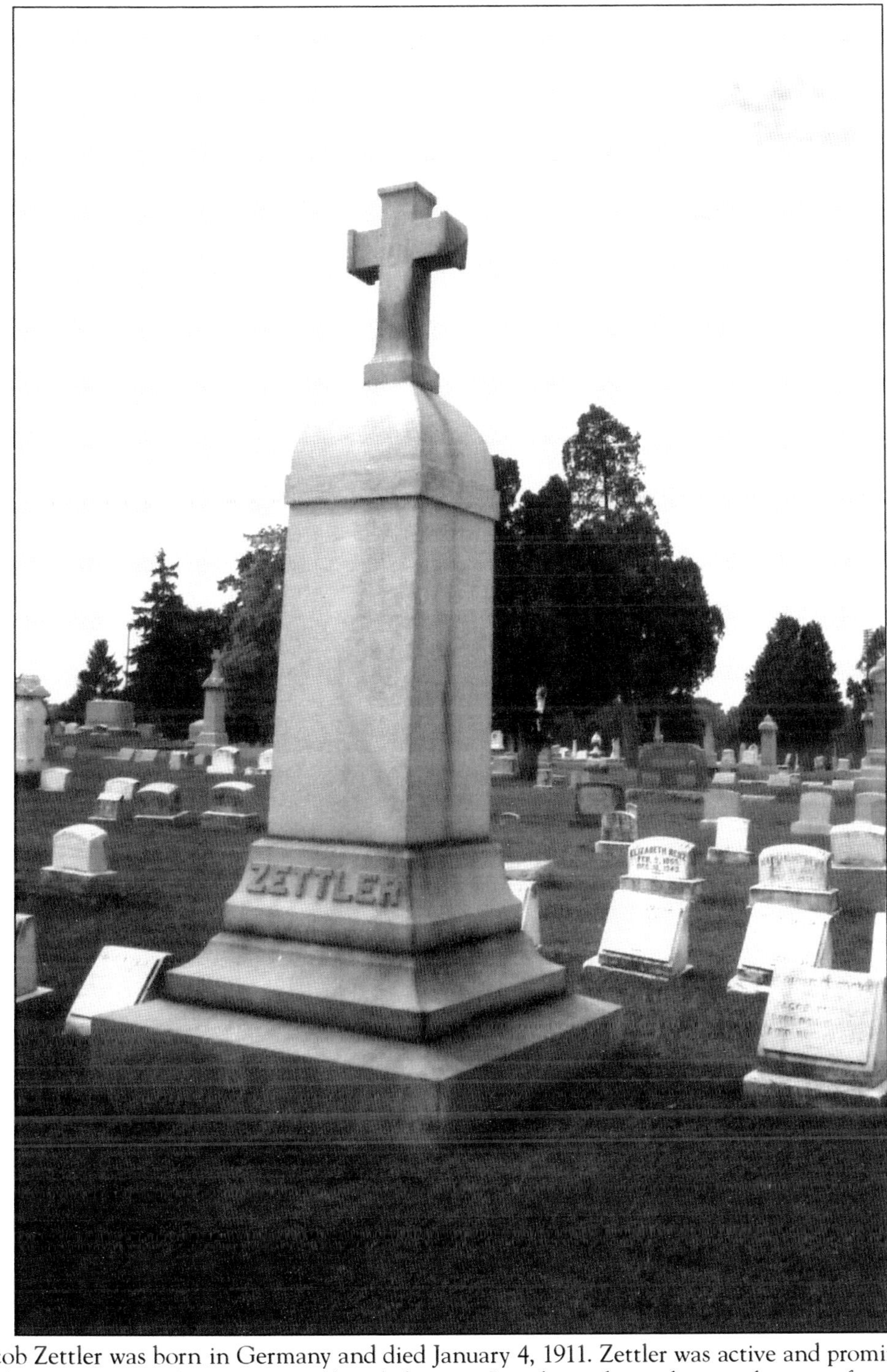

Jacob Zettler was born in Germany and died January 4, 1911. Zettler was active and prominent in businessman and was associated with his son Joseph in the real estate business for more than 40 years. With his brother Louis, he entered into the grocery business. Louise, his wife, was born December 7, 1843, and died December 23, 1892. Zettler Road was named after the Zettler family.

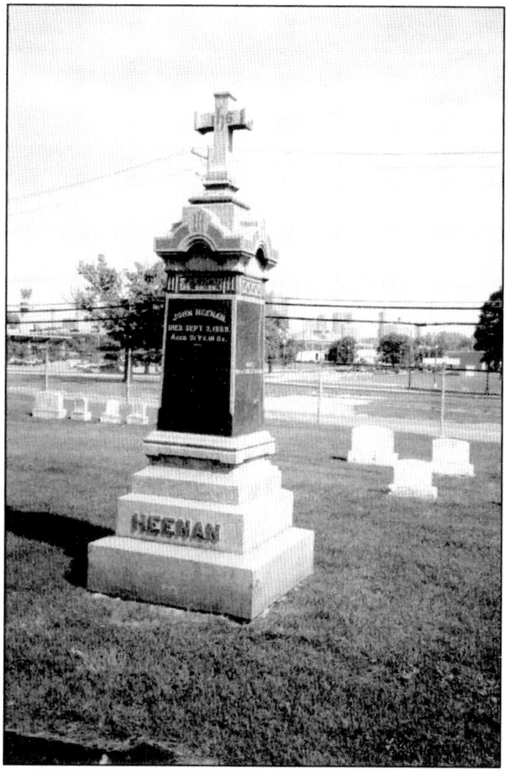

This monument marks the final resting place of the John Heenan and his family. Interred is his wife, Margaret, who died October 1, 1887. Anna Heenan died September 12, 1845, at the age of 89 years. John Heenan Sr. died September 2, 1888. Both John and Margaret were born in Ireland. John operated a grocery store on North Third Street.

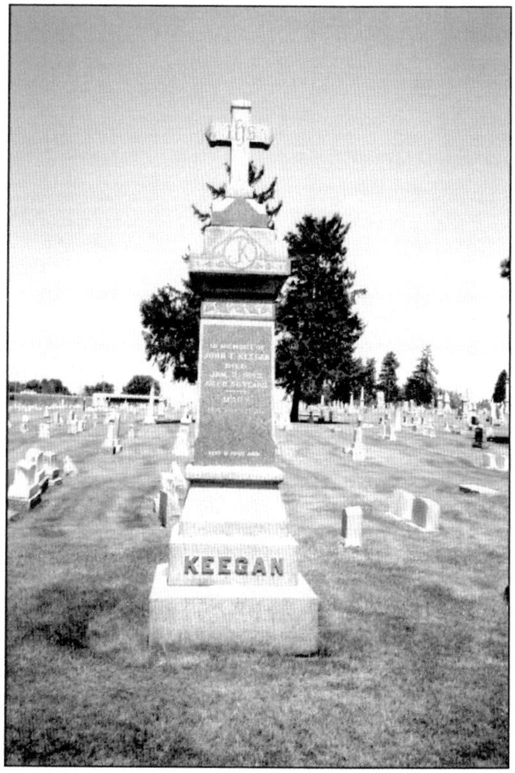

John T. Keegan died January 2, 1892, and Mary Keegan died February 23, 1926. Interred on same lot are Josie M., Ellen Broderick, and William, who was with the Griswold-Sohl Company, Carriage and Blacksmiths Hardware. John W., who was born in 1887 and died in 1944, was a stenographer in the city law department and later accept a position with a business firm. He was secretary of the board of health. Elizabeth L. died August 10, 1944.

Levi F. Swarts was born May 12, 1844, and died January 5, 1901. He served with Company K, 69th Regiment, Ohio Volunteer Infantry (OVI). The regiment took the field in Tennessee in April and guarded the railroads. In March 1864, the regiment reenlisted and went to Ohio and joined Gen. William Tecumseh Sherman's Atlanta campaign and engaged the enemy at Resaca, Pumpkin Vine Creek, Dallas, Kenesaw, Atlanta, and Jonesboro. They proceeded to Louisville and were mustered out on July 17, 1865.

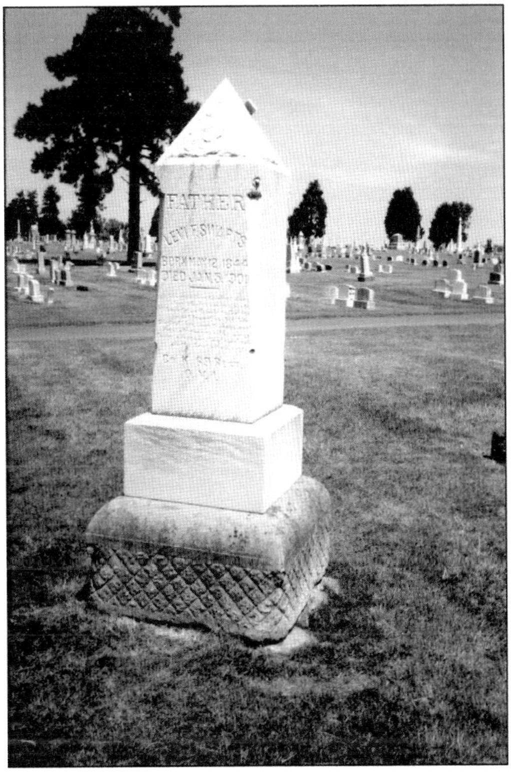

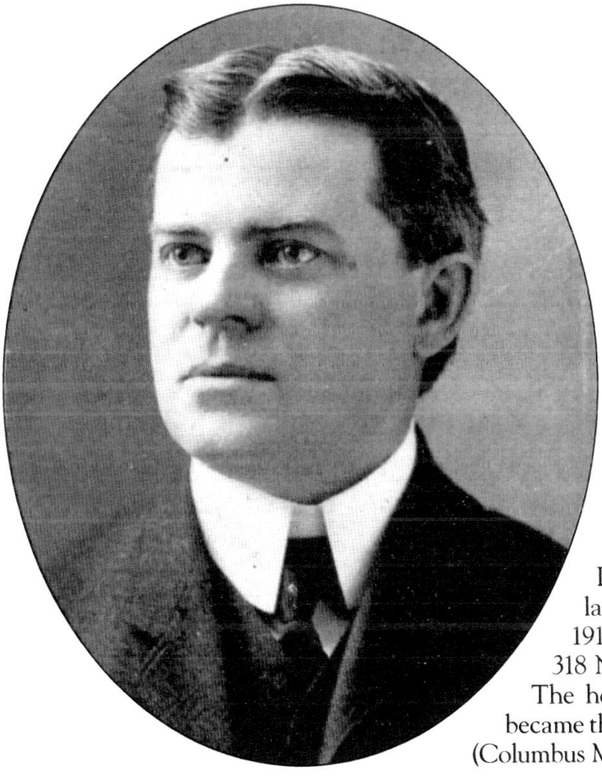

Edward J. Farley was born March 20, 1859, and died April 9, 1915. The Farleys came from Carlow, Ireland. Farley began his career in the hotel business in 1870 and was manager of Davidson Hotel from 1890 to 1908 and later the Denison Hotel from 1909 to 1912. The Davidson Hotel was located at 318 North High Street and Naghten Street. The hotel operated from 1878 to 1916, then became the Waldo Hotel, and Farley was manager. (Columbus Metropolitan Library.)

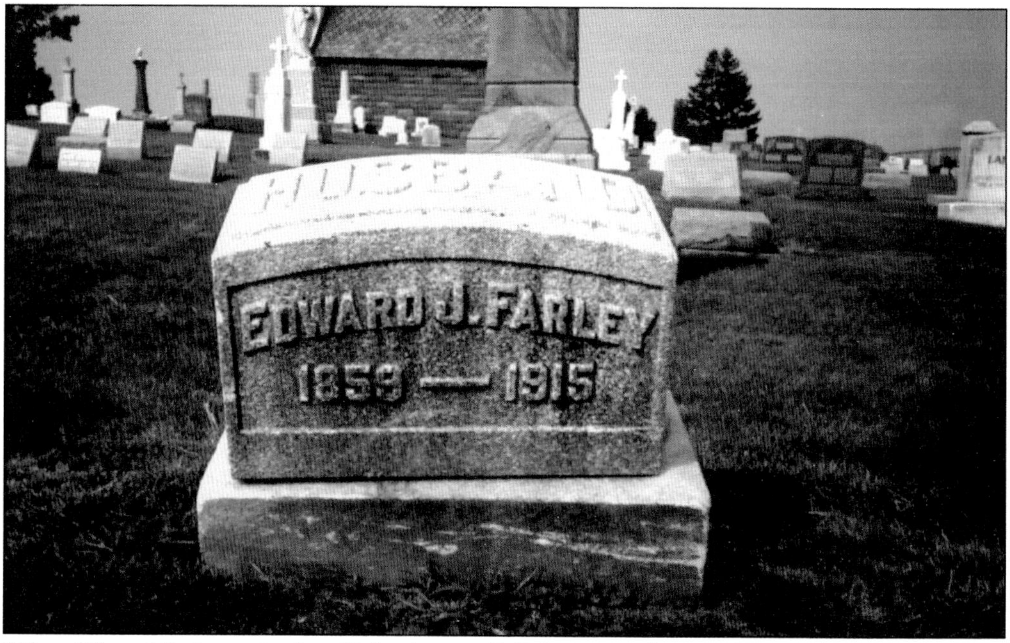

When Edward Farley arrived in Columbus in 1869, he secured a position as a bellboy in the old United States Hotel, later buying the hotel. He sold that hotel and bought the Davidson Hotel, also known as the Waldo, and later the Denison. In August 1970, demolition began on the Davidson Hotel. Farley was president of the Hound Club of Columbus and treasurer of the State Hotelmen's Association.

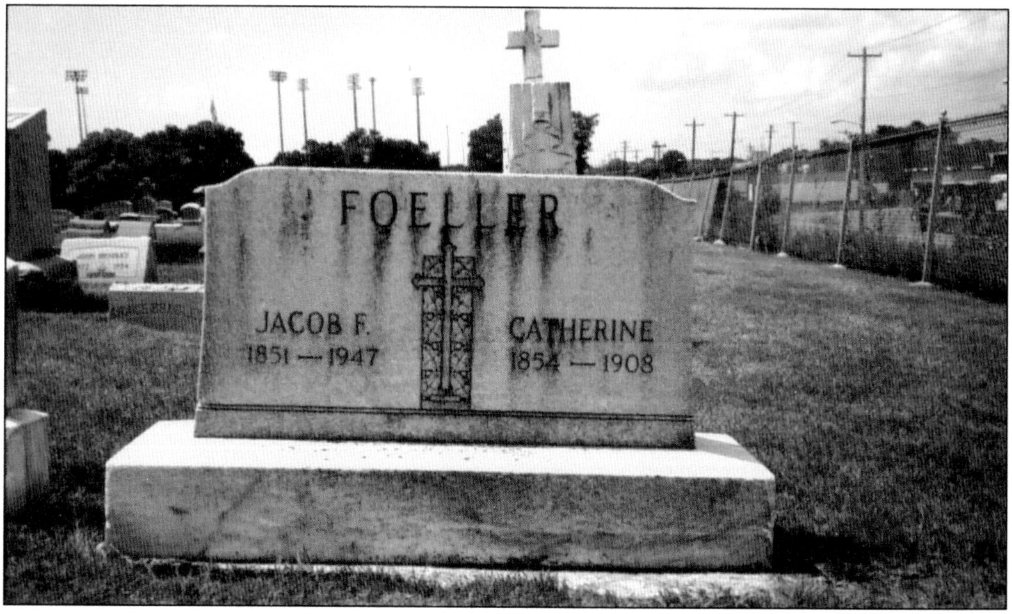

Jacob F. Foeller was born 1851 in Germany and died September 5, 1947. Foeller was associated with the Foeller Drug Company, located at Goodale and High Streets. In 1904, Letty Lally, working at the Foeller soda fountain, created what was the first "Banana Royal" sundae, made with banana slices rather than a banana split lengthwise. It is believed that Letty invented the true banana split.

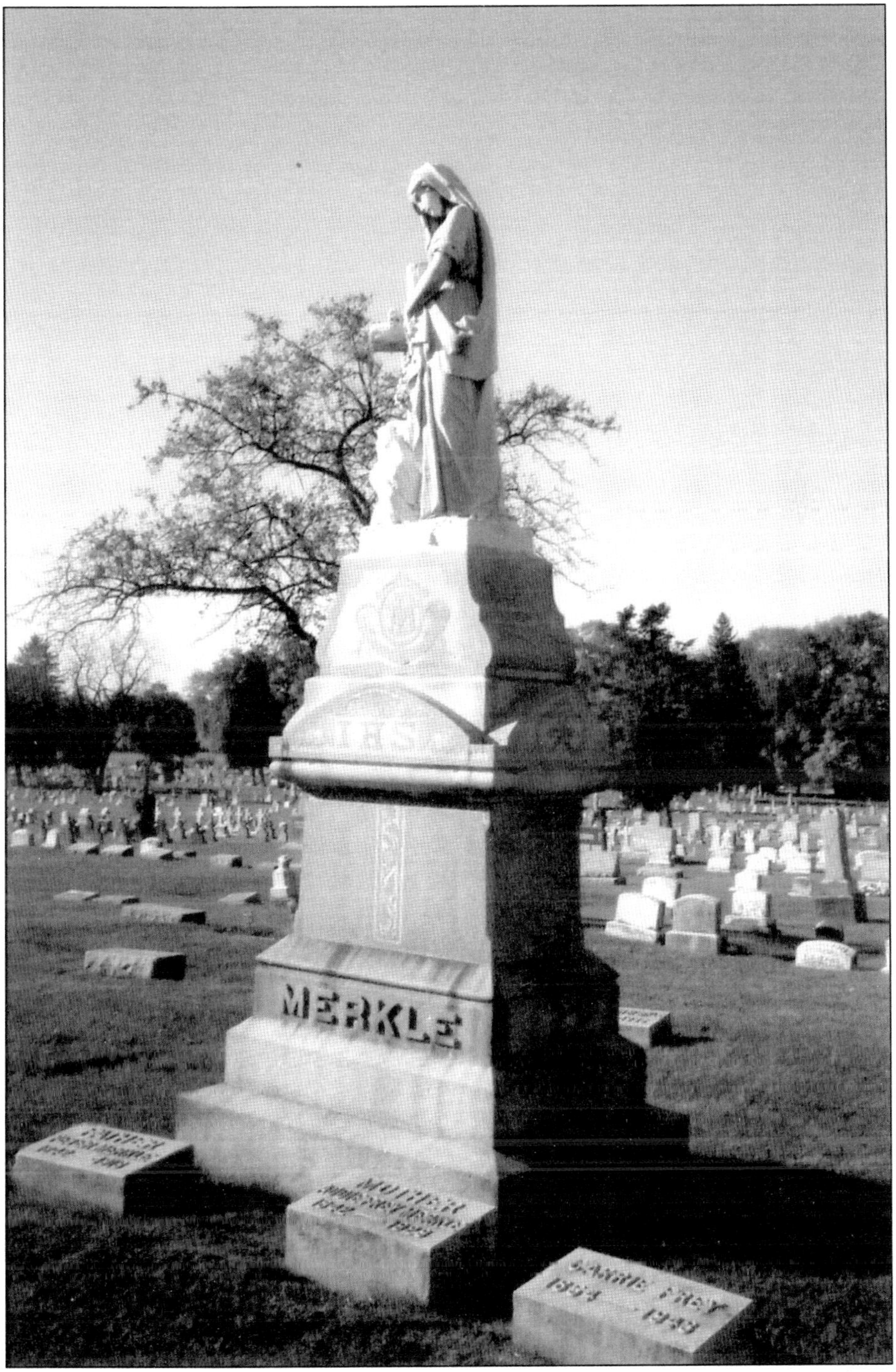

Peter Merkle was born in 1842 and died August 26, 1913. He entered the restaurant business, and purchased the Union Station Restaurant in Columbus. He established restaurants in Chicago, Toledo, Indianapolis, Dennison, and Richmond, Indiana. He held financial interests in the Columbus Railway-Light Company and the New First National Bank. His wife, Adelaide (Addie) Fredy Merkle, was born 1842 and died September 15, 1929.

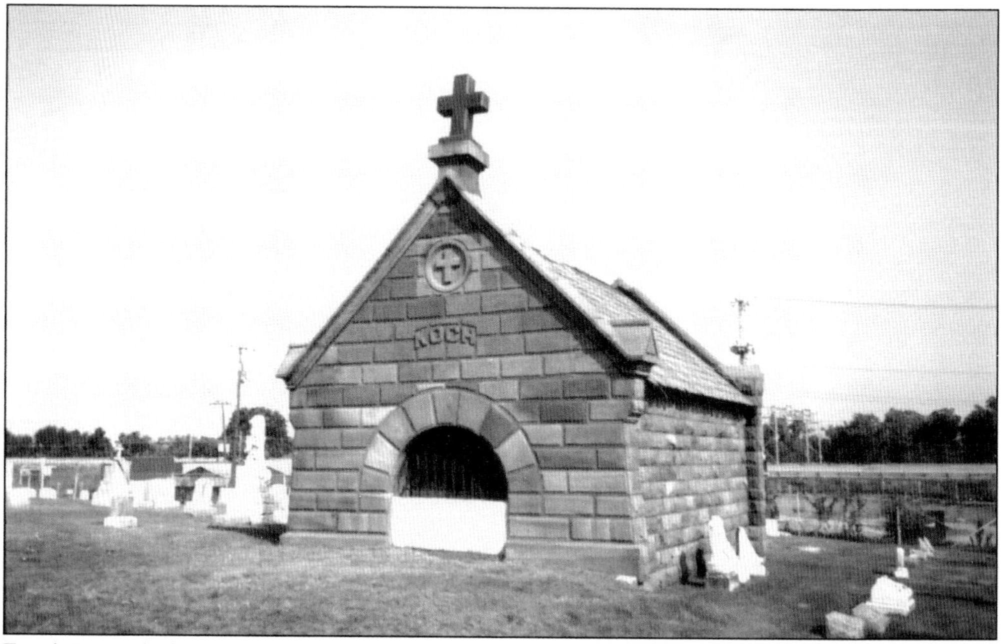

Frank B. Koch died on July 14, 1925. Aboveground entombment was an option reserved for the wealthy and prominent. Interred in the Koch mausoleum are Frank, his wife, Emma, who died August 3, 1902, and their children, Herbert, Jacobine, Josephine, Katherine, Marie, P. M., Peter, Thomas William, and Catherine. Interred at the east side of the mausoleum in earth burial are two other children, Frank Charles and Herbert Walter.

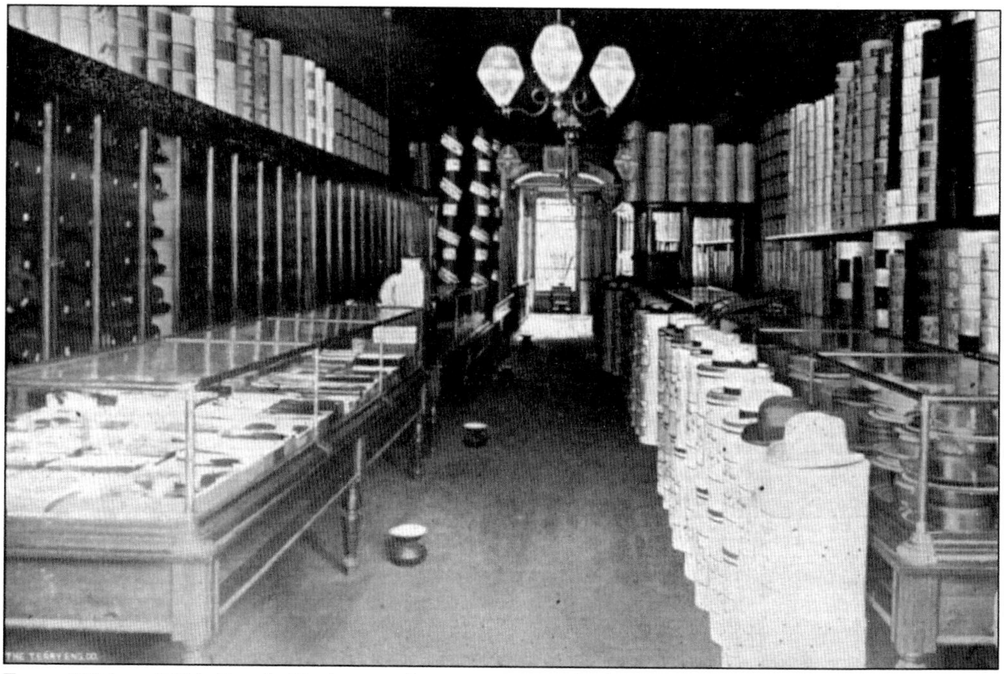

From 1904 to 1914, Frank Koch was the proprietor of a hat store located at 280 North High Street. He was a member of the Knights of Columbus and the Elks Lodge. (Columbus Metropolitan Library.)

The open column monument symbolism "Noble Life" is pictured here. This monument is the final resting place for John Murphy, who died July 9, 1884, at the age of 52 and his wife, Anna, who died July 25, 1885, at the age of 48.

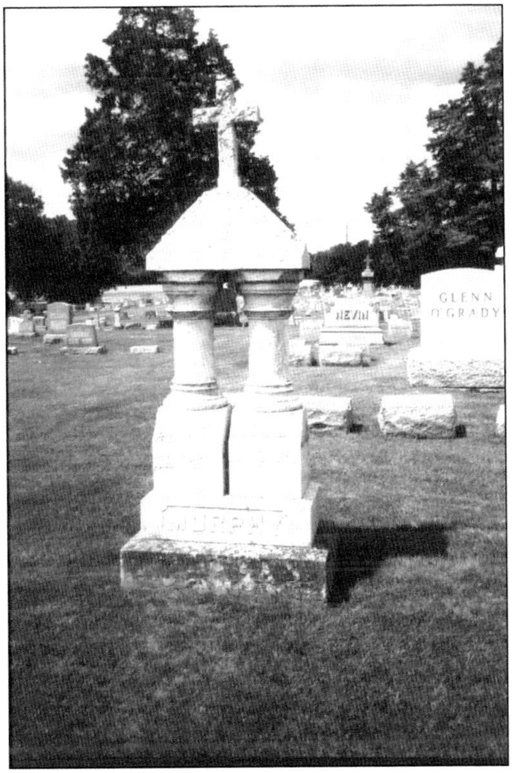

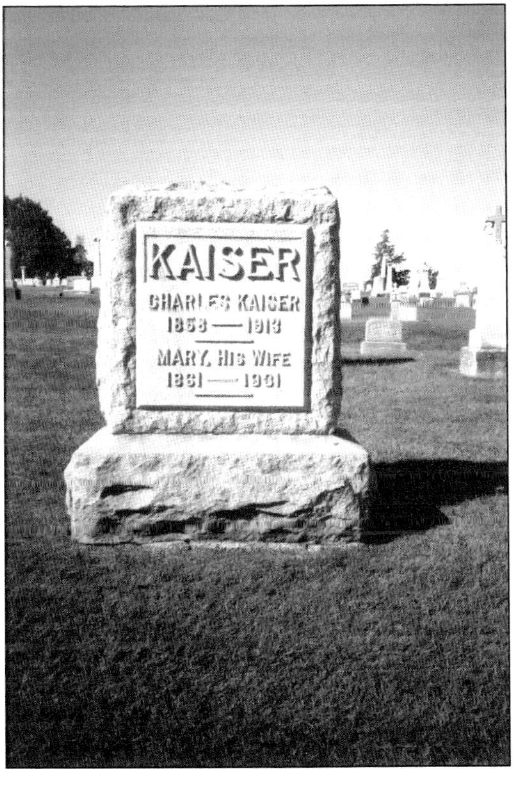

Charles Kaiser was born in 1858 and died August 9, 1913. For 25 years, he was a drum major for the Columbus Battalion Band. He was a former plaster contractor and a director in the Franklin Brewing Company and later became a director in the Pastime Amusement Company, owners of the Pastime and Hippodrome Theaters on High Street. His wife, Mary Kaiser, died November 18, 1931.

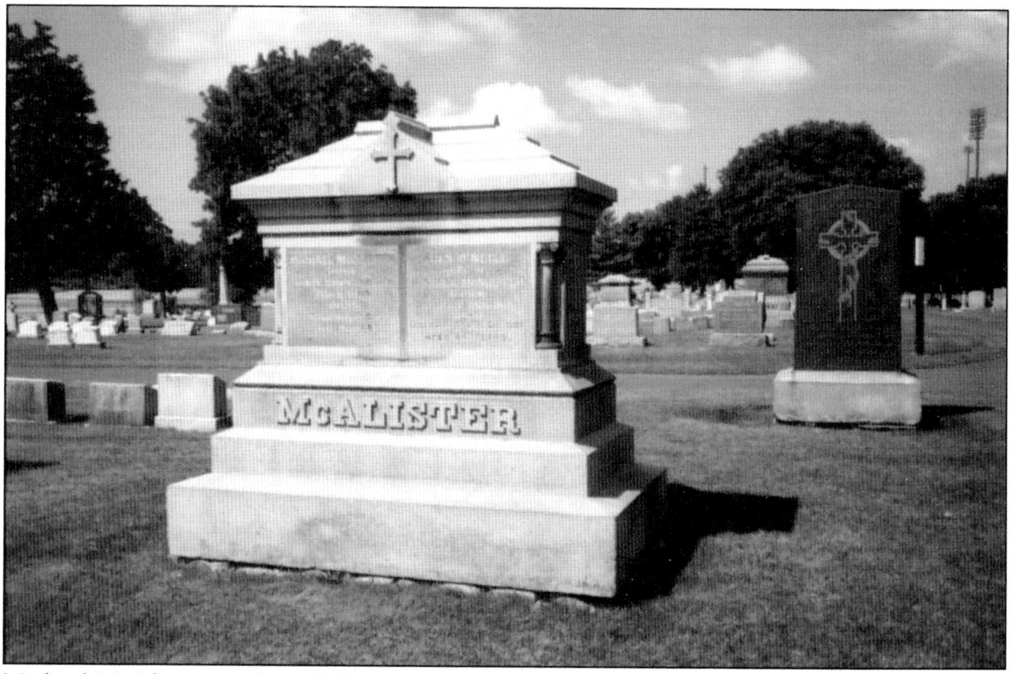

Michael McAlister was born February 1, 1809, in County Down, Ireland, and died August 9, 1886, in Columbus. McAlister was a frequent contributor of articles of intense interest and value to the press and was author of an abridged history of his native Ireland. Ann O'Neil McAlister, wife of Michael, was born in Belfast, Ireland, and died in Columbus on August 28, 1888.

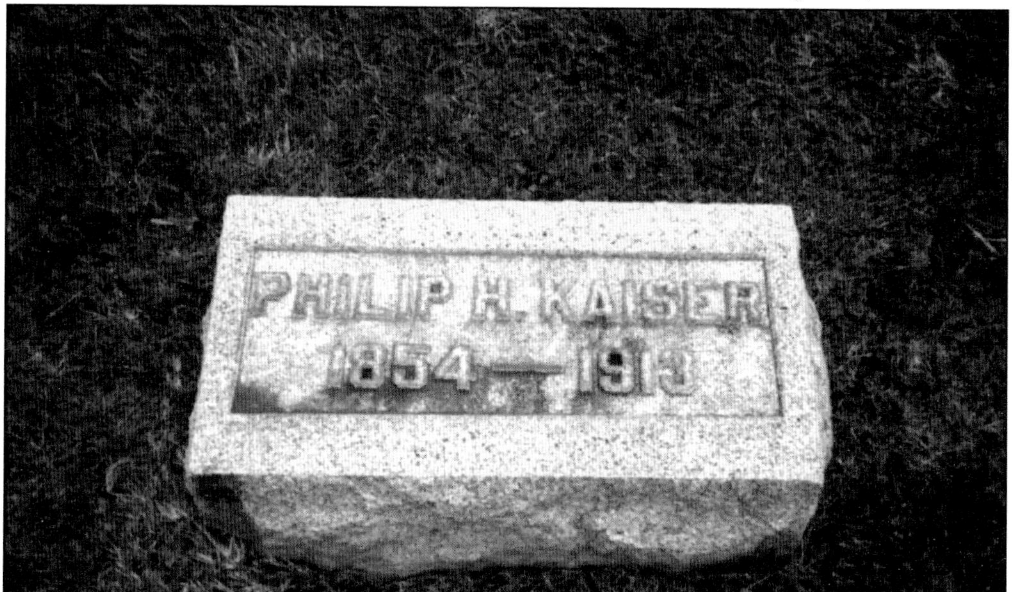

Philip H. Kaiser, for 25 years the head of the wholesale firm of liquor dealers Philip H. Kaiser and Company, died February 16, 1913. His wife, Rosina Koebel Kaiser, died November 12, 1945. Prior to 1918, there was a Kaiser Street in German Village, which was later changed by city council to Gear Street. It is not known if Kaiser Street was named for this family.

Anton Ruhl was born October 11, 1832, in Germany and died September 3, 1886. He was one of the oldest citizens and a member of the firm of Ruhl, Corbett and Company. He entered the employment of Peter Ambos and remained there until the time of his death and owned 90 acres. His wife, Caroline Ruhl, was born in 1836 and died in 1872. Ruhl Avenue is named after Anton, and Caroline Avenue was named for his wife.

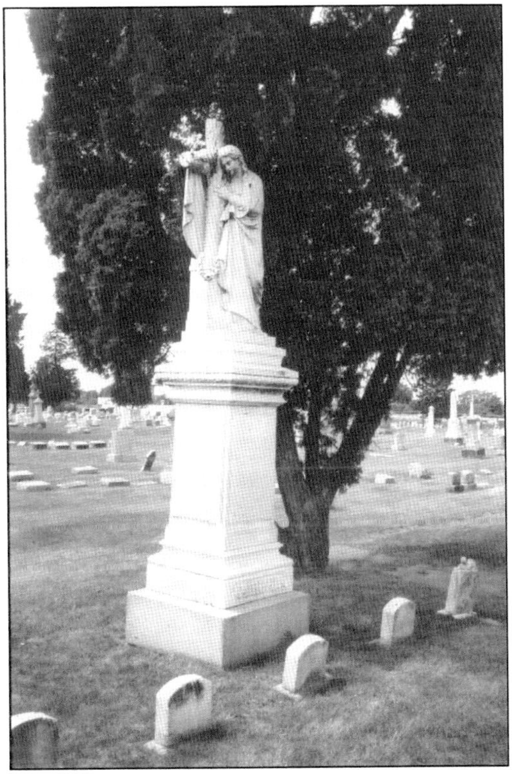

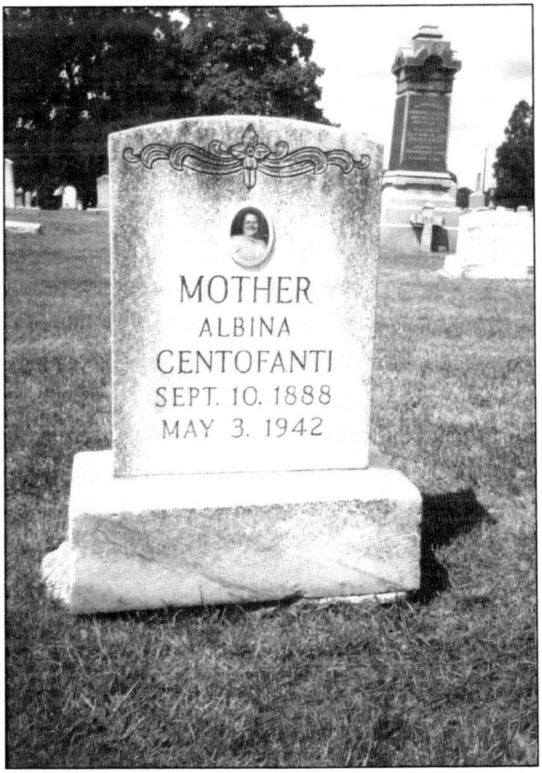

"Mother" Albina Centofanti was born September 10, 1888, and died May 3, 1942. Centofanti was the wife of Dominic Centofanti, and she was a member of Holy Rosary and Mother of Sorrows congregations of St. John the Baptist Church; the auxiliary of Introdacquese Society; and Foggia Benevento Society. Her porcelain portrait has been inserted into her monument.

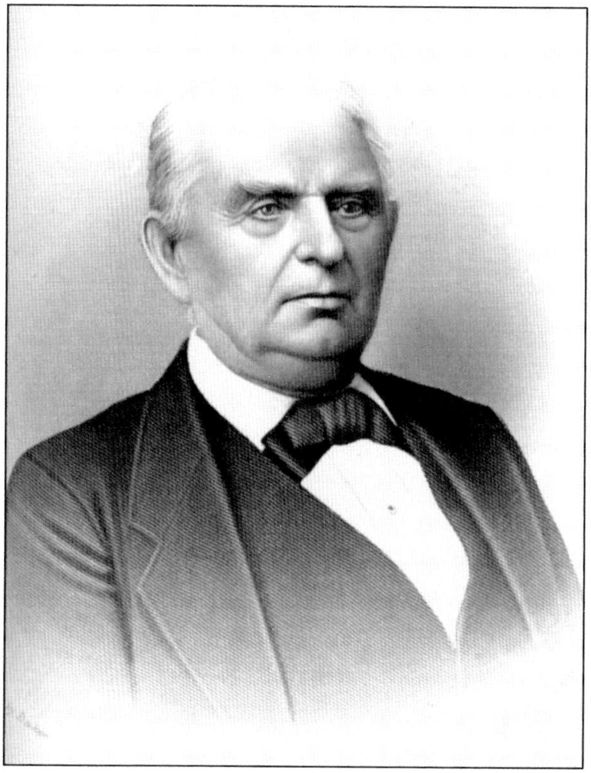

Jacob Reinhard Sr. was born April 28, 1815, in Germany and died October 13, 1893. He was the son of Michael (1788–1879) and Barbara Geis Reinhard. (Columbus Metropolitan Library.)

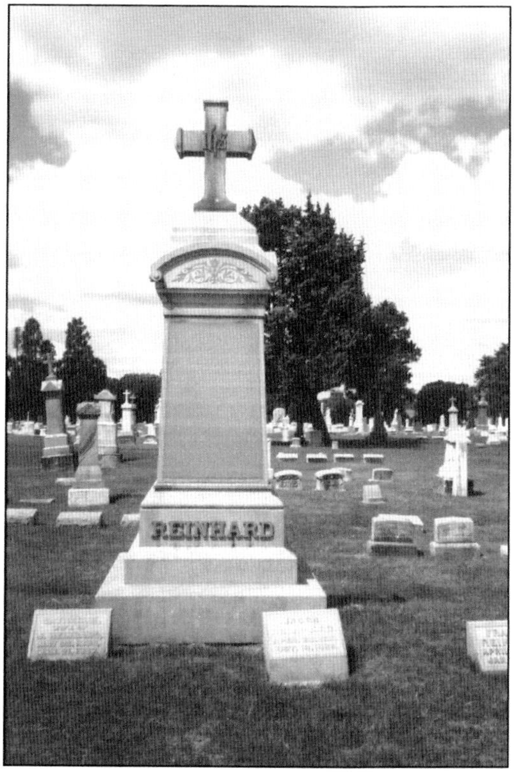

Jacob came to Columbus in 1836 as a contractor for the national road. He founded the *Westbote* newspaper in 1843 and was a Columbus city councilman from 1853 to 1872 and founded the bank of Miller, Reinhard Feiser in 1868. His wife Catherine Reinhard was born May 25, 1823, and died March 21, 1887. Reinhard Avenue was named after Jacob.

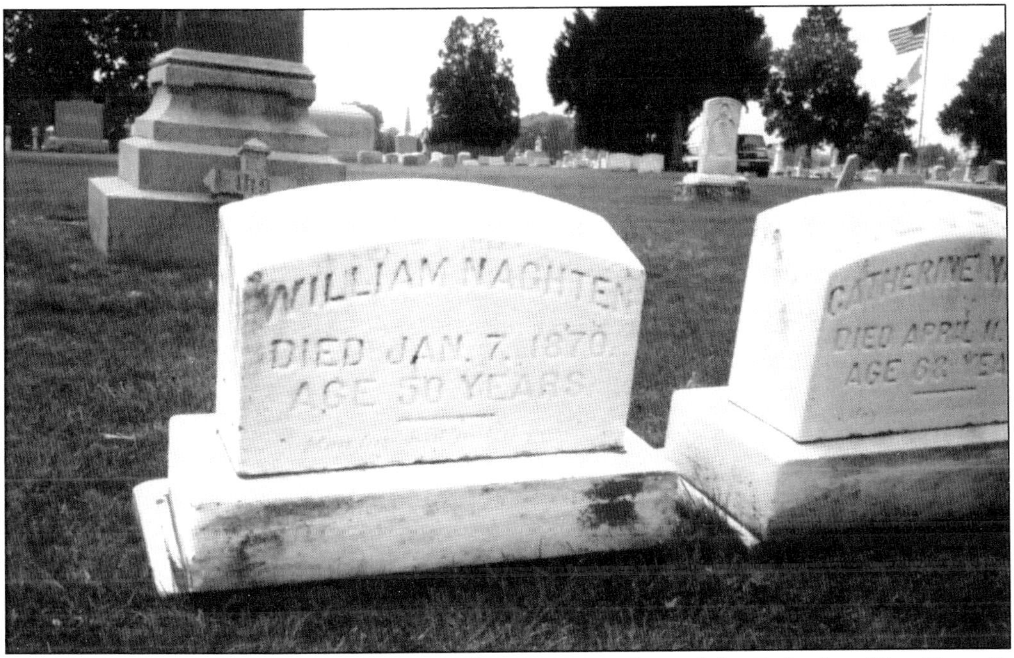

William Naghten died January 8, 1870. Naghten was president of the Columbus City Council. Naghten came to America in 1849 and located in the city of Columbus. In 1853, he was employed with the Piqua Railroad Company and remained with them until his sudden death. At one time, he served as timekeeper in the CC&IO Railroad shops. His son William A. Naghten died March 27, 1922.

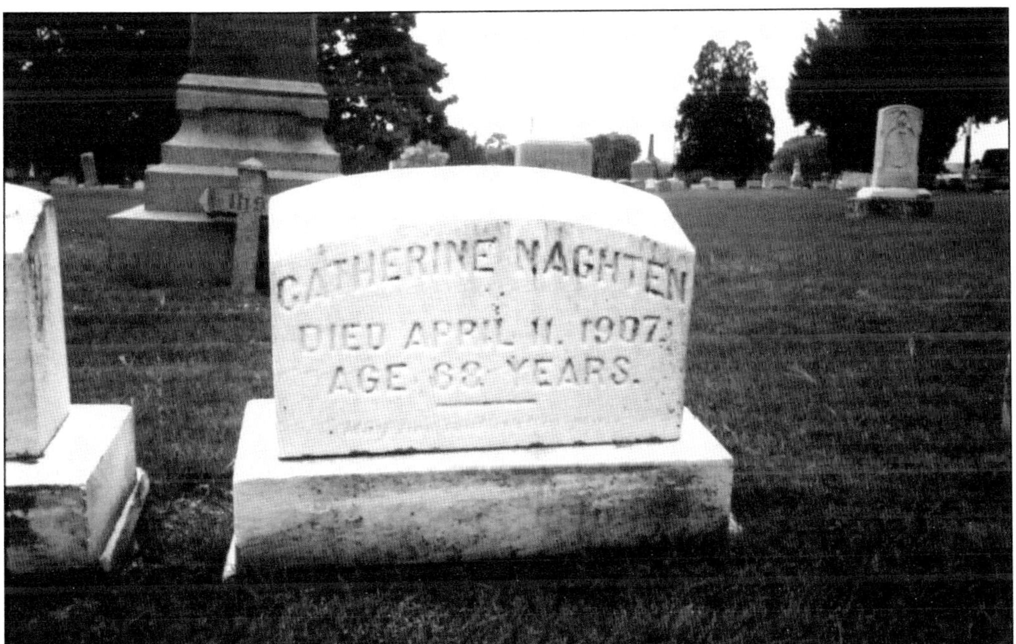

William's wife Catherine died April 11, 1907, at age 68 years. Her monument reads, "May She Rest In Peace." Naghten Street is named after her husband, William Naghten.

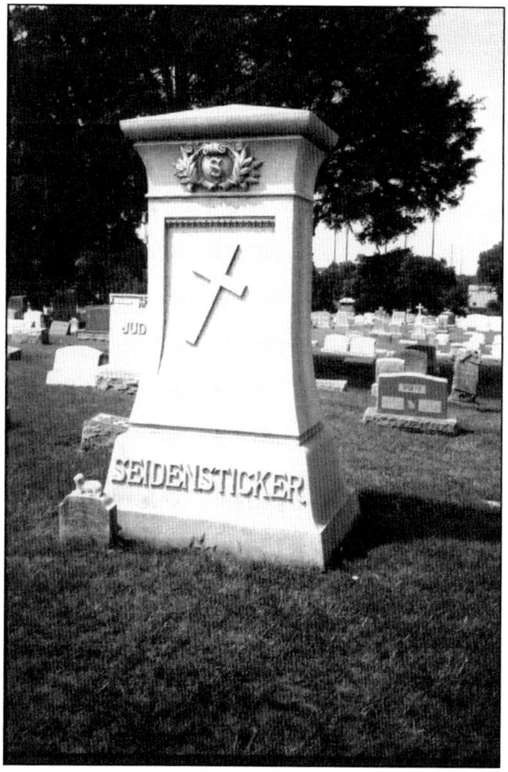

William Seidensticker was born in 1853 in Columbus and died in 1924. Seidensticker operated a dry good store at Fourth and Main Streets, under the firm name of L. Seidensticker and Brother, founded in February 16, 1882. In 1924, the company name was changed to Seidensticker Dry Goods Company. Seidensticker retired four years prior to his death. His wife, Elizabeth Seidensticker, was born in 1856 and died in 1912.

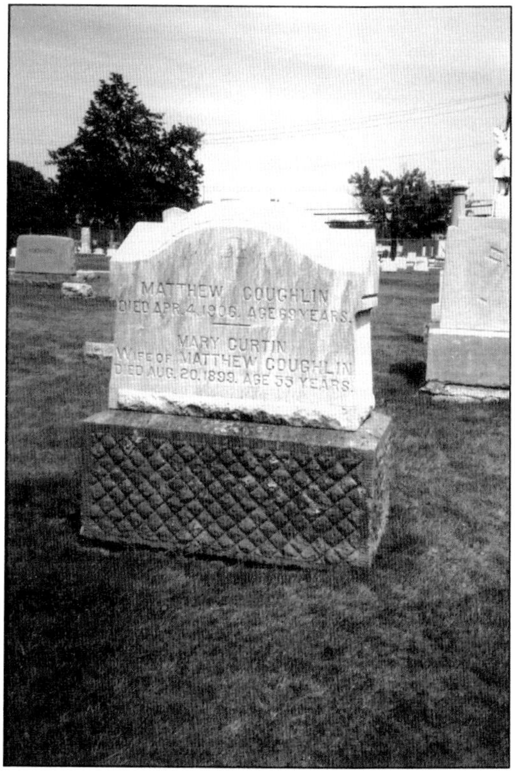

Matthew Coughlin died April 4, 1906, at the age of 69 years, at his residence on Mount Vernon Avenue. His funeral was from St. Patrick's Catholic Church. His wife, Mary Curtin Coughlin, died August 20, 1899, at the age of 55 years.

Samuel Borger was born September 15, 1854, and died September 17, 1905. He was the son of Peter Borger, founder of the Borger Brothers Boiler Works, who were manufacturers and repaired steam boilers. In 1849, his parents were among the first settlers of the west side of Columbus. (Columbus Metropolitan Library.)

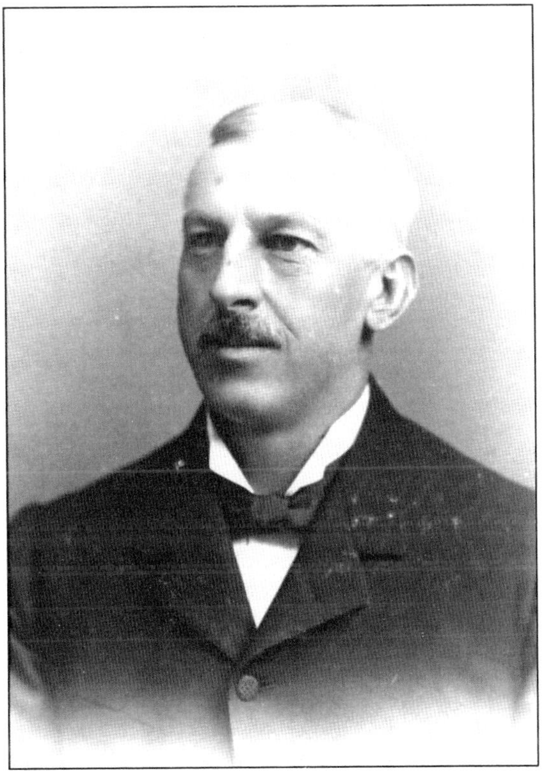

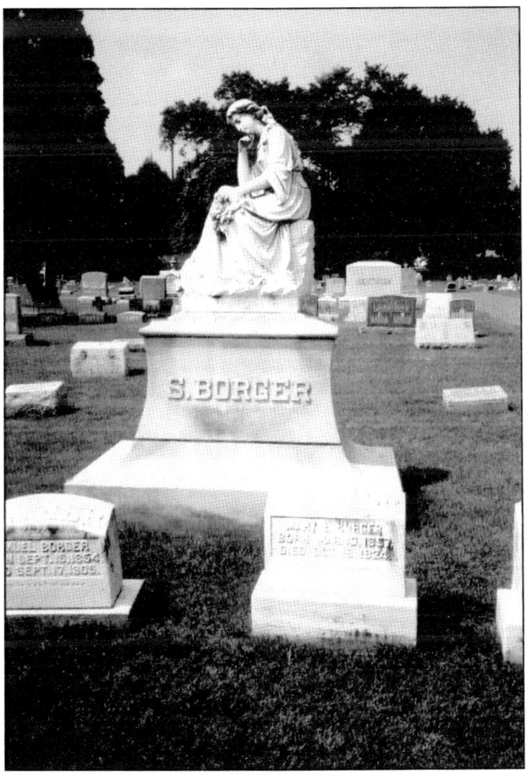

Samuel was a trustee of the Columbus Metropolitan Public Library and president of the Borger Company. He was treasurer of the Hanover Pressed Brick Company and director of the West Side Dime Savings Bank Company and the West Side Building and Loan Association. His wife, Mary E. Borger, was born in 1857 and died October 16, 1924. She served as president of the Borger Brothers Boiler Works. The works operated from 1852 to 1970.

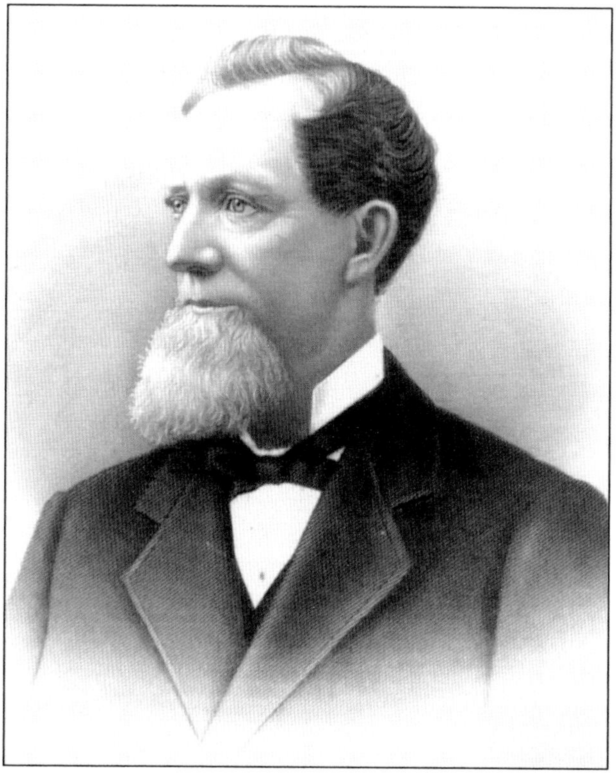

Patrick A. Egan was born September 14, 1820, in Ireland and died October 12, 1890. P. A. Egan Undertaking and Livery was a "Dealer in all kinds of burial cases and all styles of coffins." Later it became Egan Ryan Funeral Service. In 1869, Egan was a Franklin County Coroner. (Columbus Metropolitan Library.)

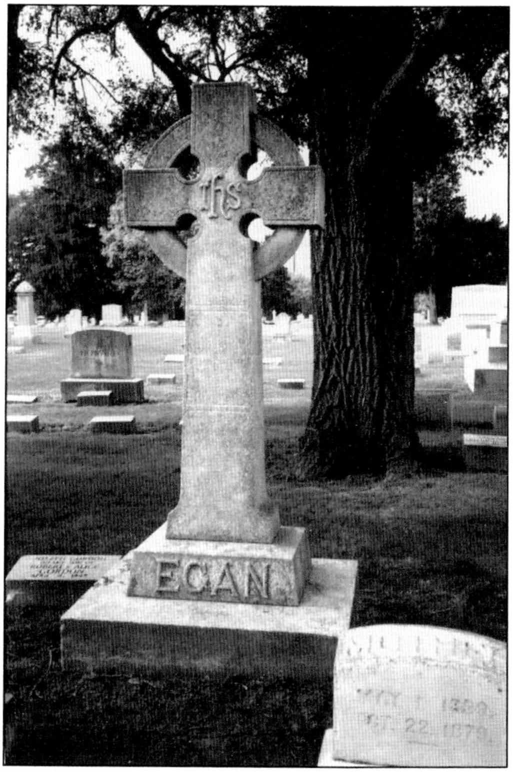

Egan arrived in Columbus in 1852. He went to work with Huntington Fitch and later was an attendant in the Central Insane Asylum until 1855, when he traveled to California. In 1859, he established P. A. Egan Undertaking and Livery and began a tradition that continues today. He married Mary Ryan, daughter of Timothy and Nancy A. Ryan. Mary died October 22, 1879.

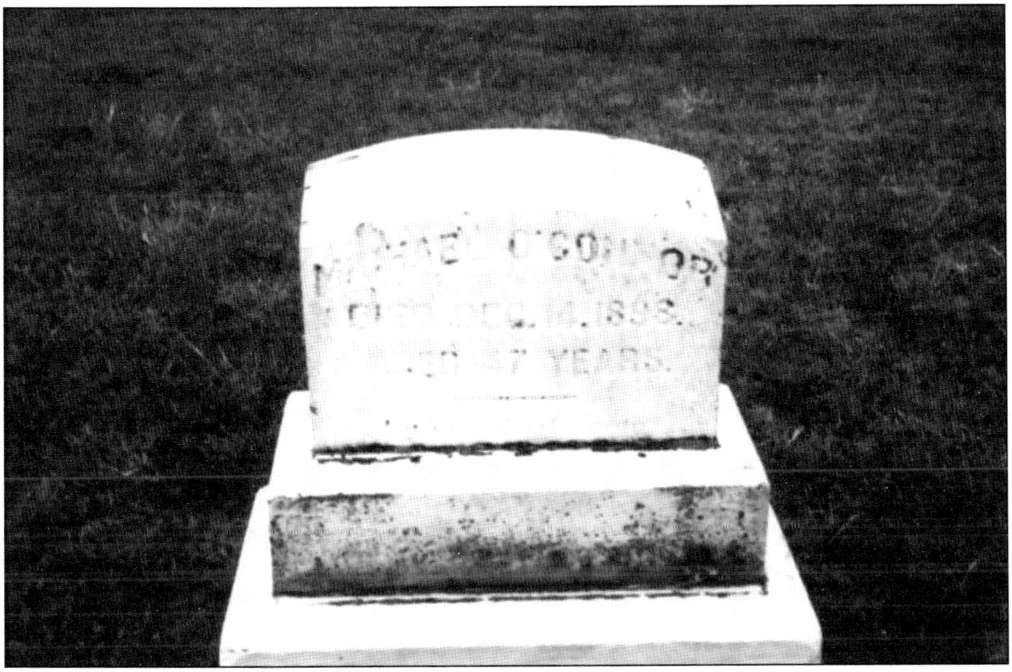

Michael Joseph O'Conner died December 14, 1898. O'Conner was an employee of the PanHandle Railroad Company and was killed in an accident that occurred on the yards of the Little Miami Railroad. Found on his body was an envelope containing a printed poem by Margaret E. Sangster. For years, he was supervisor of track in Columbus yards and knew every foot of ground as no other man.

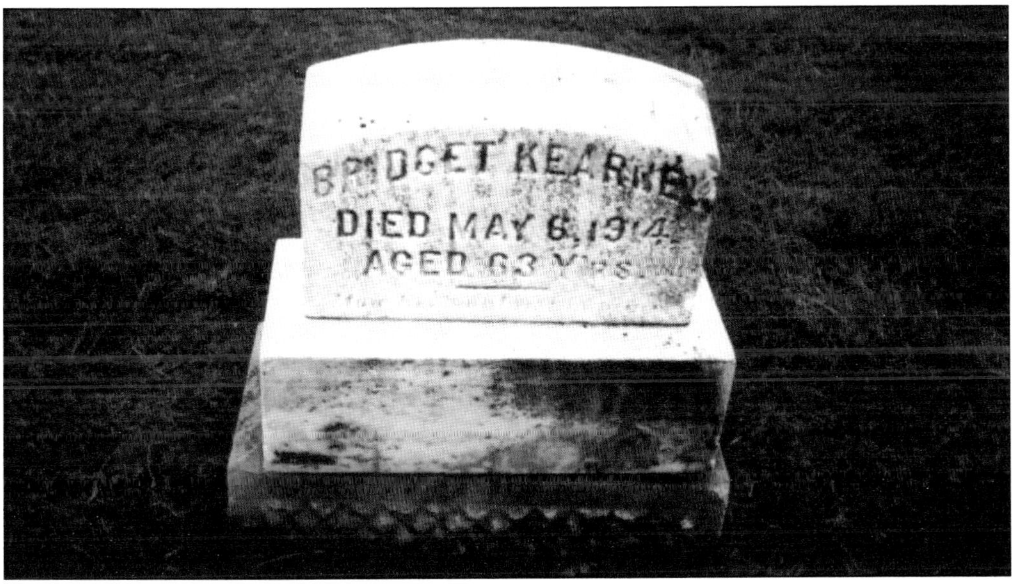

In 1913, grocer James M. Kearney drove his grocery wagon into the waters of the Olentangy River to wash it off. The force of the water swept over the wagon and Kearney. The dead horse and sections of the wagon were recovered, but no trace of Kearney. Kearney operated a grocery store at Sullivan and Central Avenues. Kearney purchased six grave lots in 1882 for $25. His wife, Bridget Kearney, died May 6, 1914.

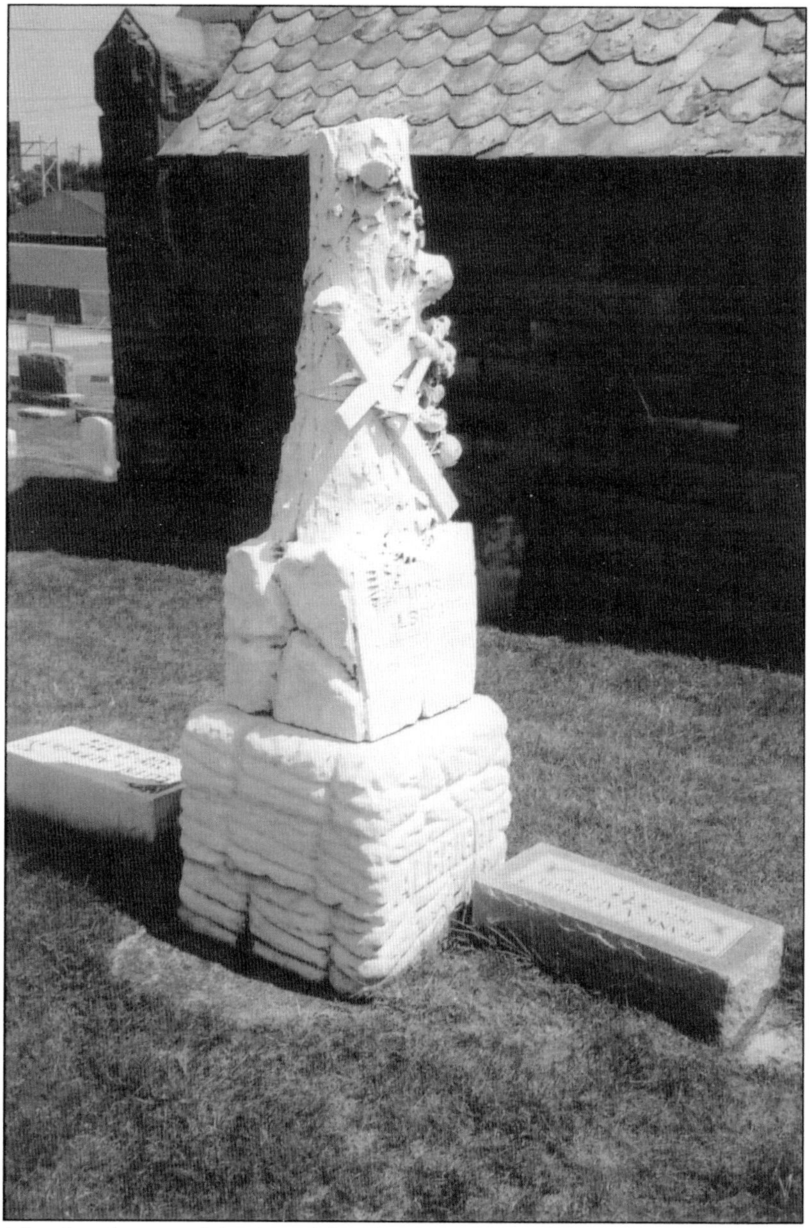

Jacob H. Albright, the son of Andrew Albright, a pioneer wagon maker, was born February 28, 1848, in Ohio and died February 26, 1894. Albright was determined to become a soldier during the Civil War but was rejected. In 1862, he and a friend joined a wagon train and traveled to Pittsburg Landing, Tennessee, a few days after the battle. He returned to Columbus, and with his parents' final consent, Albright enlisted in Company I, 133rd Regiment, OVI. In August, the regiment was mustered out and then reenlisted on October 2. He was then assigned to Company E, 182nd Regiment, OVI, and served until the close of the war, being mustered out at Camp Chase on July 14, 1865. He participated in the battle of Nashville and other engagements in Tennessee. In 1870, he entered the employment of the Columbus Machine Company and was later a subcontractor on the Toledo branch of the Columbus, Hocking Valley and Toledo Railway. His wife, Ellen, was born August 15, 1848, died August 16, 1928.

Celestino Pignatelli, shown in his porcelain portrait that is inserted into his monument, was born December 8, 1900, and died January 18, 1936. His epitaph reads "Rest In Peace." The symbol "IHS" appears above his portrait.

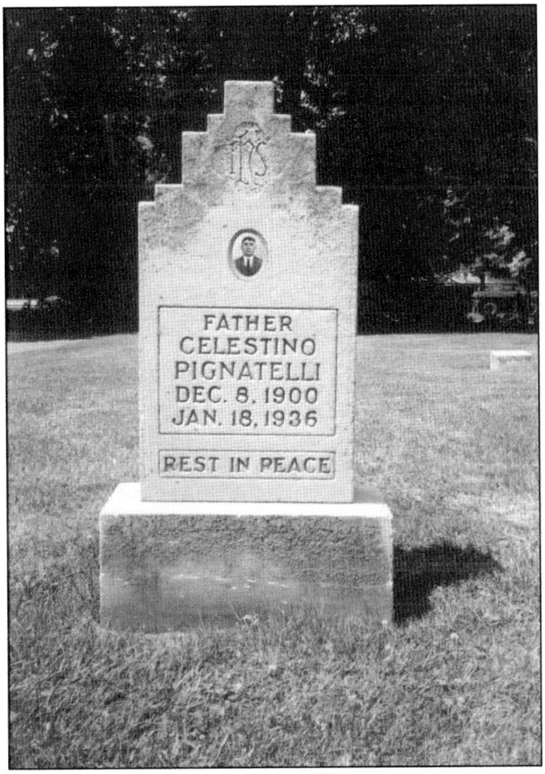

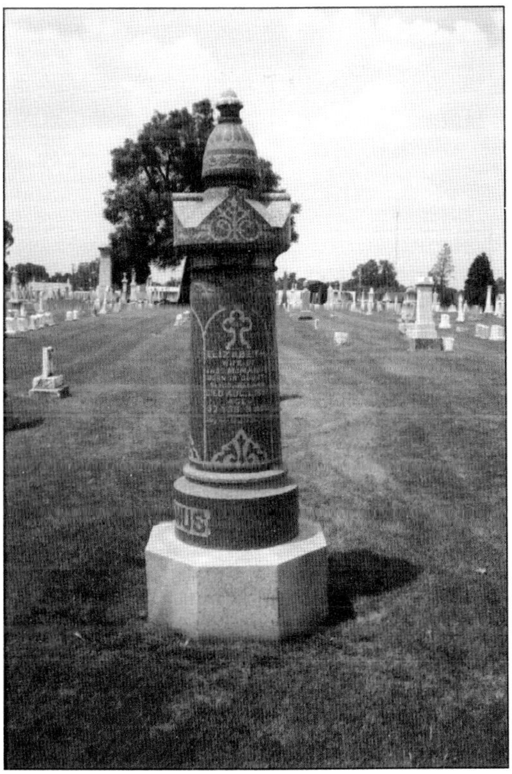

Thomas McManus died November 9, 1900, at his farm in Chatham, Virginia. For more than 20 years, he was a member of the Columbus police force. Columbus City Directory for 1890–1891 lists McManus as living at 115 East Goodale. He was the father of Capt. Jeremiah D. McManus of Engine Company No. 6. His wife, Elizabeth McManus, died August 1, 1892.

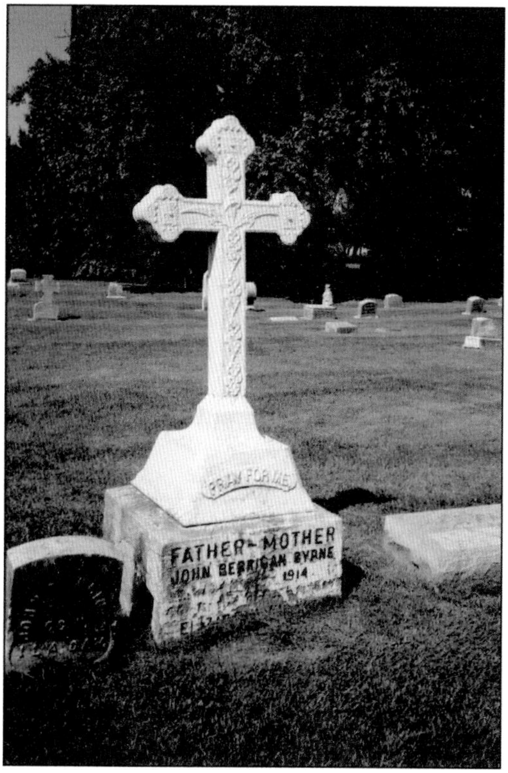

John Byrne died in 1914; his wife, Elizabeth, died in 1929. Metal monuments such as this were cast from pure zinc, forming a coating of zinc carbonate. When exposed, it is rust resistant, and the monuments take on a bluish-gray color that is a result of the zinc carbonate. The term "white bronze" was used to make the monuments sound more appealing. Monuments can range in shape and size.

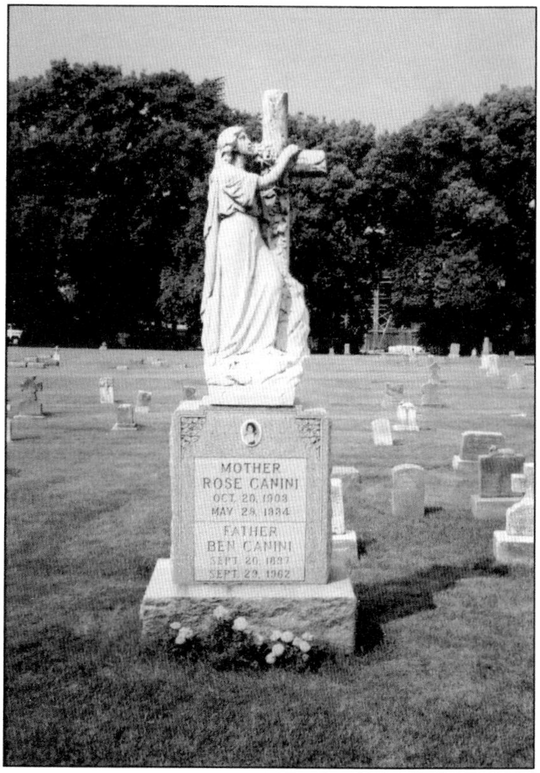

Benny Canin was born September 20, 1897, and died September 29, 1962. Canin was a retired sewer contractor, and his Requiem Mass was held at St. John the Baptist Church. His wife Rose DiSieno Canini was born October 20, 1903, and died May 28, 1934, following an operation. This cemetery is very fortunate to have many beautiful pieces of statuary and many porcelain portraits can be found throughout this historical cemetery.

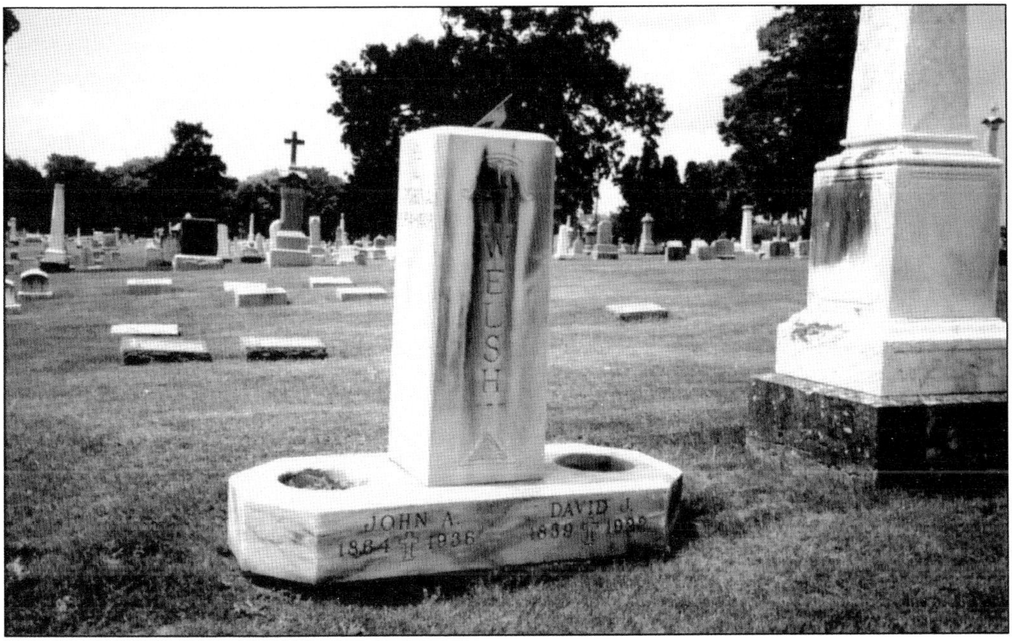

John A. (Jack) Welsh was born in 1865 and died July 14, 1936. Welsh was the patriarch of the Columbus Fire Department, becoming a fireman in April 1884, appointed captain in 1890, and later assistant chief. He was head of the Fire Prevention Bureau and, according to his obituary, "one of the bravest firemen that ever lived." Welsh was a bachelor and lived in firehouses. Welsh is interred beside his brother David J. Welsh, who was born 1859 and died in 1922.

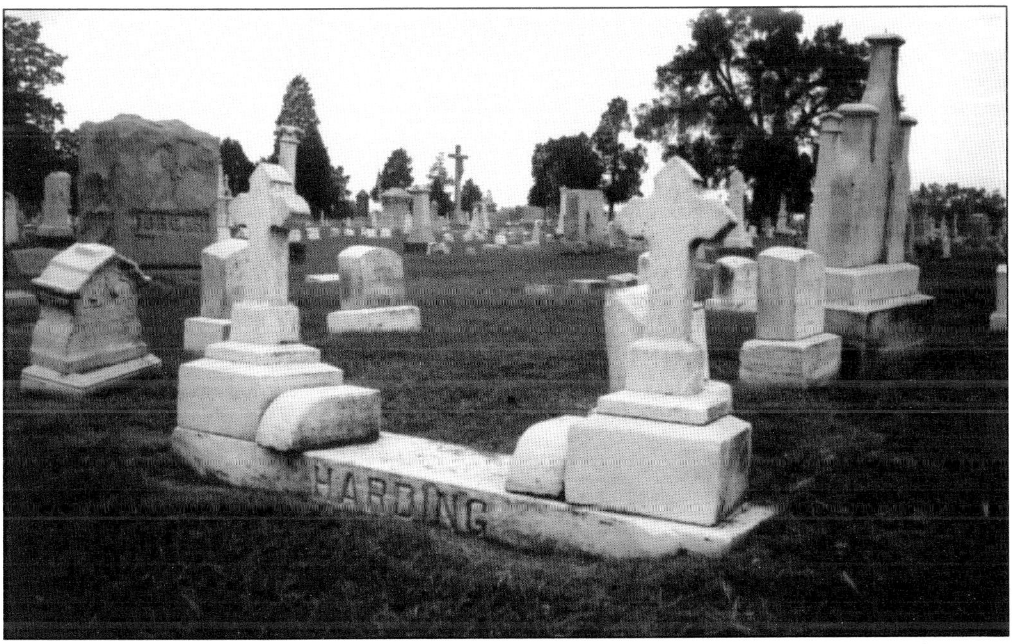

Not ones to get their skirts dirty, Victorian ladies would step from a carriage onto the stone engraved with the patriarch of the family name. David P. Harding was born in 1851 and died March 20, 1931. Harding was a retired contractor. He was the son of Michael Harding, architect of St. Patrick's Catholic Church. His wife, Mary Jane, was born in 1852 and died April 21, 1922.

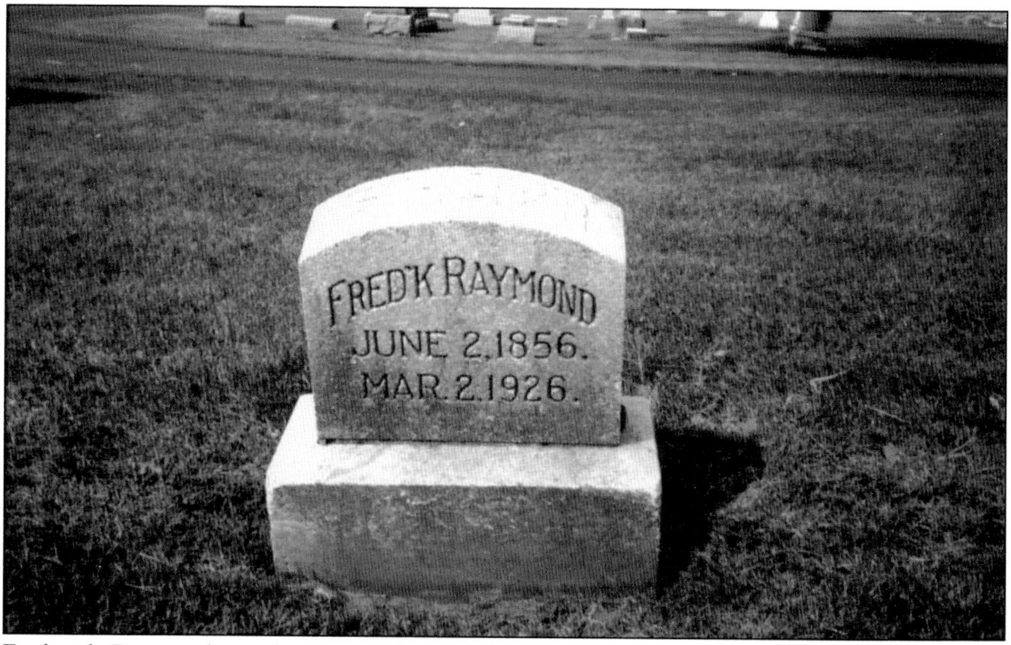

Frederick Raymond was born in 1856 and died March 2, 1926. His first wife, Laura Gale Raymond, died in 1897. After her death, he married Mary Wood Garrett in 1901. Raymond operated a horse-drawn taxi service from the railroad station to local hotels. He made bricks to build his house across from the fairgrounds, operated a saloon out of his home, and assisted in clearing the land for Minerva Park.

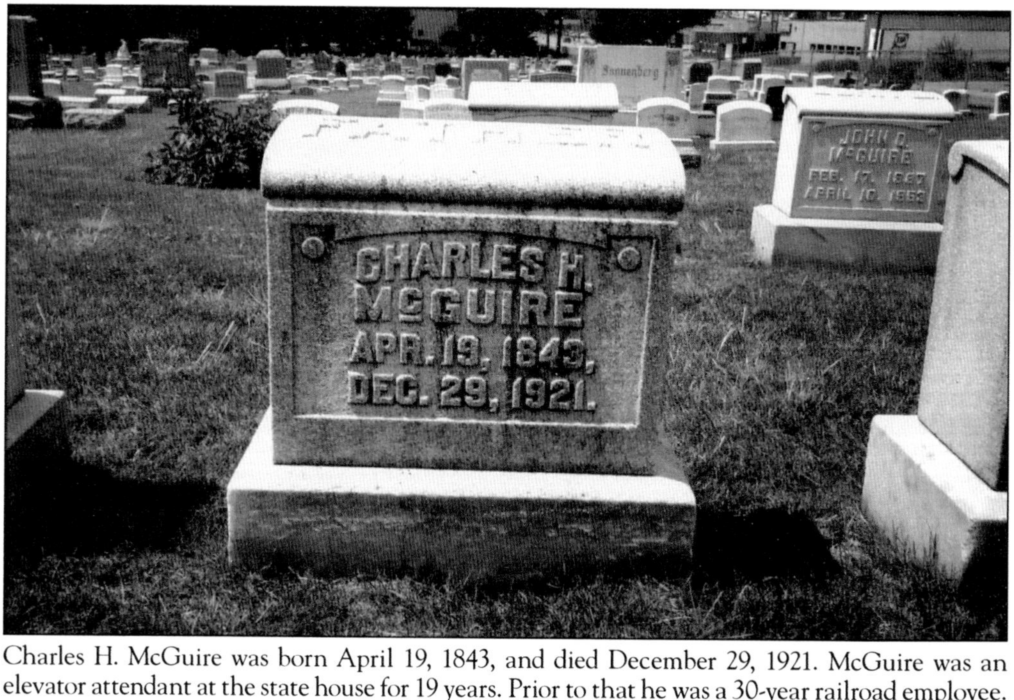

Charles H. McGuire was born April 19, 1843, and died December 29, 1921. McGuire was an elevator attendant at the state house for 19 years. Prior to that he was a 30-year railroad employee. He served with the 103rd Ohio Infantry during the Civil War and was a member of the Union Veteran Legion and the Buckeye Republican Club.

This image of Frank P. Lilley with his woodwind was taken in 1910. He was born January 31, 1856, in Italy and died January 11, 1942, at the age of 85. He married Mary Belle Henthorn on October 5, 1883, and they had seven children. Mary Belle died September 25, 1933. (Virginia Smith.)

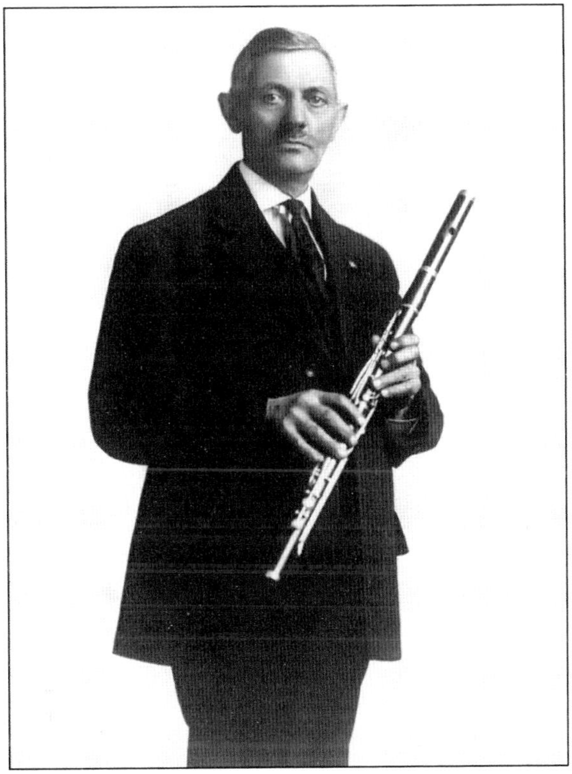

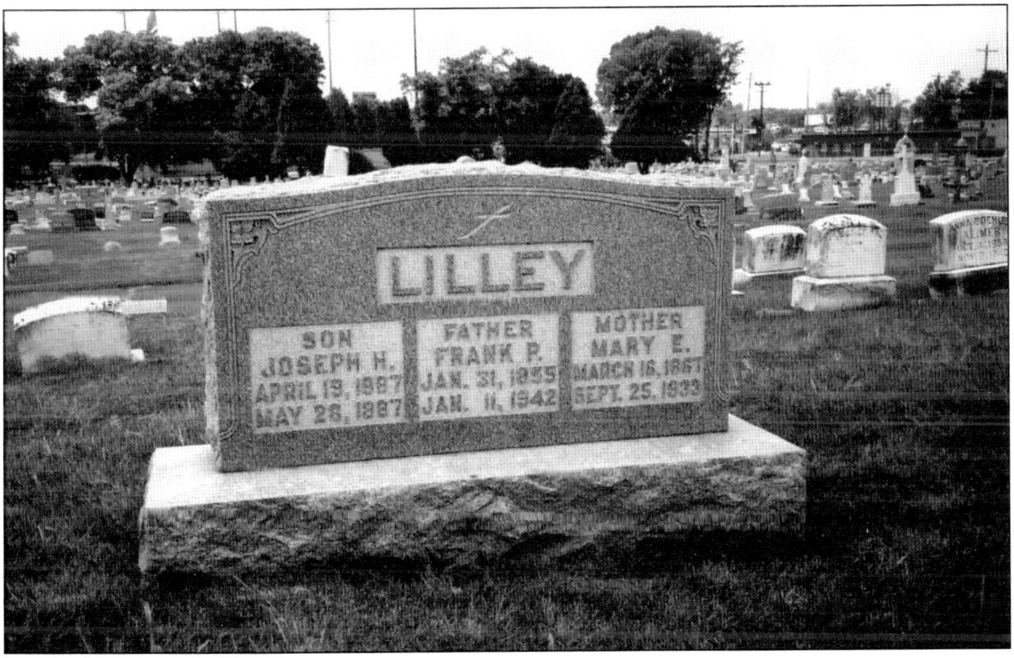

Lilley arrived in the United States in April 1881 and earned his living as a traveling musician. He enlisted in the Ohio Volunteer Infantry, 165th Regiment, May 1, 1884, and was quickly transferred to the band. He was a Spanish-American War veteran and a member of Camp No. 49, Spanish War Veterans, the Federation of Musicians local No. 103, and Woodmen of the World.

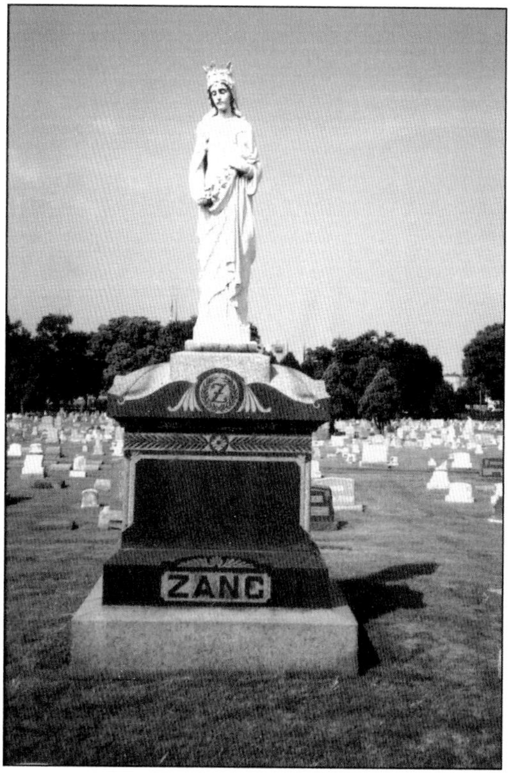

Fred L. Zang was born in Germany June 2, 1852, and died February 25, 1937. He came to Columbus from Cincinnati in 1877. In 1902, he entered the bakery business and became head of the pie concern. He was the proprietor of the first pie bakery company in Columbus, located at 1123 Hunter Avenue and in business for 35 years. His wife, Louise, was born in 1858 and died in 1909.

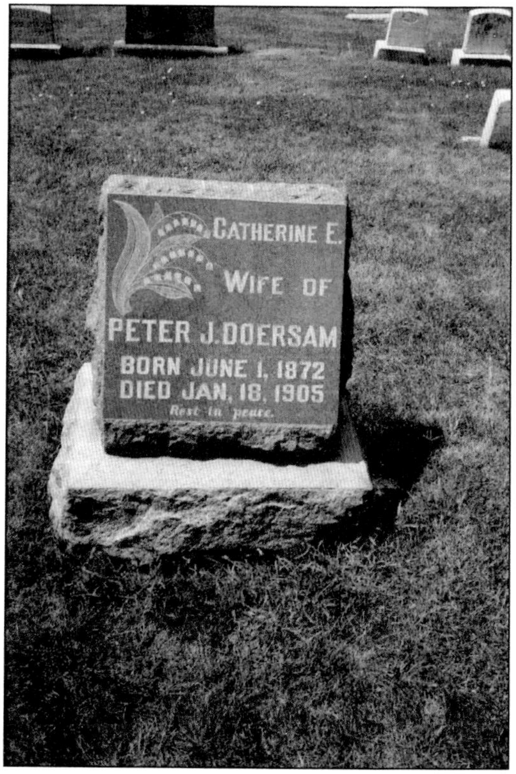

Catherine E. Doersam, wife of Peter J. Doersam, was born June 1, 1877, and died January 18, 1905. Catherine died after giving birth, as did the child. Peter was an assistant foreman in the sheet metal department of Jeffrey Manufacturing Company. Her monument is engraved with a lily of the valley, which is a symbol of the return of happiness, purity, and humility.

Sgt. Victor Churches was born February 3, 1872, in Italy and died January 10, 1917. He was an 18-year member of the Columbus Police Department. Serving five years in the United States infantry, he joined the Columbus Police Department in 1899 and was promoted to the rank of sergeant in 1905. He was a district sergeant and transferred to the position of headquarters sergeant. His wife, Rose, died March 25, 1962, at the age of 83.

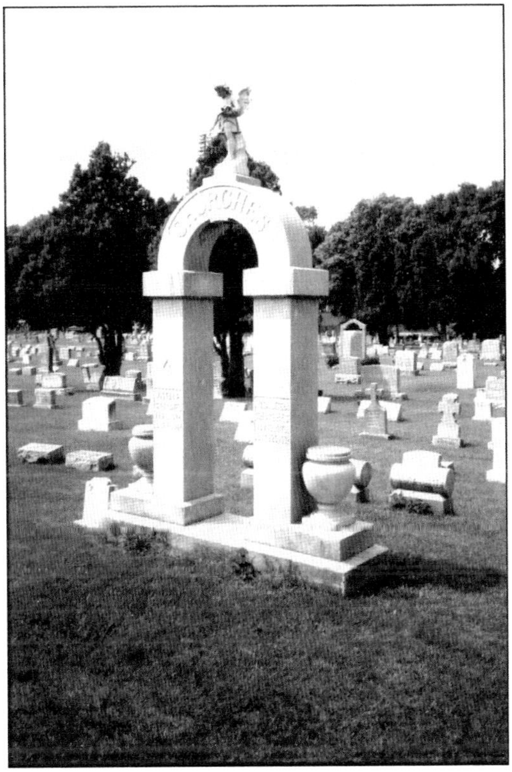

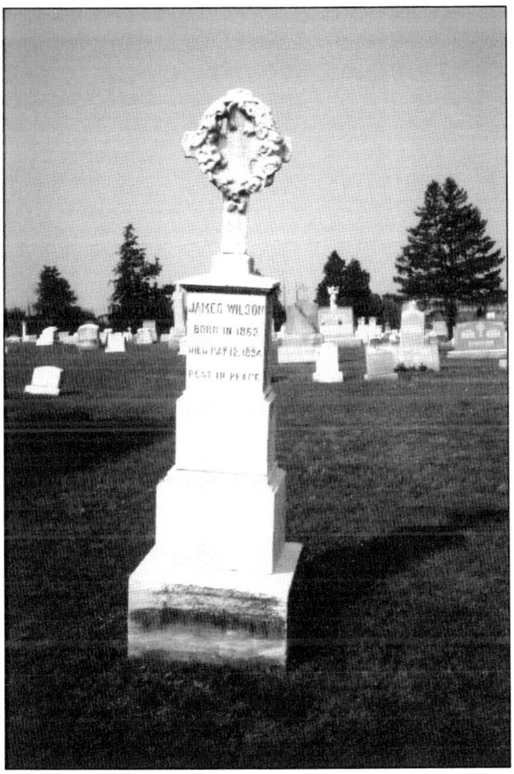

James Wilson was born in 1863 and died May 12, 1894. Wilson was the second victim of a fire at the Panhandle freight house. His body was found under the platform. His epitaph reads "Rest In Peace." The funeral of Edward Koehl, who also lost his life in the fire, took place at the German Independent Protestant Church, and his burial followed in Greenlawn Cemetery.

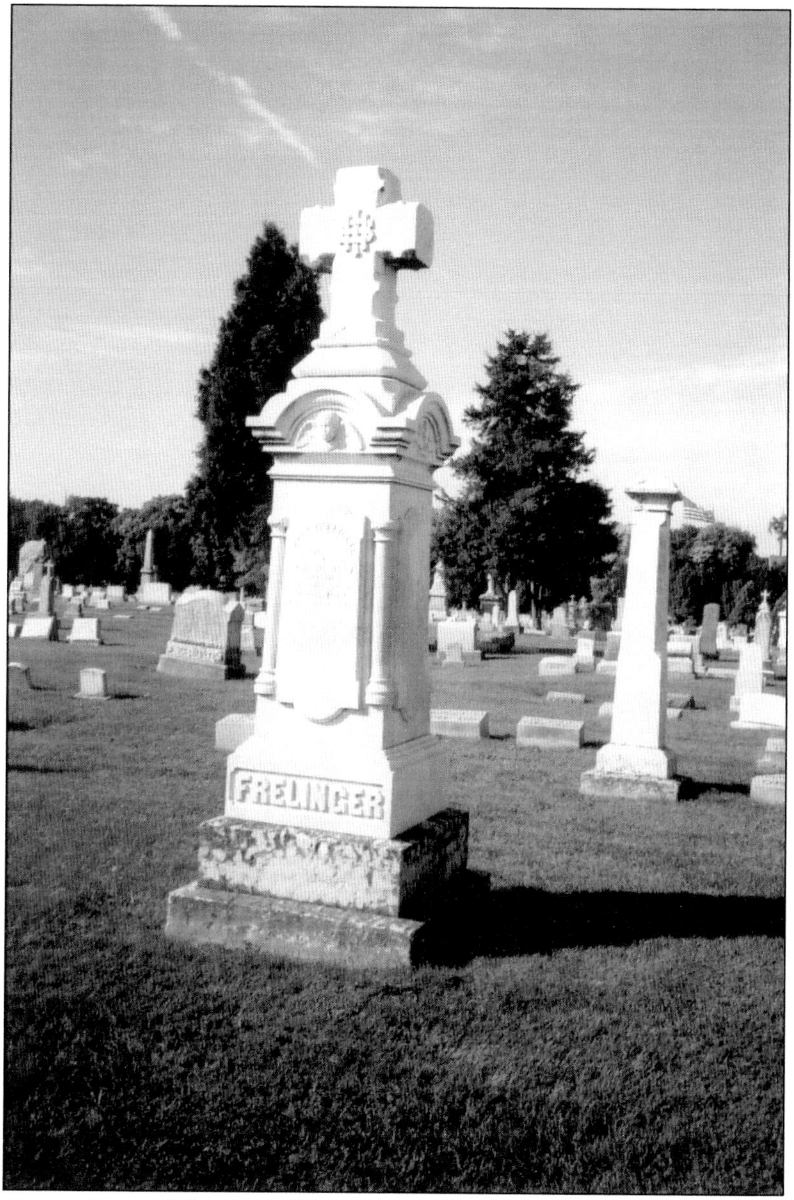

Peter Frelinger, nicknamed the "Riverboat Engineer," was born July 22, 1831, in France. Raised in Cincinnati, he spent most of his life on the great paddle-wheel riverboats while learning his trade with George Shields of Cincinnati. As an engineer, his first river trip was on the *Nina Simmes*, built in 1860. He served as engineer on the *William Burton* and the *Sir William Wallace*. He was part owner in the New Orleans and Bayou Sara Mail Line and served as its engineer. He also served the *Frank Pargoud* and the *Katie* as engineers. In 1878, Frelinger planned and supervised the construction of the engines of the Jeffersonville, Indiana, *J. M. White*. Frelinger's brother Gregory Frelinger was a Columbus blacksmith and his sister was Elizabeth Wolfel, wife of Charles Wolfel of Columbus. Peter owned property in Columbus and loaned money to Fr. G. H. Ahrens and Bishop John Ambrose Watterson. He died on April 9, 1880, of malarial fever at the Hotel Dieu in New Orleans where he had residence. His remains were returned to Columbus for burial, and his funeral was held at St. Joseph's Cathedral.

Luke G. Byrne was born December 7, 1847, in County Meath, Ireland, and died May 8, 1916. Byrne came to the United States when a small boy and was a resident of Franklin County for more than 60 years. (Columbus Metropolitan Library.)

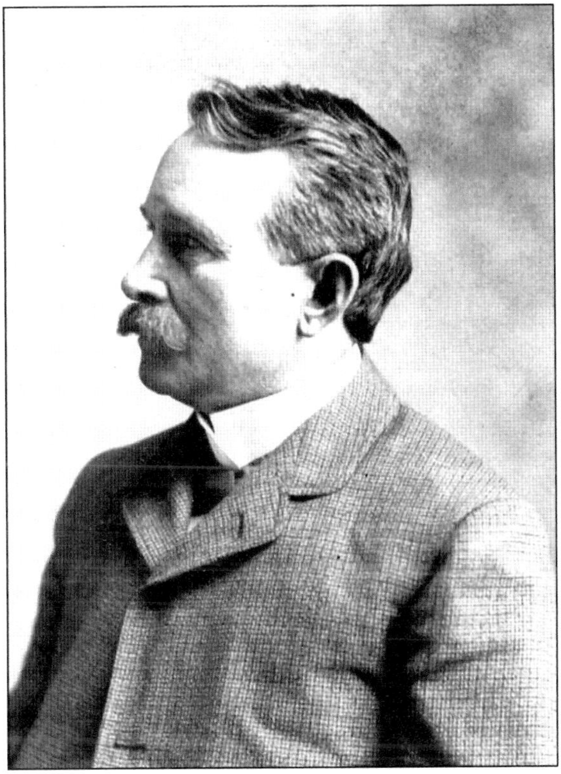

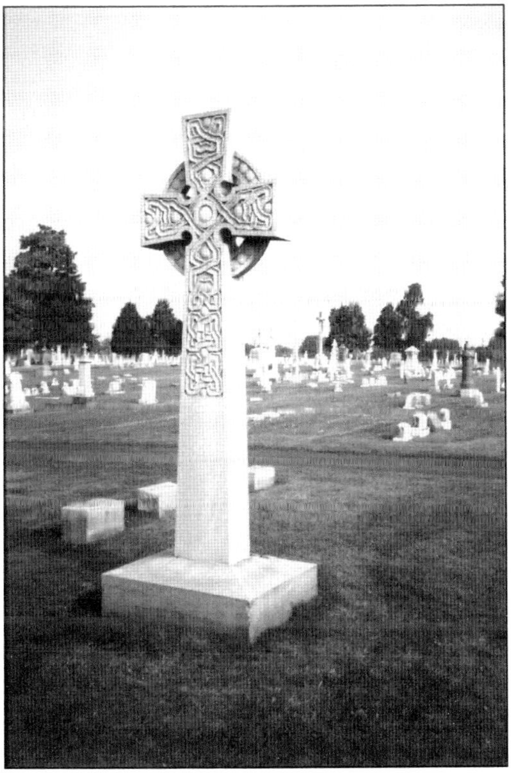

Byrne's monument is referred to as the Celtic cross. He was educated in the village school in Groveport, Ohio. For four years, he studied in the law office of Judge J. W. Baldwin and Lorenzo English. Admitted to the Ohio bar in 1873, he and G. S. Peters formed a law partnership that existed until 1880. He was also a Columbus Law Director in 1901. His wife was the former Rose M. Leonard.

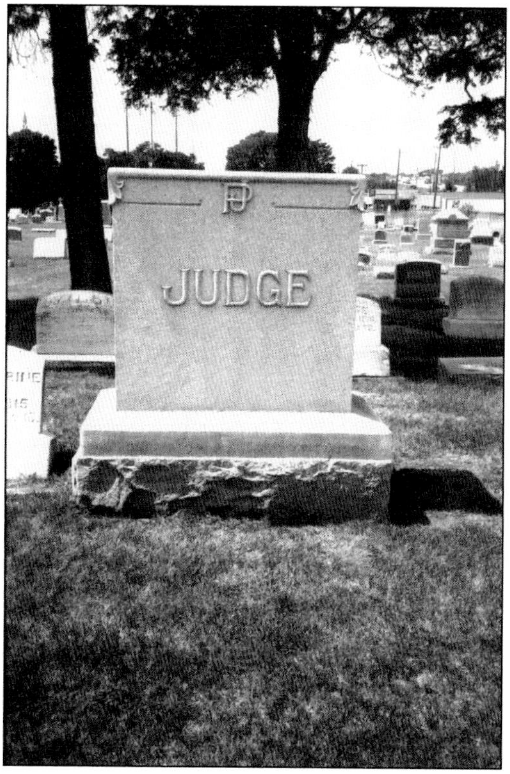

This splendid monument is the final resting place of Paul Judge. Judge had suffered for eight months with paralysis and died December 13, 1910. He was a retired contractor who lived at 1167 Neil Avenue and had retired four years prior to his death and was a widower. His only son and a brother lived in New York City. His wife, Catherine A. Judge, died March 25, 1905, at the age of 52.

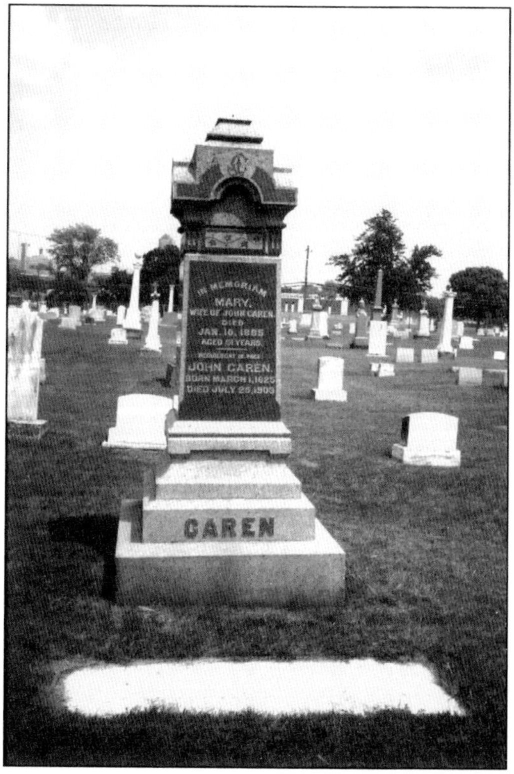

John Caren was born March 1, 1825, and died July 25, 1903. Caren was a pioneer, having resided in the city for over 50 years. A popular railroad man all his life, he was connected in one capacity or another with the Panhandle Road. He was elected to the city council in 1863 and a member of that body for four years. His wife, Mary Caren, died January 10, 1885.

Charles Medler, a driver for the Elliott Bakery, was born September 20, 1857, and died November 14, 1895. In an accident that occurred at the Broad Street crossing of the Midland Division of the Baltimore and Ohio Railroad, the passenger train struck him. He was thrown from the wagon, and the load of confectionery was scattered all over the street. There were no gates or watchman at the crossing.

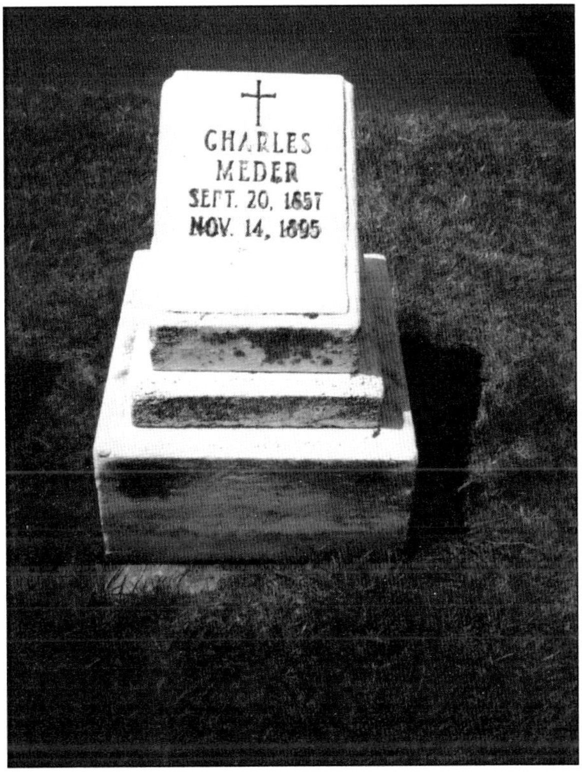

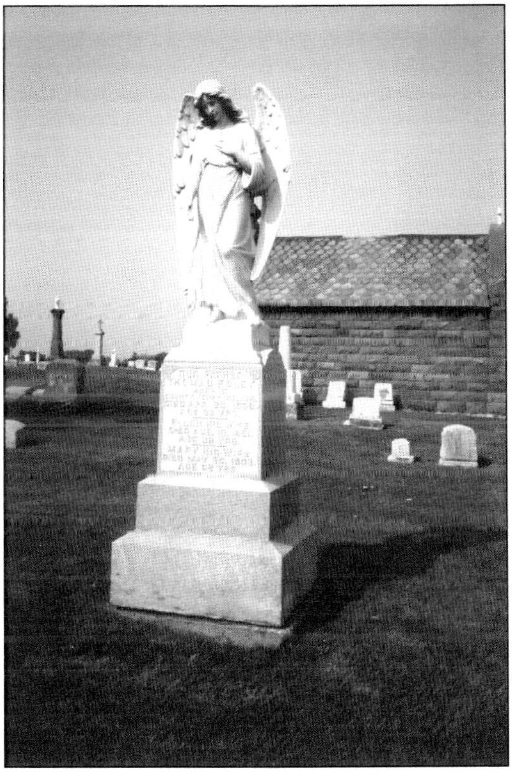

The final resting place of Thomas Foley and his two wives is watched over by this beautifully sculptured angel that represents rebirth, resurrection, protection, judgement, wisdom, mercy, and divine love. Foley was born in Ireland and died April 20, 1900. His first wife, Ellen, died August 10, 1861. His second wife, Mary, died May 30, 1903.

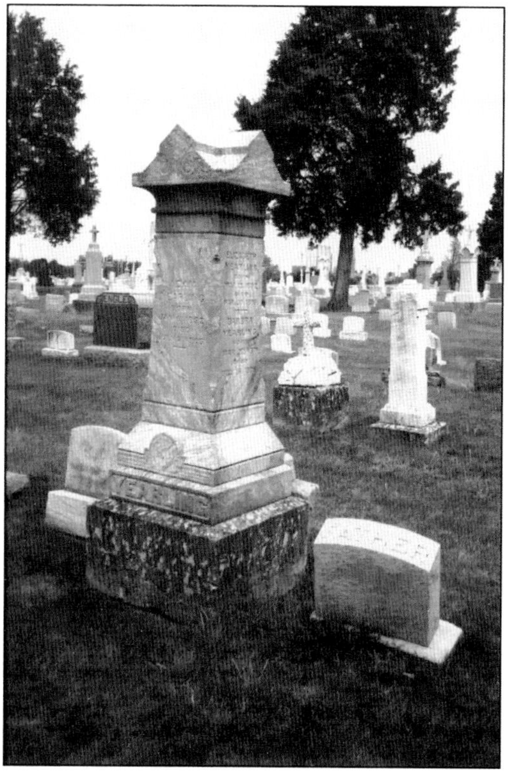

This is an example of a square-sided monument. Yearling was born in Germany, on January 6, 1832. He died in Columbus on July 2, 1905. He came to this country with his parents in 1850 and located east of Columbus on a farm. He retired from farming in 1883 and moved into the city, living at 1186 East Main Street. Yearling Road may be named after this family.

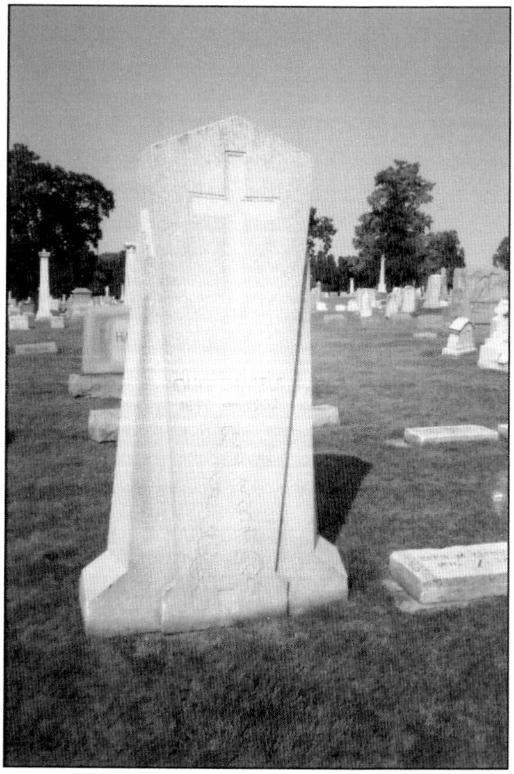

Carl O. Daniels, president of the Greendale Brick Company, was born at Magnetic Springs, Ohio, in 1890 and died September 5, 1932. He attended Aquinas College and later became associated with the accounting firm of Heller, Kershner and Martin. In 1922, he was the secretary-treasurer of the company, and later he succeeded to the presidency of the firm and also the Greendale Products Company and the Greendale Minerals Company.

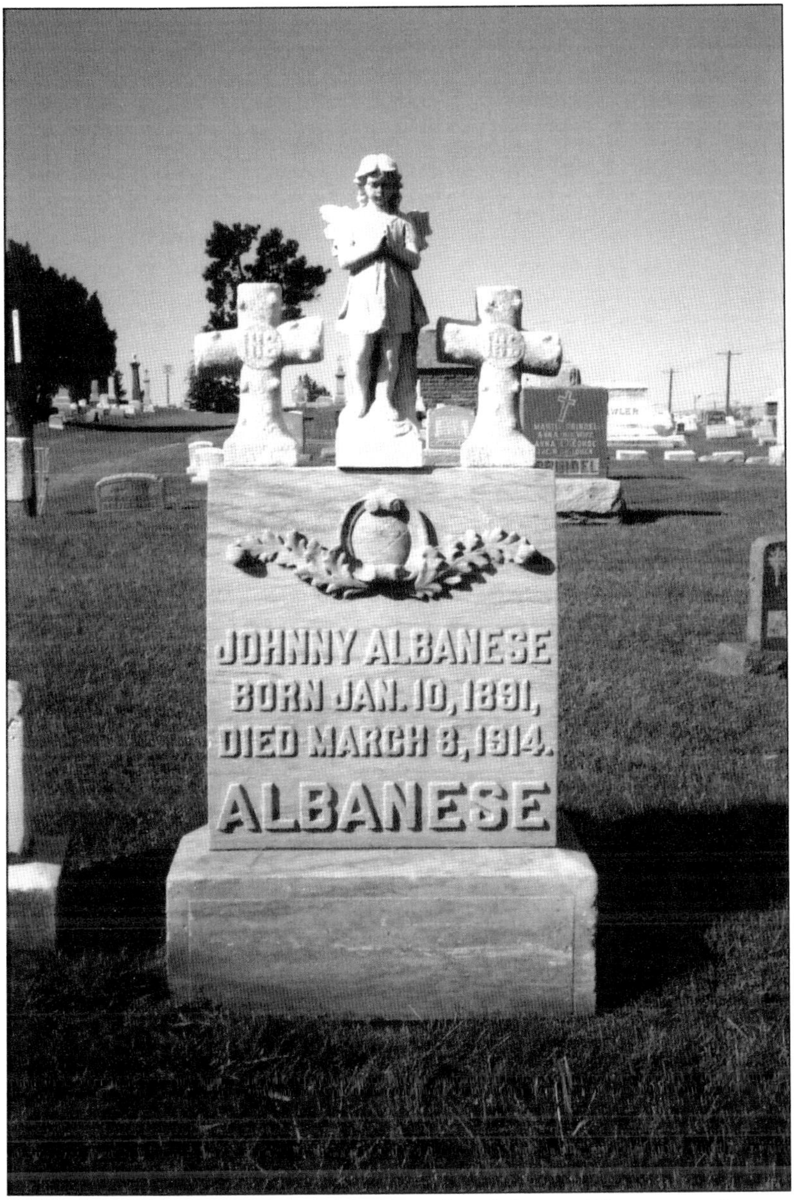

An unknown person in front of Union Station shot Johnny Albanese, a former Columbus newsboy and well-known lightweight prizefighter. Albanese was born January 10, 1891, and died March 8, 1914. He was on his way home when an altercation took place in front of Union Station. Albanese struck his assailant, and the man drew a gun and killed Albanese with a single shot. Albanese had not fought for about a year prior to his death. His last encounter was with Johnny Griffith at Akron. He had fought Johnny Kilbane, a lightweight champion, at Memorial Hall. He had fought Benny Goodman of Chicago and other well-known pugilists. Albanese had traveled with the Hagenback and Wallace's Circus the summer before. Before he entered the prize ring, he sold the *Ohio State Journal* at the corner of Broad and High Streets. He had married Esther Needles, but they had been separated, and he had been making his home with his mother, Mary Albanese. His brother Nick was part owner of the Goodale Athletic Club and a fight promoter. His uncle was Sgt. Peter Albanese of the police force.

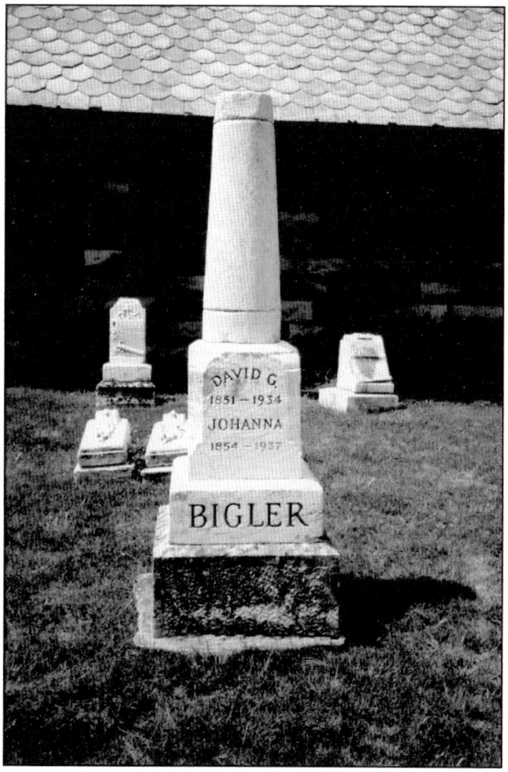

This single column monument is the Bigler burial plot. David G. Bigler was born in 1851 and died June 6, 1934. Bigler was a member of St. Dominica Court, Catholic Order of Foresters. His wife, Johanna Bigler, was born in 1854 in Columbus and died January 4, 1937. After the death of her husband, Johanna moved to Westerville. Both of their funeral services were held at St. Dominica's Church.

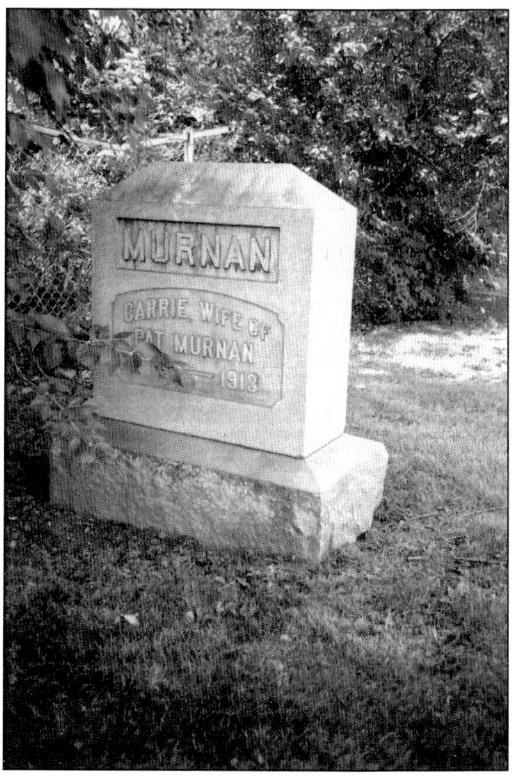

Carrie Murnan was born in 1865 and died in 1913. Her black-draped automobile escorted her cortege to Mount Calvary Cemetery. She married Maurice Pat Murnan, who operated the first taxicab service, a gambling house, and a saloon. He later married Grace Daugherty, for whom Graceland Shopping Center was named. Maurice died in 1937, and Grace died in 1939. Murnan Road was named after Maurice. They are buried in St. Joseph's Cemetery, Carrie rests alone in Mount Calvary Cemetery.

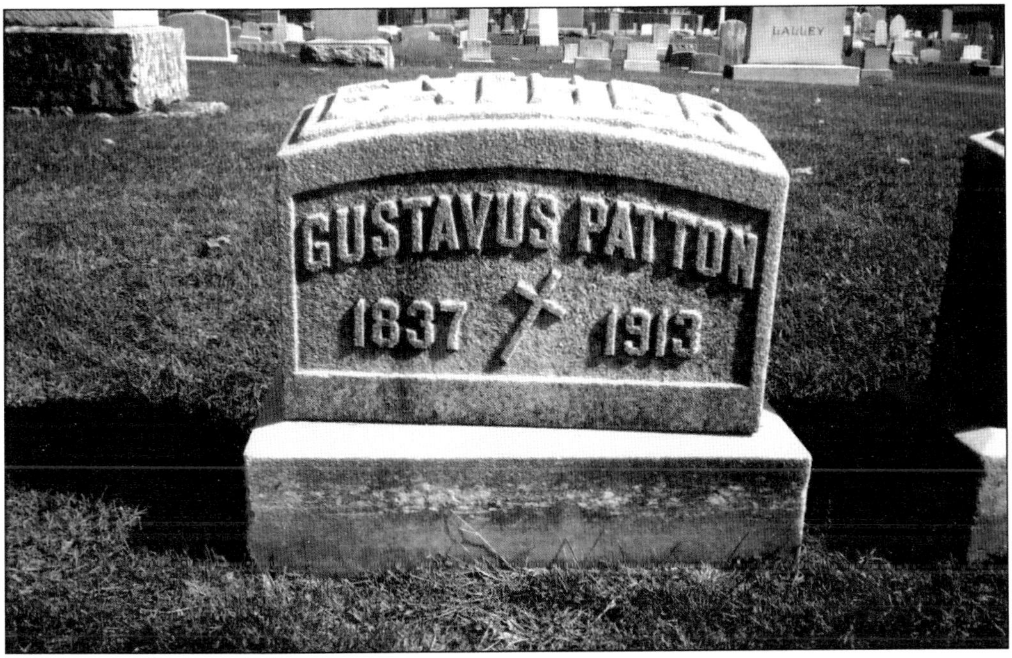

This mere headstone marks the final resting place of Gustavus Patton, who was born in 1837 in a log cabin that once stood at the corner of Town and Front Streets. He died in Franklin County on January 23, 1913, the son of Alexander Patton (1791–1858), who was the 16th mayor of Columbus serving three terms during 1847–1849.

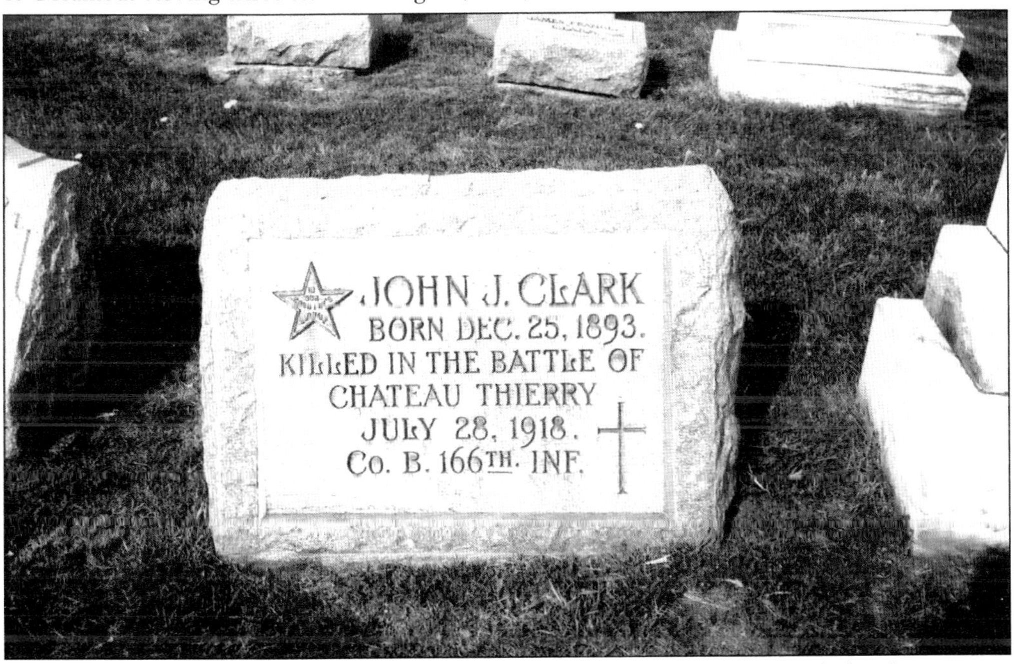

The Battle of Chateau-Thierry was fought July 18, 1919. It was one of the first actions involving the United Expeditionary Force under Gen. John J. Pershing. John J. Clark was born December 25, 1893. He was killed in the battle on July 28, 1918. Clark served with Company B, 166th Infantry.

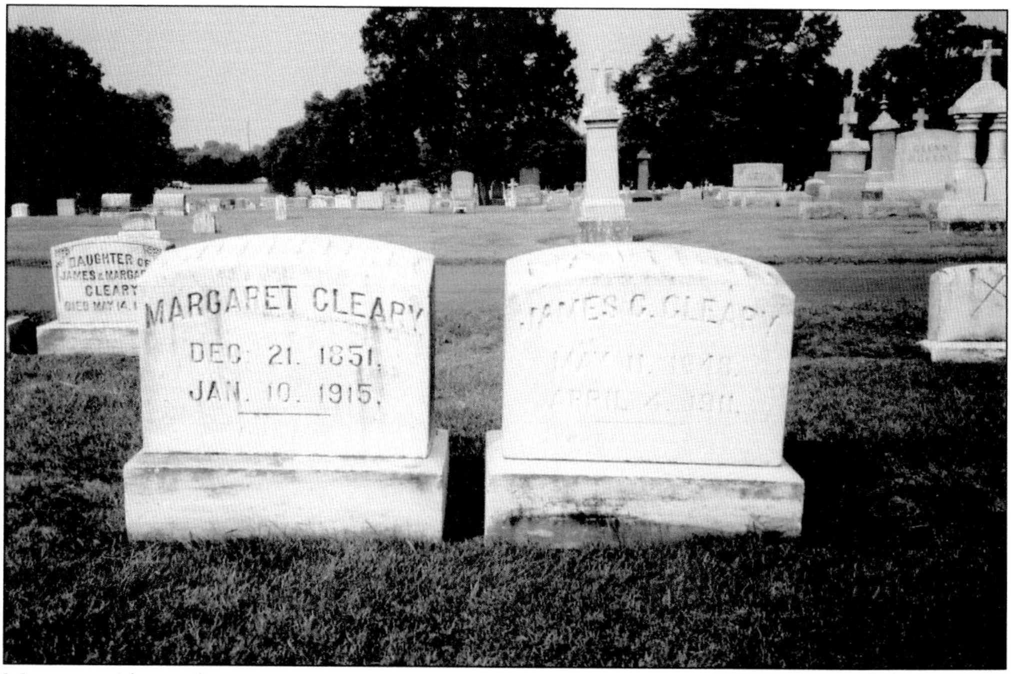

Margaret Cleary, born December 21, 1851, died at her home on North Grant Avenue on January 10, 1915. Her husband, James C. Cleary, born May 11, 1848, died at his home on Tuesday, April 4, 1911. In this family plat are daughter Margaret, who died June 23, 1945; daughter Mazie, who died May 14, 1940; and John C. Cleary, born February 2, 1871, and died January 26, 1909.

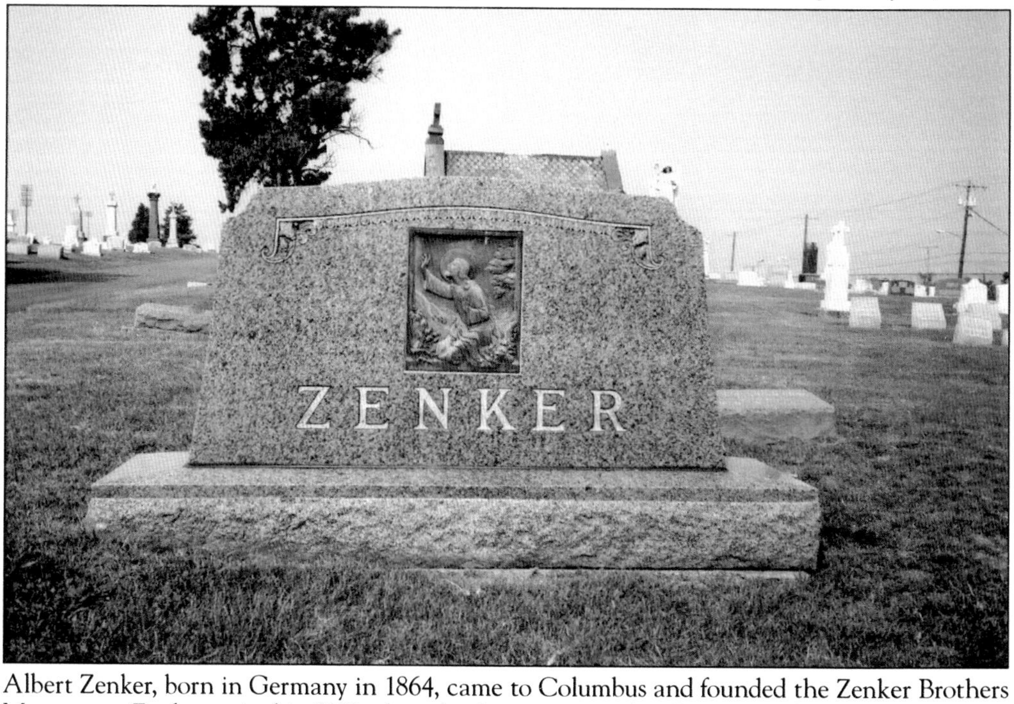

Albert Zenker, born in Germany in 1864, came to Columbus and founded the Zenker Brothers Monument. Zenker retired in 1921 when the firm was moved to East Mound Street. Zenker died October 11, 1941. His wife, Anna Zenker, was born 1868 and died February 11, 1963.

Domenico Casbarro was born June 13, 1876, and died May 28, 1940. The Woodmen of the World memorial symbol is seen above his photograph. The inspiration for the name Woodmen came from a church sermon, which touted the trees as being "God's first temple." This was an early benefit of Woodmen membership, and the headstones can be found in cemeteries across the nation, until being abandoned in the 1920s for being too expensive.

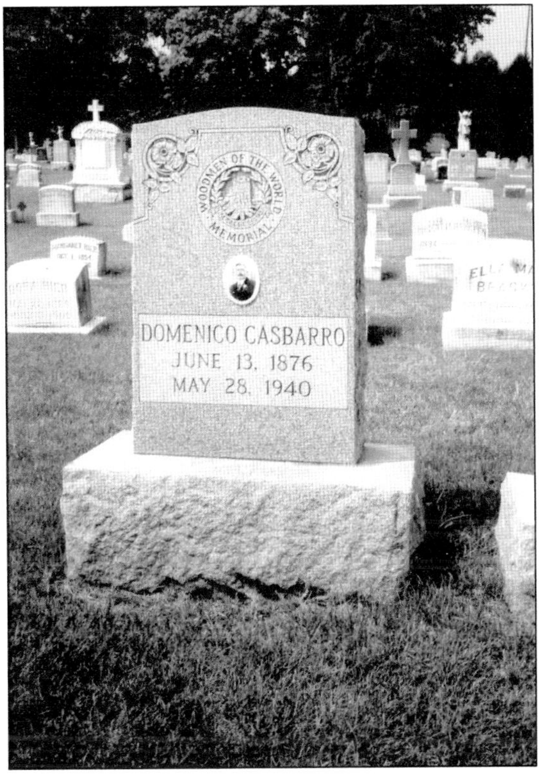

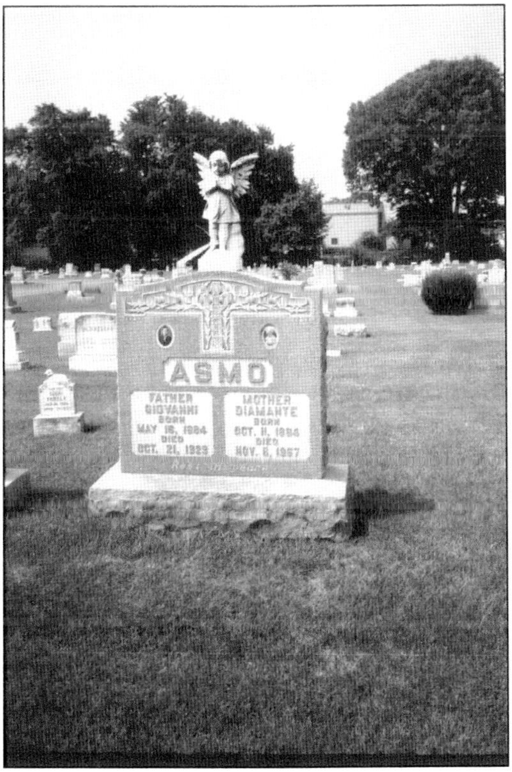

Porcelain portraits are inserted into the monument of John "Giovanni" Asmo, who was born May 16, 1884, and died October 21, 1929. Asmo was a well-known grocer, at 1024 Chase Avenue. His wife, Diamante Asmo, was born October 11, 1884, and died November 6, 1957. A beautiful cherubim stands watch over Giovanni and Diamante. The epitaph reads, "Rest in peace."

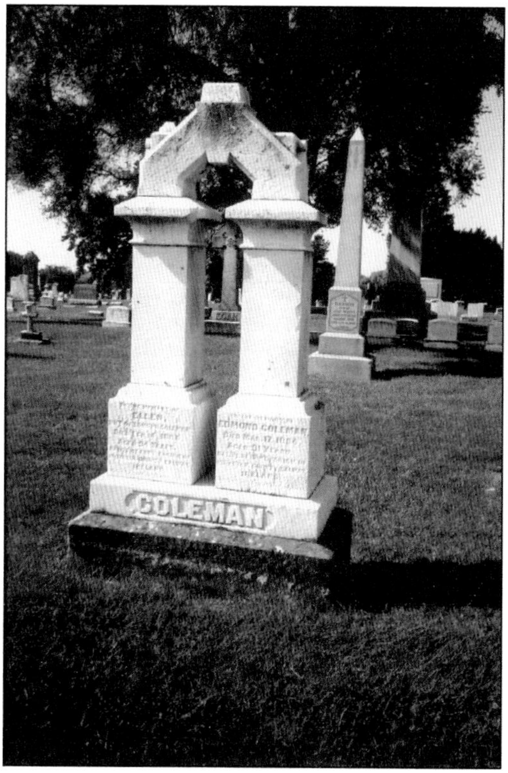

This monument was erected to the "Memory of Ellen," the wife of Edmond Coleman who died February 4, 1886. Ellen was born in Galway, Ireland, in 1793. Her funeral was held at Sacred Heart Church on Sunday, February 7, 1886. An epitaph is inscribed, "May she rest in peace." One month later, her husband, Edmond, died March 17, 1886, at the age of 91 years. A column monument represents noble life.

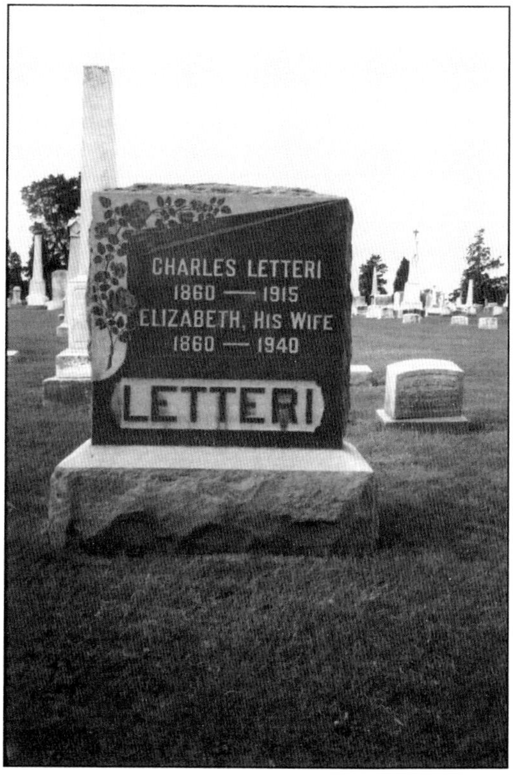

Charles Letteri was born in 1860 and died May 20, 1915. Letteri was employed by the Pennsylvania Railroad, as a foreman of the boiler works at the PanHandle shops. His wife was Elizabeth Kelley Letteri, born 1860 and died January 26, 1940. She was a native of Hardin County and came to Columbus as a child.

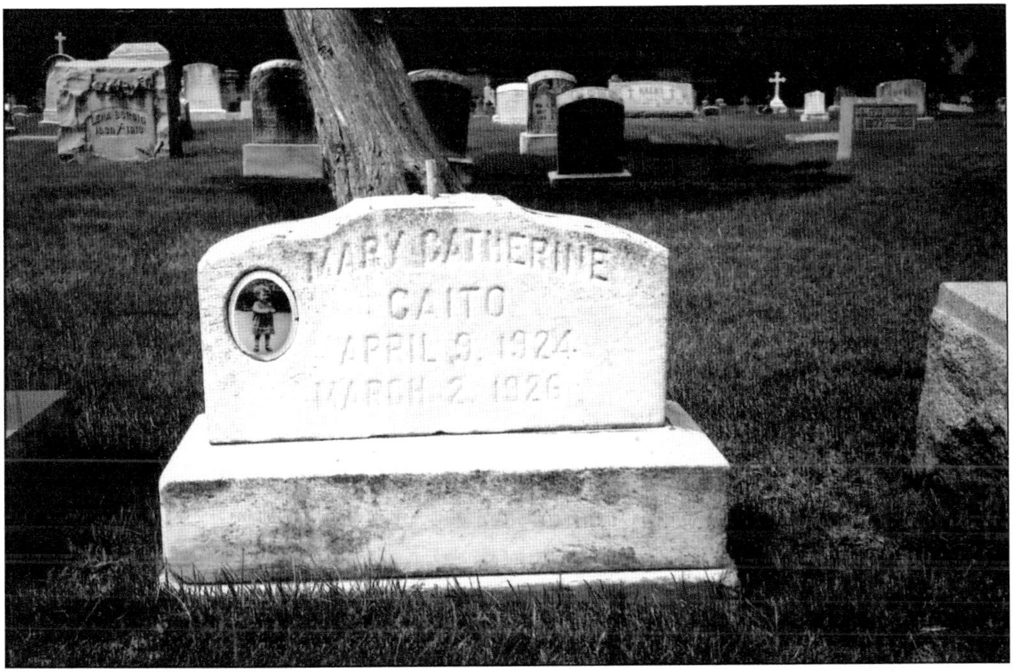

Mary Catherine Caito was born April 9, 1924, and died March 2, 1926. Caito was only two years old. Her photograph appears on her monument. Grieving for the loss of a child is often a life-long painful process. Mary Catherine was the two-year-old daughter of Mr. and Mrs. Philip Caito.

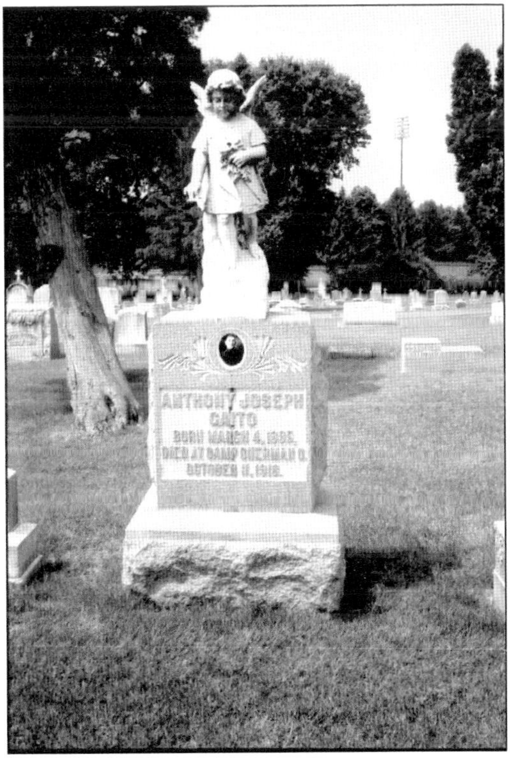

Anthony Joseph Caito was born March 4, 1895, and died at Camp Sherman, Ohio, on October 11, 1916. His photograph appears on his monument. The angel on this monument represents "Rebirth, resurrection, protection, judgment, wisdom, mercy, or divine love." Under no circumstances should a sacred symbol be place below the family name and never used as a mere ornament.

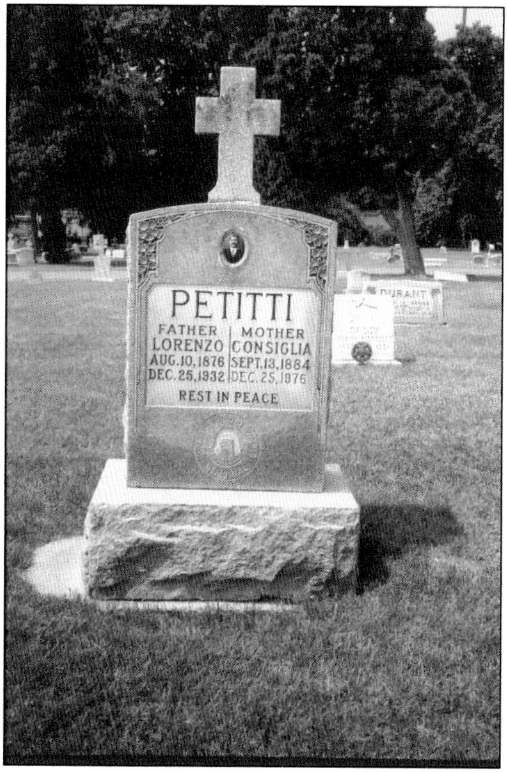

Lorenzo and Consiglia Petitti's monument epitaph reads, "Rest In Peace." Lorenzo was born August 10, 1876, and died December 25, 1932. His wife, Consiglia, was born September 13, 1884, and died December 25, 1976. Lorenzo was a member of the Woodmen of the World, a fraternal insurance society for persons over the age of 16.

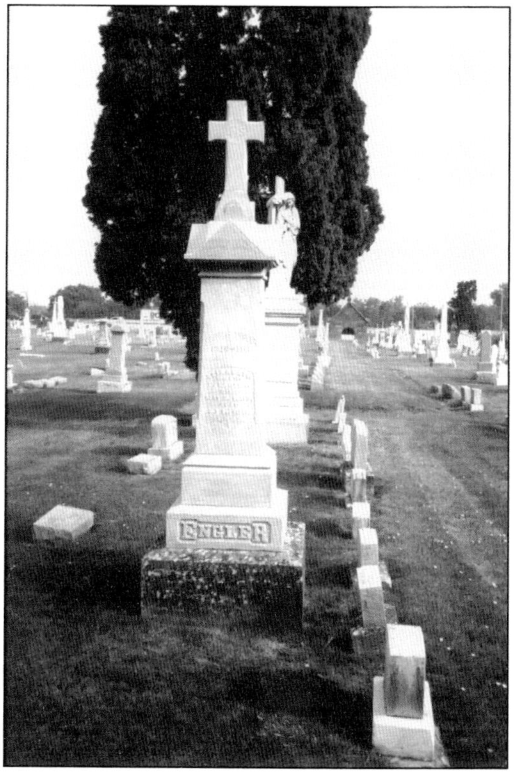

This monument is the Engler family plot. The patriarch, Francis I. Engler, was born in 1825 and died October 26, 1918. His wife, Elizabeth, died May 3, 1883, at the age of 47. Interred also is Marie J. Engler, their daughter who died December 6, 1866; Francis A., born in 1863 and died in 1897; and George P. Engler, born in 1873 and died in 1929.

In this beautiful setting is the final resting place of Aponia "Pauline" Cardinale, wife of Frank Cardinale. She was the daughter of Salvatore Montese. The porcelain portrait inserted into her monument is of her in her wedding attire. A baby son, Alfonse Cardinale, born in December, only lived a few hours after birth and died December 28, 1921.

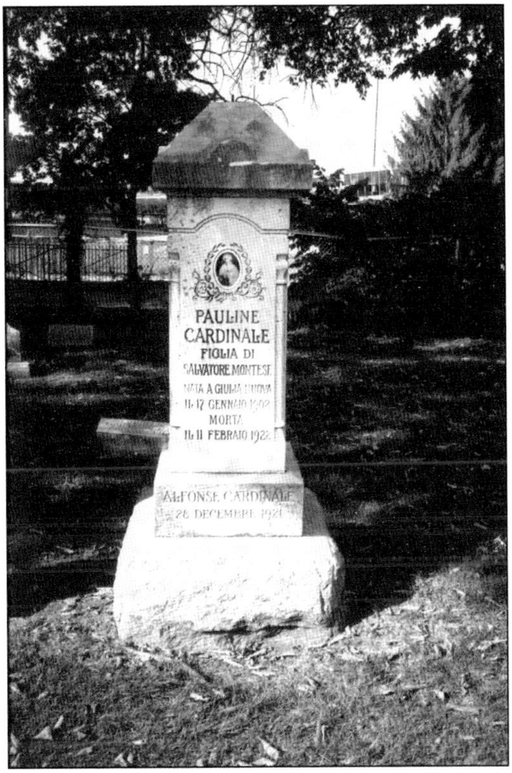

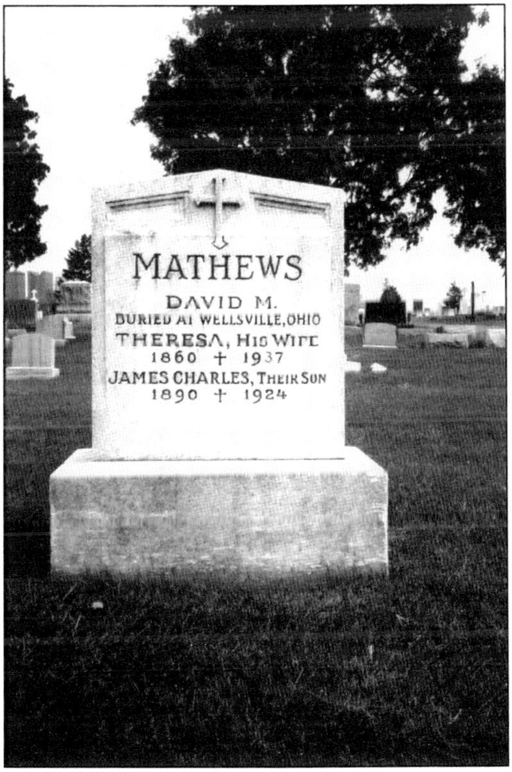

David M. Mathews was buried at Wellsville, Ohio. This is referred to as a cenotaph, a grave where the body is not present or an engraved memorial erected at a grave where the body has not been interred. A cenotaph may look exactly like any other grave in terms of marker and inscription. Theresa, his wife, was born in 1860 and died in 1937. Son James Charles was born in 1890 and died in 1924.

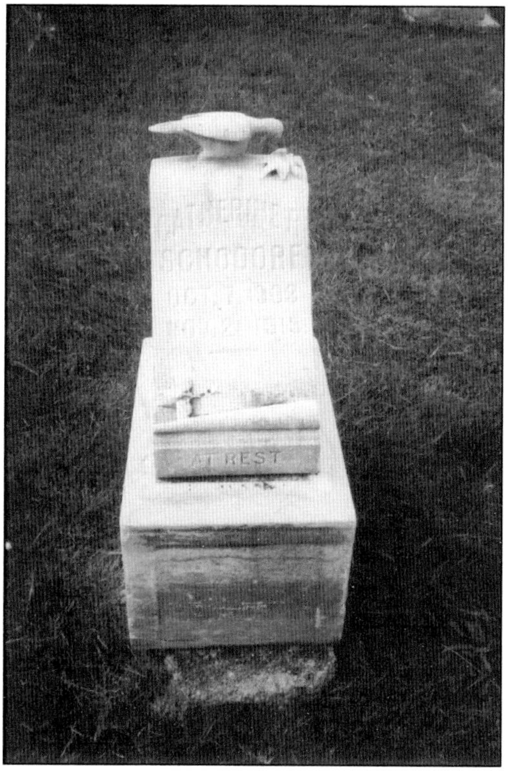

The bird on this monument symbolizes external life, a winged soul, and spirituality. Katherine Schodorf was the 12-year-old daughter of Mr. and Mrs. A. C. Schodorf of 83 Martin Avenue. Katherine was born October 7, 1903, and died November 21, 1915. Her funeral was held at Holy Family Church.

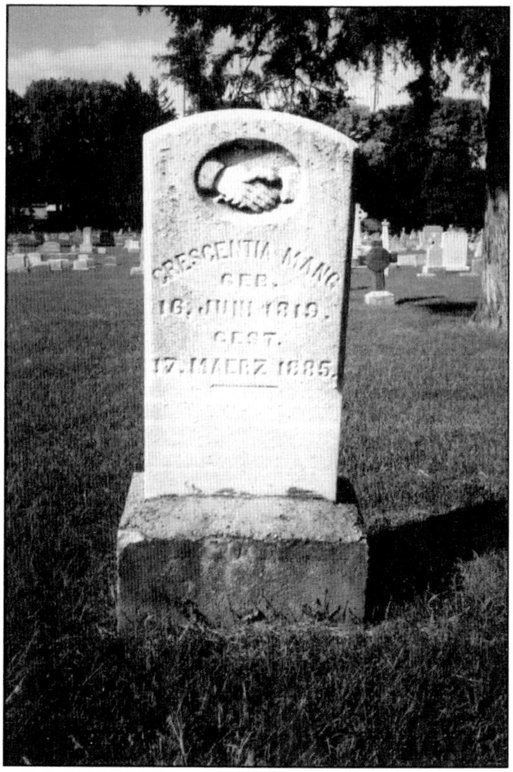

Carved into this monument are clasped hands that represent farewell or hope to meeting in eternity. This monument marks the grave of Crescentia Mang, born *Juni* (June) 16, 1819, and died *Maerz* (March) 17, 1885.

The Connecticut Monumental Bronze Company produced the Thomas Monahan monument (who died December 10, 1891). The company began in 1874 and was incorporated as the "Monumental Bronze Company" in 1879. They stopped the production of metal grave markers in 1914. It was the only company in the United States to make these markers, and all the casting was done at the Bridgeport Company.

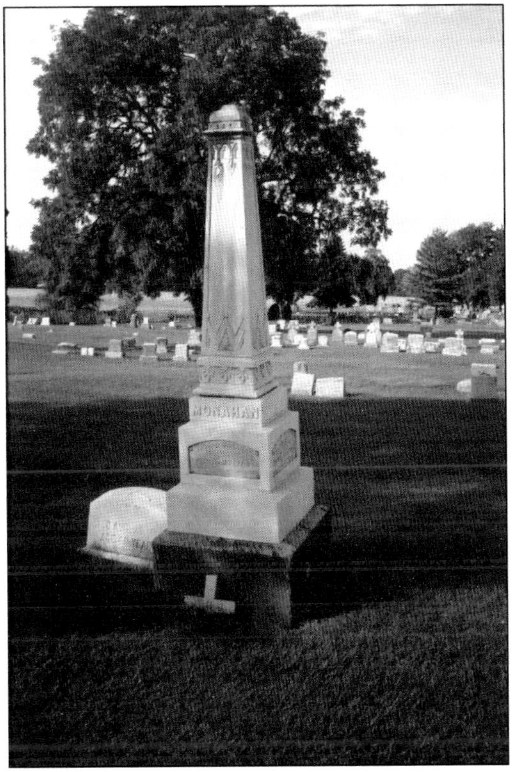

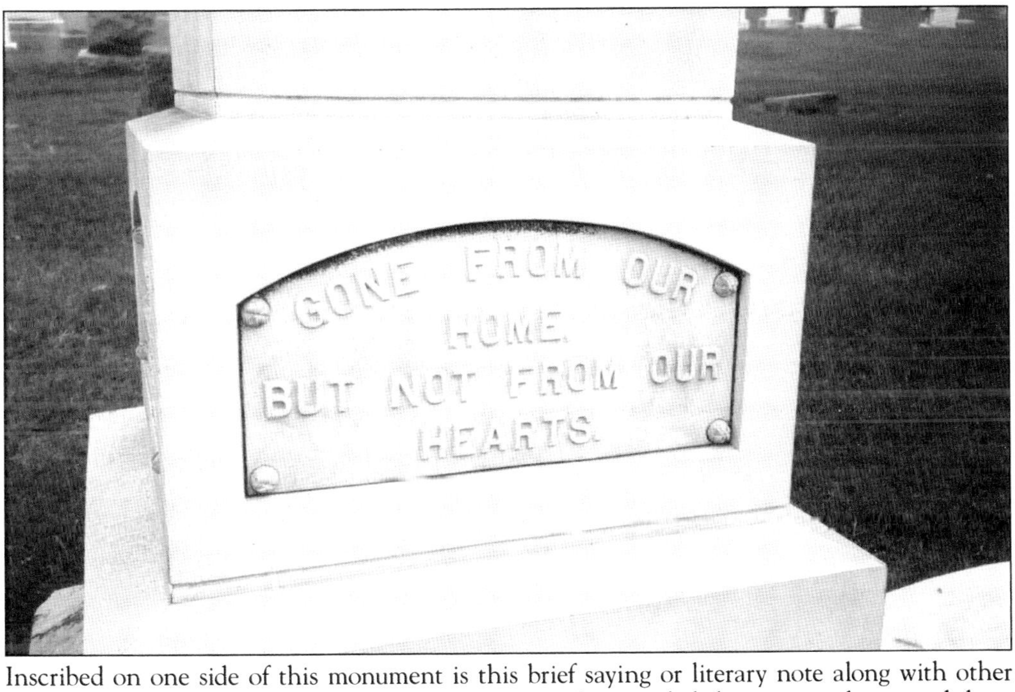

Inscribed on one side of this monument is this brief saying or literary note along with other epitaphs that appear elsewhere. Most monuments only provided the names, places, and dates of birth and death and other biographical information. The company continued casting bronze and other metal moldings until they filed bankruptcy in 1939.

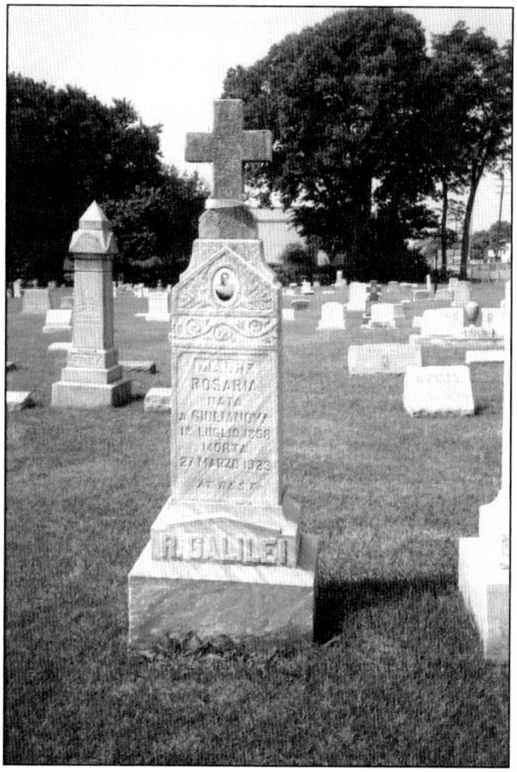

This impressive monument was constructed for Rosaria Galilei, born in 1858 and died March 27, 1923. Her funeral services were held at St. John's the Baptist Church. A porcelain portrait of Galilei is inserted into her monument. Placed around the top section of her monument is a dried palm leaf.

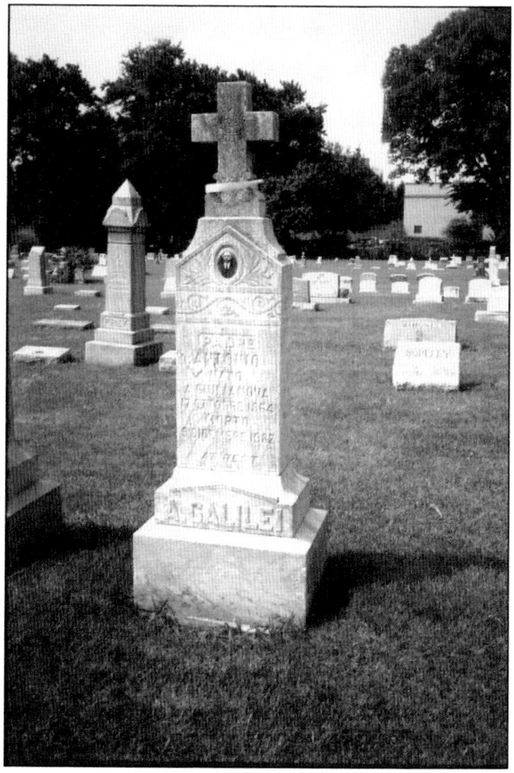

Interred next to Galilei is her husband, Antonio, born in Italy on October 17, 1864, and died December 9, 1932. Antonio was a car repair helper for the Norfolk and Western Railroad. He was a member of St. John the Baptist Church and Holy Name Society. His portrait in porcelain is inserted into his monument, and a dried palm leaf encircles around the top of his monument.

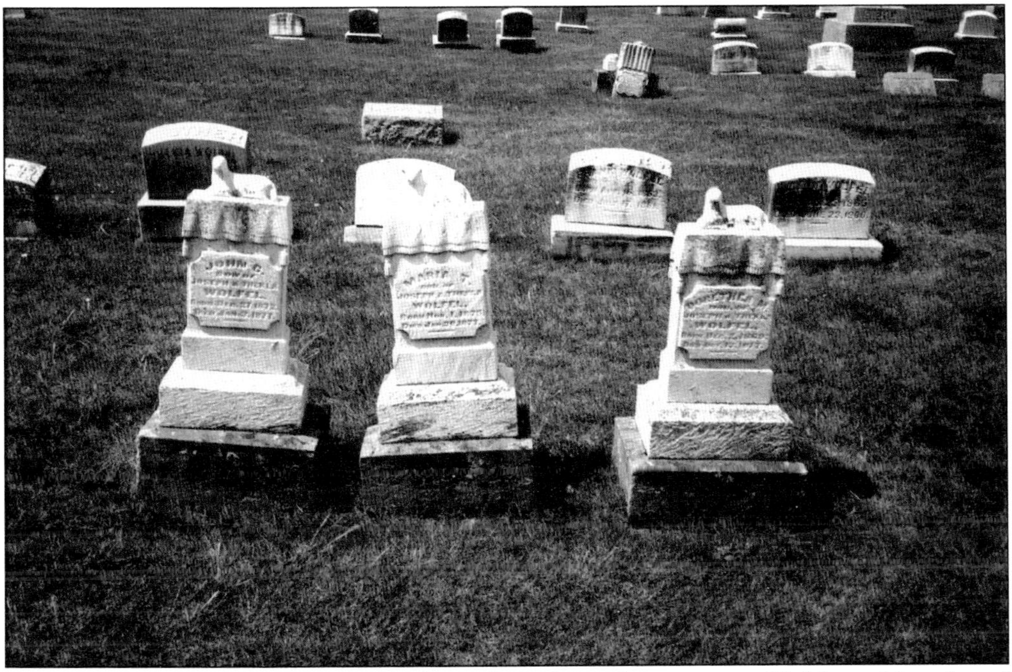

Parental mourning has been a universal one throughout the centuries. Children of Joseph and Thekla Salle Wolfel are interred here. Son John C. Wolfel, daughter Maria T., and daughter Dorothea M. all died in 1877. Joseph died in 1914, and Thekla died December 27, 1928. Joseph was a retired Columbus grocer.

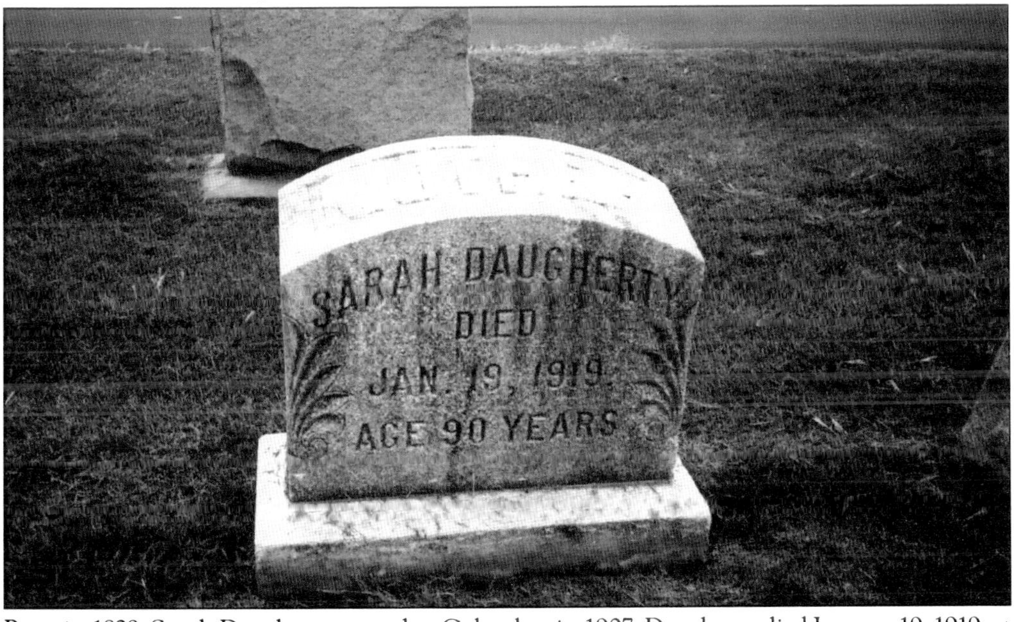

Born in 1829, Sarah Daugherty moved to Columbus in 1907. Daugherty died January 19, 1919, at the age of 90 years old, of senility at her home. Senility is a disease with symptoms of dementia that includes mental deterioration, loss of memory, bodily function, strength, and energy. A daughter, Grace Daugherty, a son, and 12 grandchildren survived her. Her funeral was held at Holy Name Church.

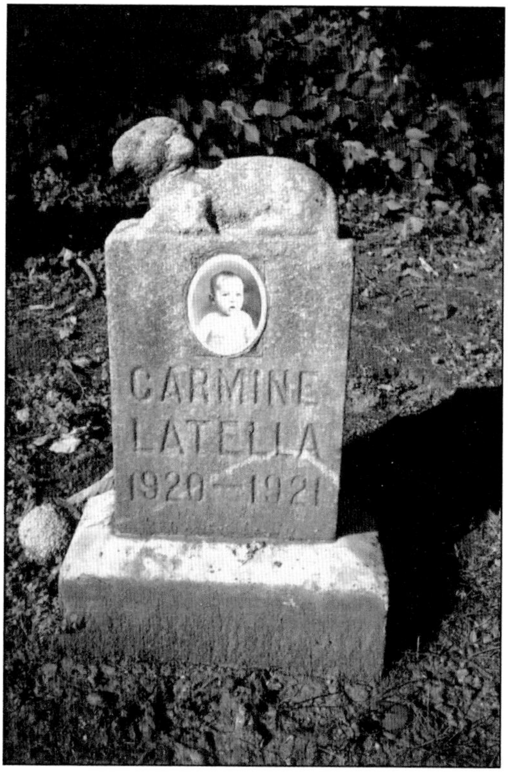

The lamb is a Biblical symbolism, representing innocence, sacrifice, and resurrection and often used on the headstones of children. Carmen "Carmine" Latella died March 6, 1921, at the aged one year; he was the son of Mr. and Mrs. Joseph Latella. His porcelain portrait is inserted into monument.

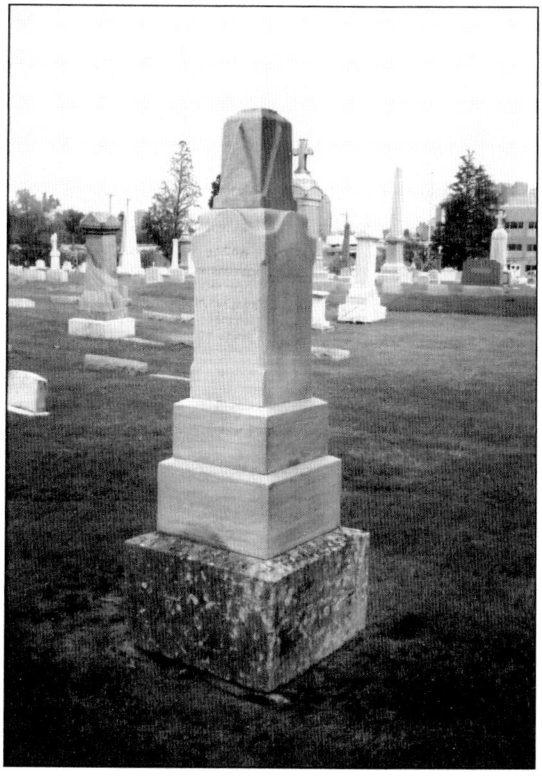

The first record of a burial in the Holycross section, or the German side, of Mount Calvary Cemetery is the daughter of Jacob Roehrenbeck, Katharine Roehrenbeck, who died April 26, 1867. Katharine is buried in the family plot, Holycross section B, lot 121. The next recording of a burial was that of Friedrich Ross, who was interred in the single grave section on April 25, 1867.

Thomas F. McDonald was born 1847 and died in 1902. His wife, Annie T., was born in 1853 and died February 1, 1925. Annie was preparing to go to church and suffered a heart attack. Her funeral was held at St. Joseph's Cathedral, and flowers were omitted. Omitting of flowers is popular today with many funerals. The carved flowers on this majestic monument symbolize "Life's frailty, immortality."

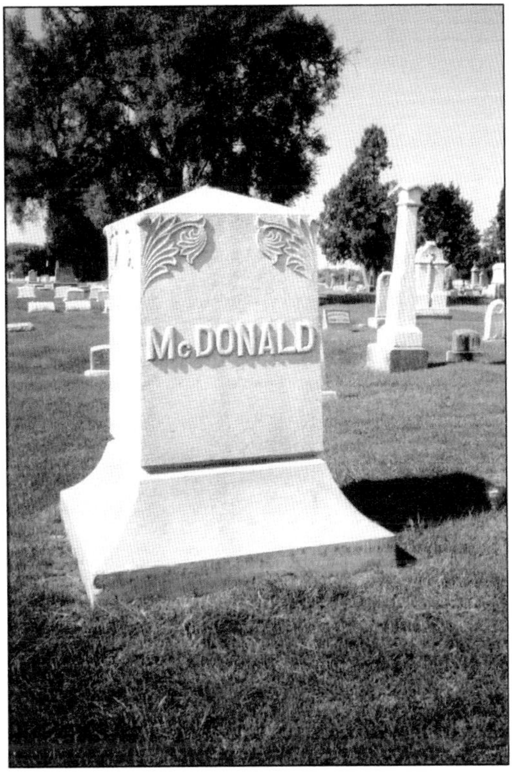

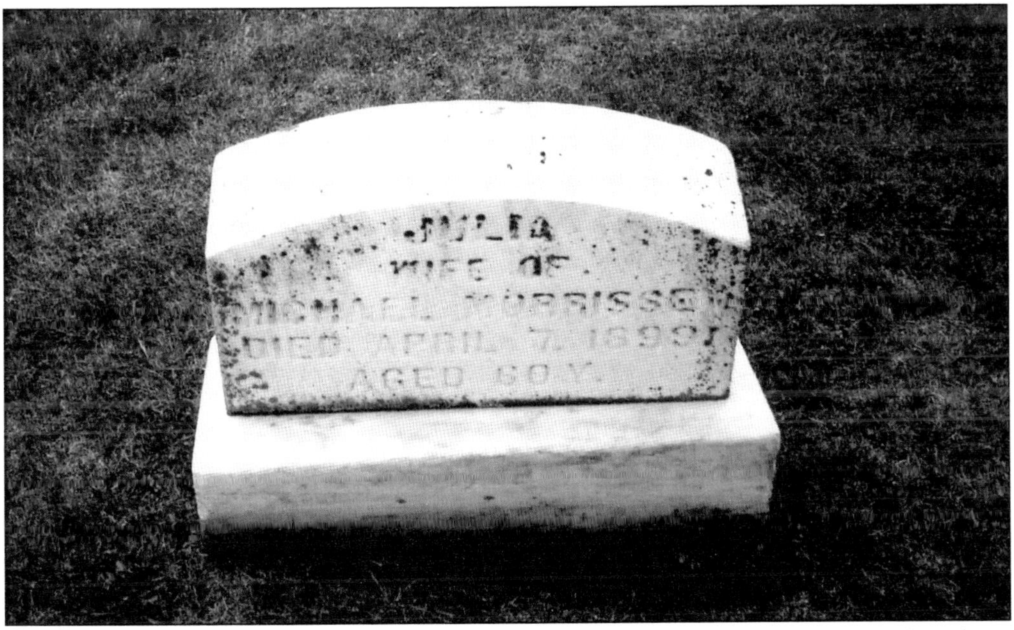

Michael Morrissey died April 1907. Born in Ireland, he immigrated to America in 1857 and was employed with the PanHandle Railway Company as a lampman in the yards. His funeral was from the Church of the Sacred Heart, which he was a member of and had witnessed the laying of the corner stone of that church in 1874. His wife, Julia, died April 7, 1899. Morrissey is buried next to his wife in an unmarked grave.

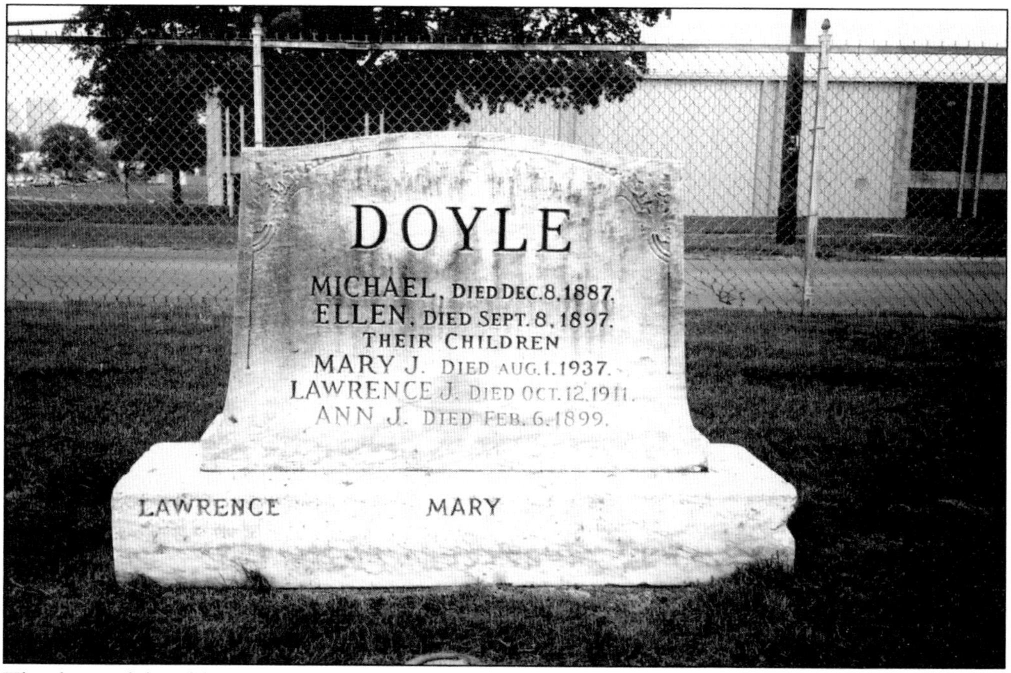

This beautiful "tablet" memorial is the final resting place of Michael and Ellen Doyle and their family. Michael died December 8, 1887, at the age of 63. His wife, Ellen, died September 8, 1897. Their children were Mary Josephine, who died at the age of 75 on August 1, 1937; Lawrence Doyle, who died October 12, 1911; and Ann J., who died February 6, 1899.

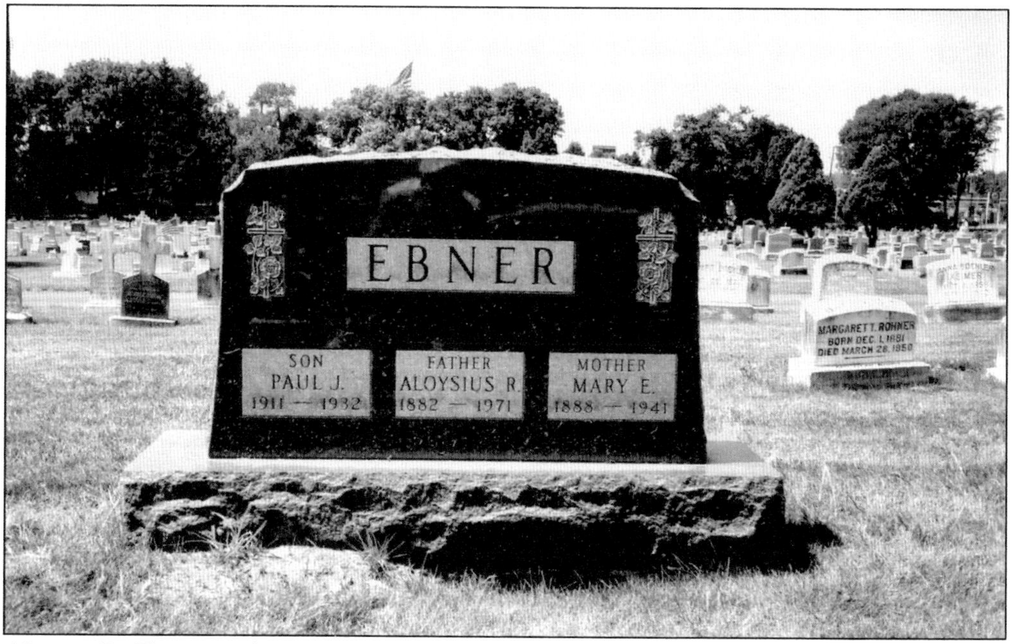

Aloysius R. Ebner was born in 1882 and died March 6, 1971. Ebner was a veteran of World War I; he had retired from Columbus Auto Parts after 25 years. His wife, Mary Ellen Ebner, was born in 1888 and died May 7, 1941. A son, Paul Ebner, born 1911 and died January 26, 1932, is interred beside them.

Policeman Joseph L. Loschiavo was born September 26, 1864, in Sicily, and he died August 14, 1912. He served on the Columbus Police Department for 13 years and was president of the McKinley Italian Society. His wife, Frances Loschiavo, was born October 8, 1871, in Italy, and died June 1, 1946. The M. J. Seelig and Company, Sculptors and Metal Founders of Williamsburg, New York, constructed the beautiful zinc statue atop this monument.

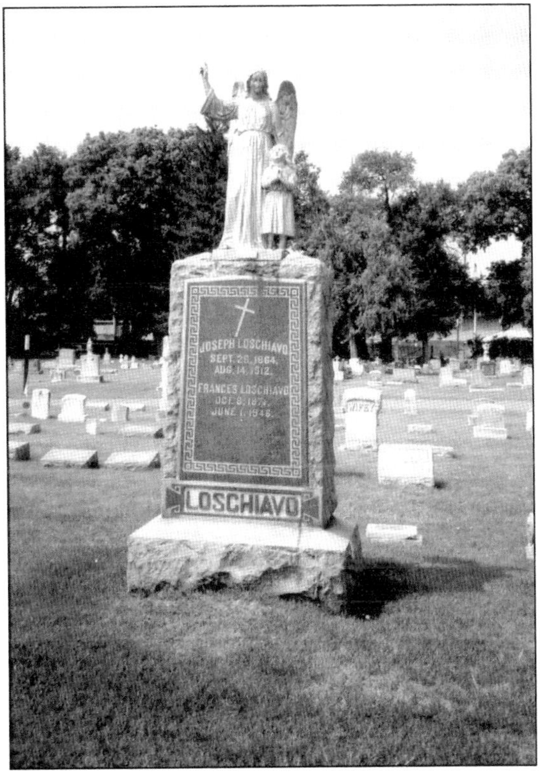

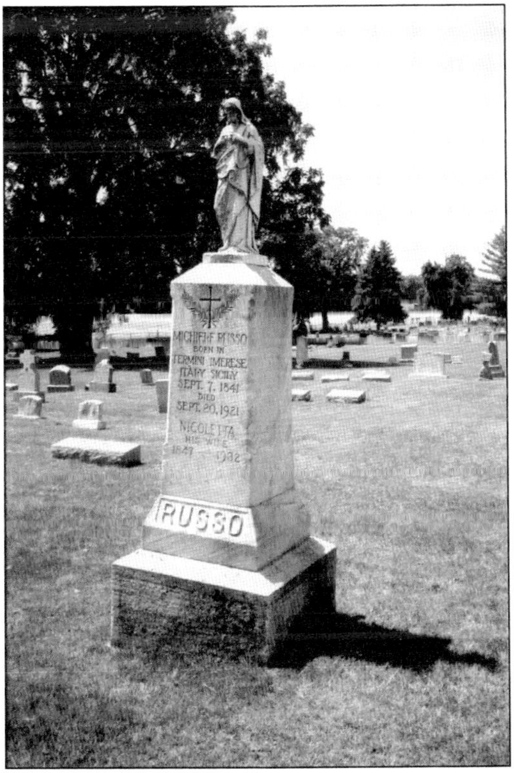

This beautiful memorial stands today as a tribute to Michiele and his wife, Nicoletta Russo. Russo was born September 7, 1841, in Termini Imerese Italy, Sicily, and died September 20, 1921. Nicoletta was born in 1847 and died May 24, 1932. Michiele was a retired fruit dealer and was survived by 40 grandchildren and 21 great-grandchildren. His funeral was held at St. John the Baptist Church.

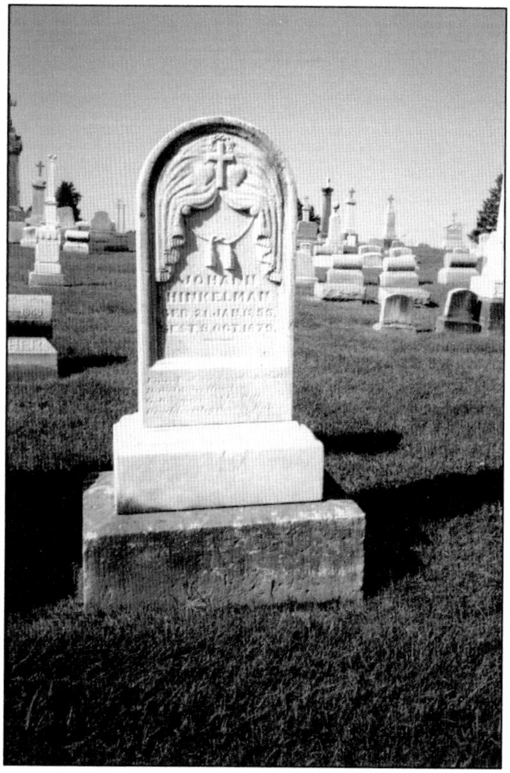

Johann Hinkelman was born February 21, 1855, and died October 8, 1879. The funerary symbol "Drapery or Pall" carved into her monument represents mourning or mortality. Erosion is destroying the epitaph that appears near the base of the monument.

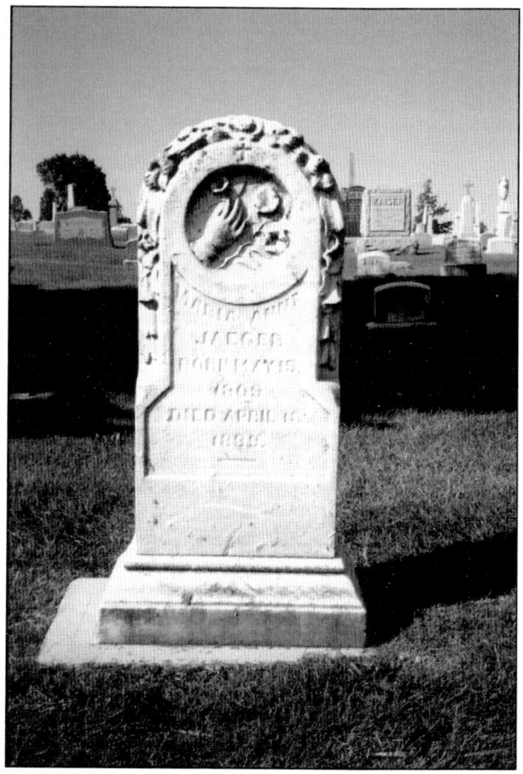

Maria Anne Jaeger was born May 15, 1809, and died April 18, 1889. Her lavishly carved monument displays a motif of flowers surrounding a circle enclosing a hand holding a flower. The carved decoration on this monument symbolizes life's frailty or immortality.

This "tablet" memorial was erected on the Padden plat in memory of Michael Padden (1836–1910) and Catharine Padden (1842–1908). In the 1901–1902 city directory, Michael and a Katherine are listed as boarding at 769 Sullivant Avenue. In 1905, Michael E. is listed as a machinist, and Katherine as a cashier.

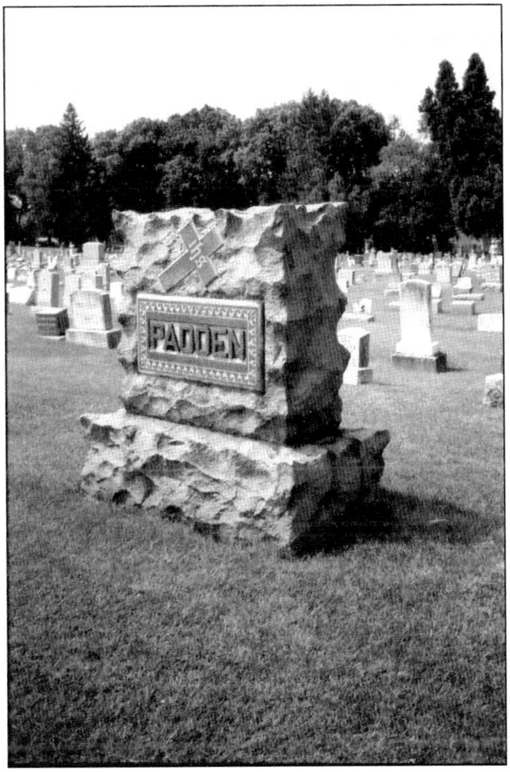

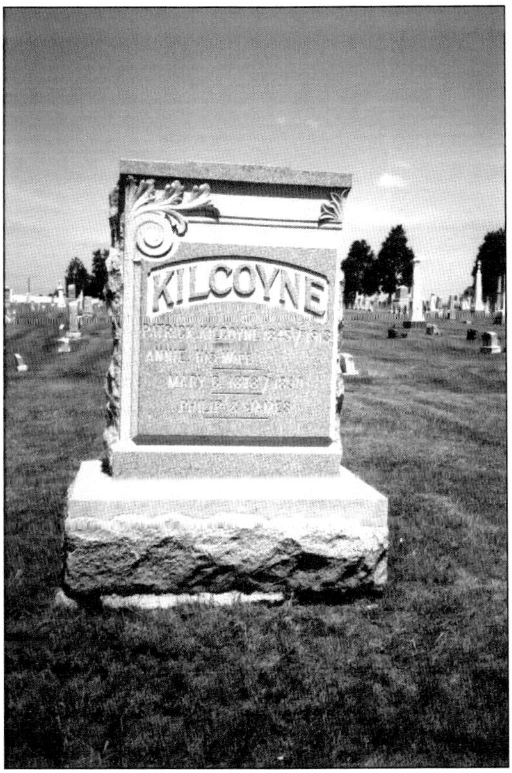

This "upright" monument is the resting place of Patrick Kilcoyne, who was born in 1845 and died May 26, 1913, and his wife, Anna, who died March 9, 1920, at the age of 84 years. Anna made her home with her son, John P. Kilcoyne. Requiem High Mass was held at St. Francis Church. Also interred are Mary C., born in 1878 and died in 1890, Philip, and James.

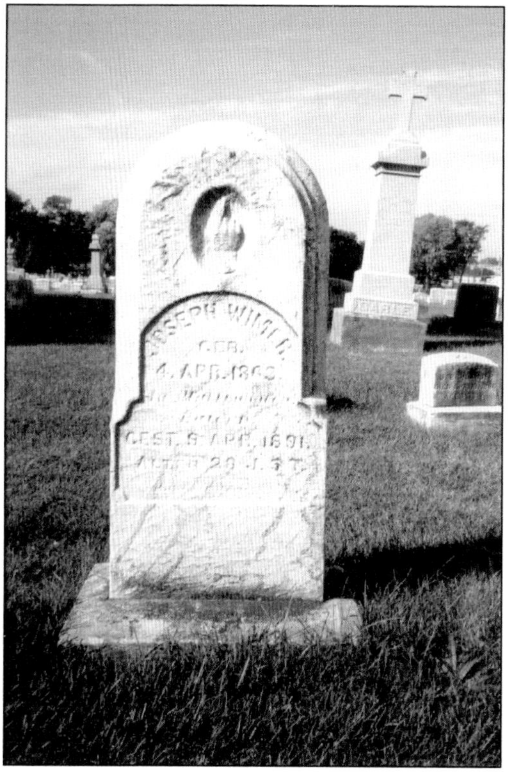

Joseph Wimer was born April 4, 1863, and died April 9, 1891. The symbol of the finger pointing upward represents the pathway to heaven or heavenly reward. Symbols contribute to the significance and beauty of the memorial and convey a definite message for all times.

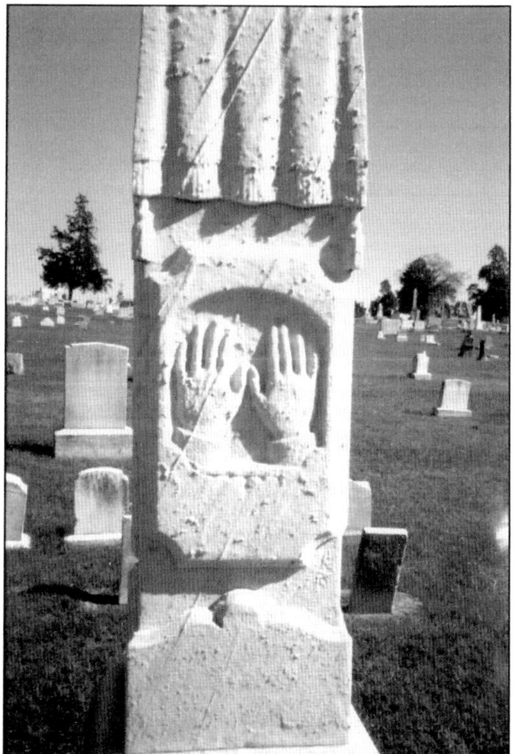

Hands pointing upward indicate a heavenly bound soul. Joseph Widmaier was born March 19, 1835, and died August 27, 1905, and Mary was born in Germany on April 13, 1825, and died August 11, 1912. She came to American as a child, living in Zanesville, later coming to Columbus, where she married Joseph. Mary purchased six graves on August 22, 1905, at a cost of $55. In a 1901–1902 city directory, Joseph is listed as a car inspector.

John J. Ranally was born October 4, 1913, and died December 6, 1924, at the age of 11 years old. His epitaph reads, "Gone but not forgotten." Angels often grace children's and adult's monument as shown here. This child was remembered.

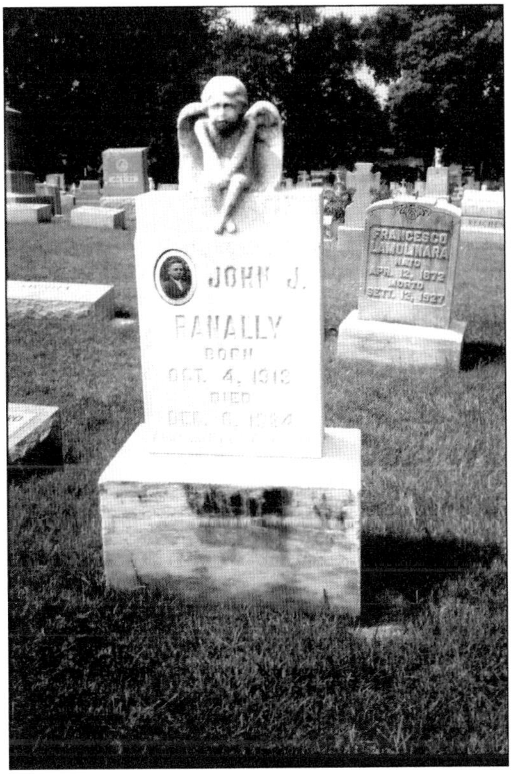

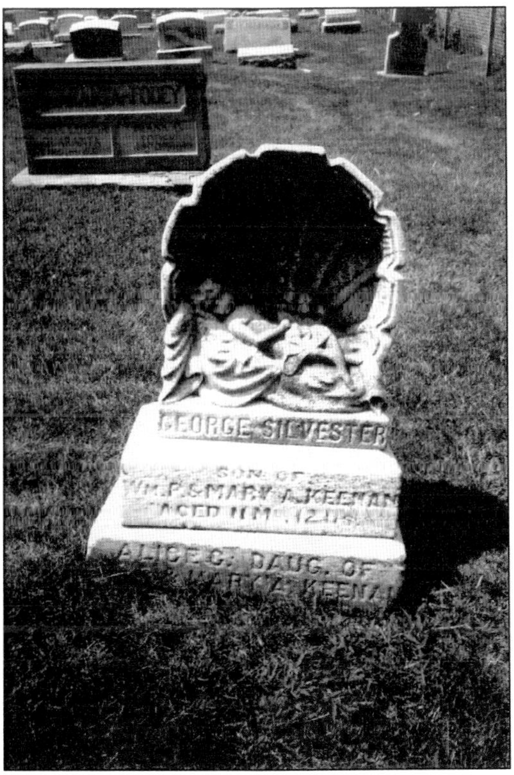

An inscription on this reads, "In heaven there is one angel more." George Silvester Keenan, son of William P. and Mary A. Keenan, died at the age of 11 months, 12 days. Also interred is a daughter, Alice C. Keenan. This monument is also referred to as, "Rock A Bye Baby."

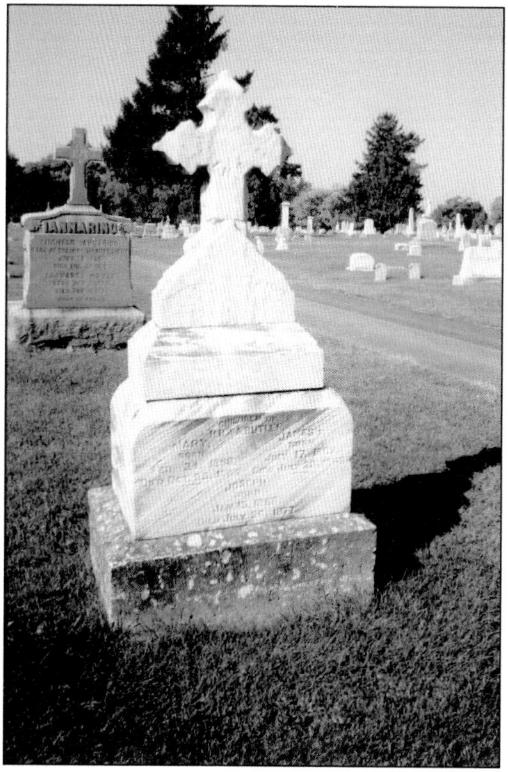

Interred here are the children of H. B. and A. Butler. Mary was born February 24, 1858, and died October 25, 1862; James T. was born July 17, 1862, and died July 23, 1863; and Joseph was born January 15, 1866, and died July 26, 1877.

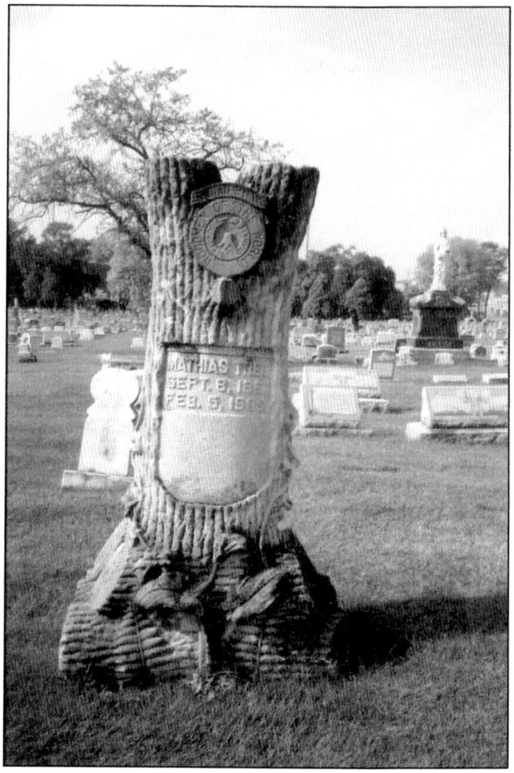

This monument was erected by the Woodmen of the World. Mathias Treib was born September 8, 1861, and died of typhoid pneumonia February 5, 1905, at the age of 45. Treib was a prominent member of the Columbus Liederkranz and the Maennerchor.

Edward L. Tanian was born July 16, 1858, and died March 28, 1929. He was president of the Tanian Brothers Grocery and Bakery Company. This was the first chain store system in Columbus. With one store, Tanian and his brother Joseph established a chain of 22 stores. Joseph was born January 21, 1854, and died October 18, 1910. Edward retired in 1917, when the firm was sold to the Kroger Grocery and Bakery Company.

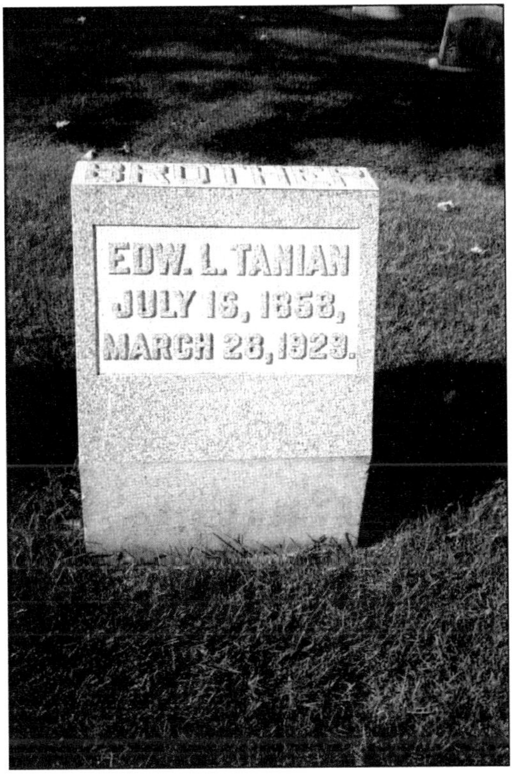

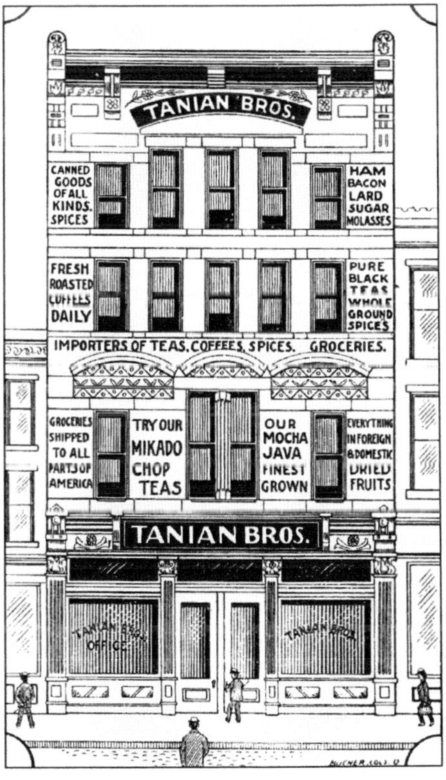

The Tanian firm controlled 12 stores in Columbus and its four-story wholesale building at 136–138 East Town Street. The Tanian company built a large mail order department and carried a complete line of groceries. They were able to fill and ship directly to the homemaker. They were importers of tea, coffee, and spices, and specialized in a large selection of canned goods, ham, bacon, lard, sugar, molasses, and domestic dried fruits. (Columbus Metropolitan Library.)

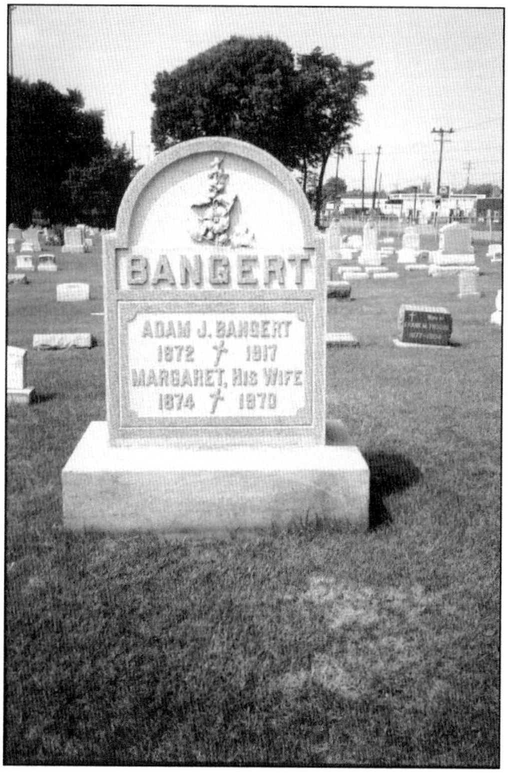

The engraved flower represents life's frailty or immortality. Adam J. Bangert, born in 1872, was a meat dealer and local butcher at the Central Market. He died April 28, 1917. His wife, Margaret Bangert, was born in 1870 and died January 23, 1970, at her Kossuth Street home. Margaret was a lifetime member of Tabernacle Society and Altar-Rosary Society.

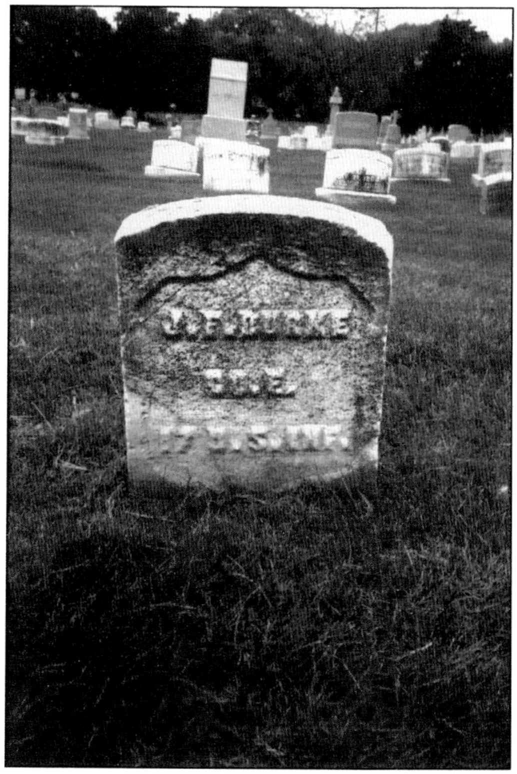

John "Don" Francis Burke was born 1879 and died July 3, 1899. Burke was one of the American heroes of the war with Spain and was the first Columbus boy killed in the fighting around Santiago. After his death, Columbus boys in his regiment saw to it that his grave was properly marked, in the hopes of recovering his remains once orders were given by government officials to disinter and transfer bodies.

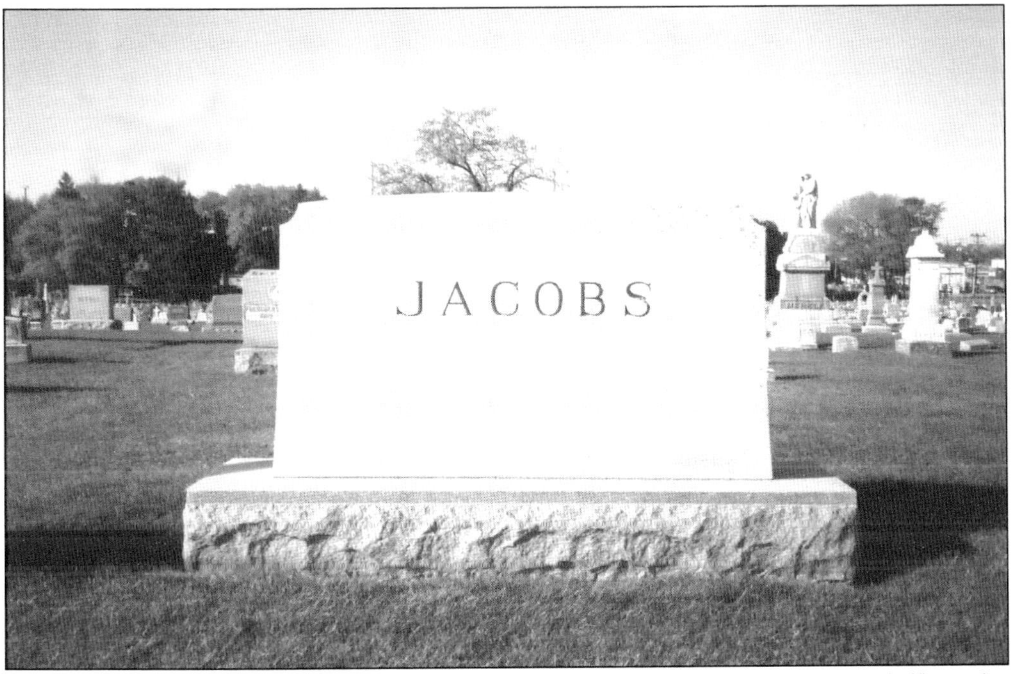

Felix A. Jacobs was born August 3, 1840, the son of Cornelius and Christenia (Gangloff) Jacobs. Felix died March 2, 1926. His father was a native of Germany, and his mother was from France. Cornelius took a prominent part in building the first Catholic church in Columbus, known as the Little Stone Church.

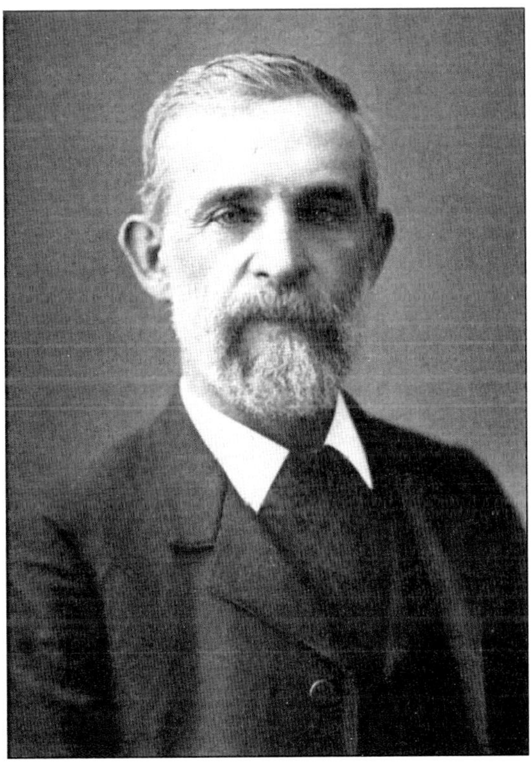

In 1866, Felix with his brothers, Henry L. and William E., formed the firm of Jacobs Brothers in the manufacturing and sale of agricultural implements, later becoming the Kilbourne and Jacobs Company. Felix was a former member of city council and a director of public improvements under Mayor Samuel L. Black. He was a director and vice president of the Columbus Brick and Terra Cotta Company, and a director of the Columbus Machine Company. (Columbus Metropolitan Library.)

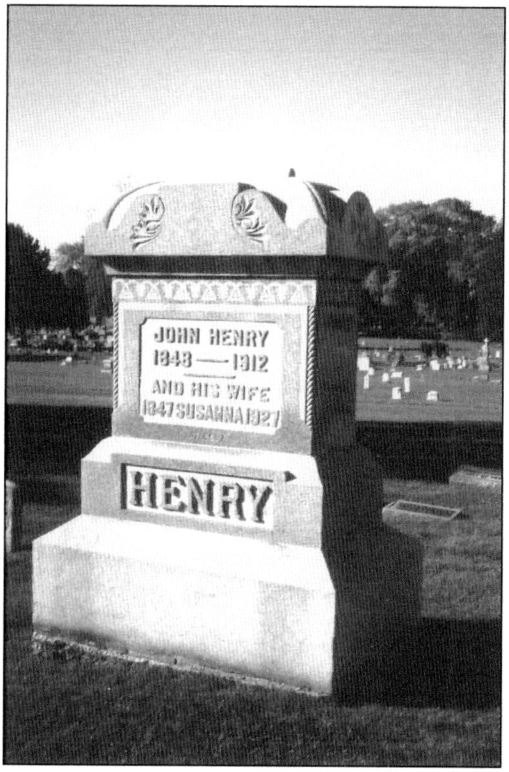

In 1872, John Henry arrived on the shores of America. For 21 years, he was a tailor on the west side. In 1880, he married Susanna Loy; they had one daughter who died in infancy. Fond of children after the loss of his only child, he always provided Christmas for the children of the area, and it was his custom to give children who came into his store little gifts.

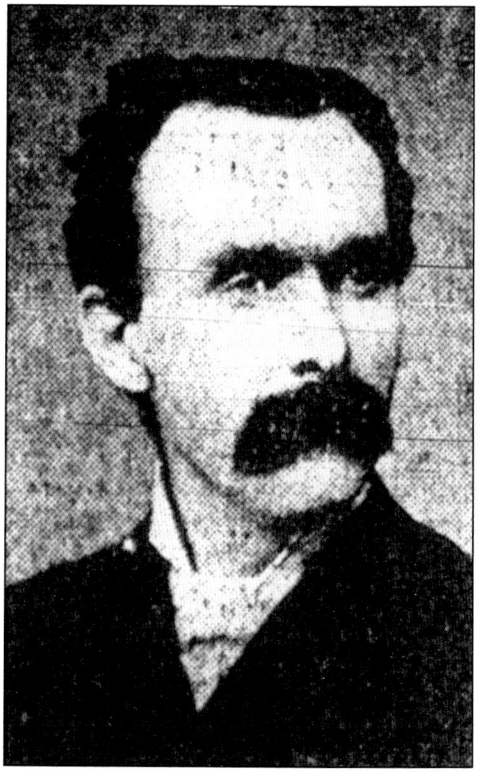

Henry was born in Ireland in 1849 and died January 22, 1912, at his home located at 295 West Broad Street. He was a true friend of all children and at his funeral many of those neighborhood children were present. His wife, Susanna, died in 1927. (Columbus Metropolitan Library.)

Frederick Wittenmeier Sr., interred in this section, was born in 1854 and died on September 27, 1921. For years, he was a stone contractor and had retired a year before his death. During his career as a stone contractor, he was active in the construction of the prisons, such as Franklin County Court House and State House Annex, several buildings on the Ohio State University campus, and many residences. He was a former member of the Builders' Exchange. His wife, Agnes, died July 15, 1919.

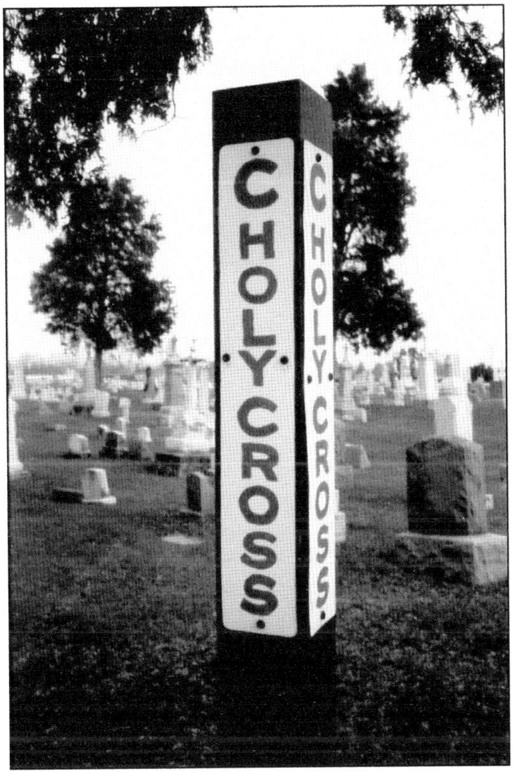

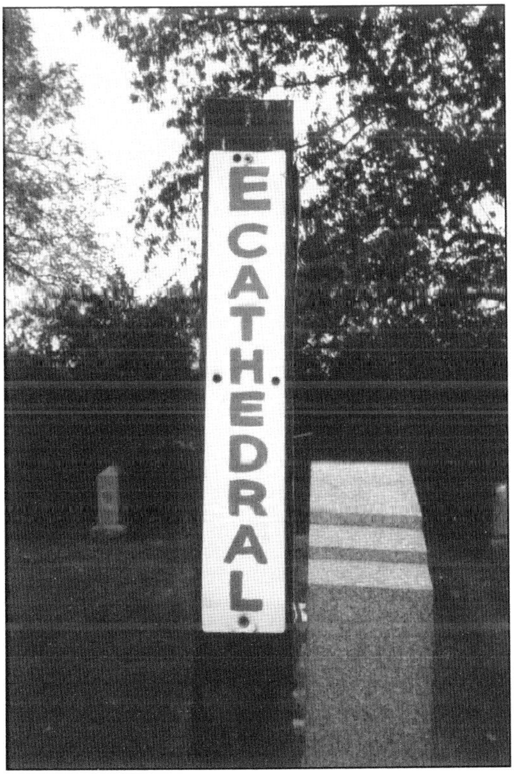

John A. Fleming, interred in this section, was born in 1876 and was killed by a train in January 1904. Fleming had been employed with the Hallwood Cash Register Company as a salesman. He was engaged in issuing a new city labor directory. His wife was the daughter of Columbus mayor Phil Bruck. Hallwood Cash Register Company was known as "A Marvel of Mechanical Skill" and opened in 1897. It was a leading competitor of National Cash Register Company.

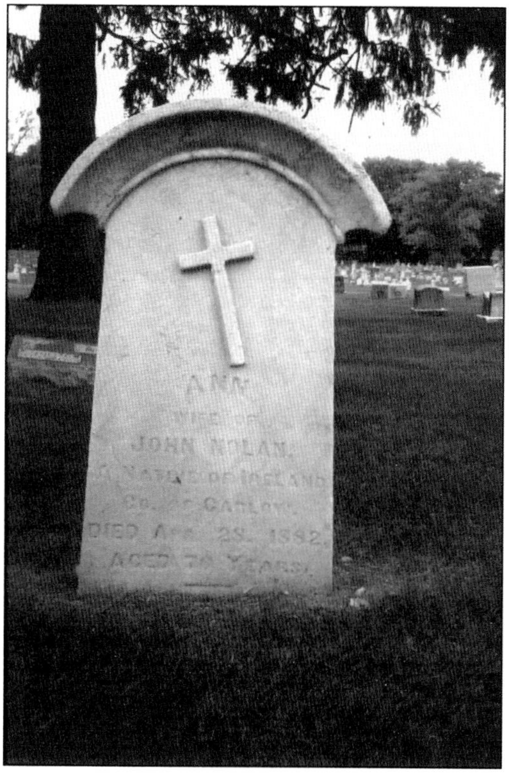

John Nolan was born in 1812 and died December 14, 1910. Nolan was engaged in the dairy business. He used tobacco and alcohol, ate whatever he liked, and insisted on an abundance of fresh air. He refused to stay in a stuffy room, drank water, never wore eyeglasses, and read newspapers every day. Nolan does not have a monument, only his wife, Ann, does.

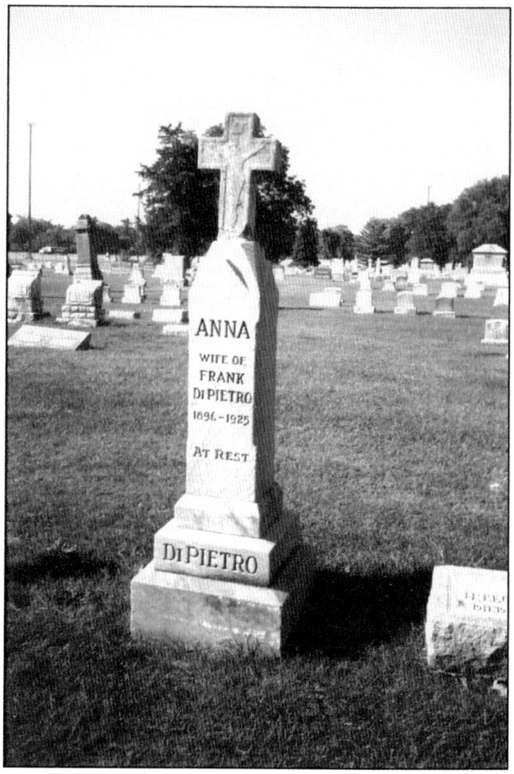

Anna DiPietro was born in 1896 in Italy, and died March 12, 1925. Anna was the wife of Frank DiPietro and mother of three sons and two daughters. Her mother, three sisters, and four brothers survived her. Her funeral was held at St. John the Baptist Church.

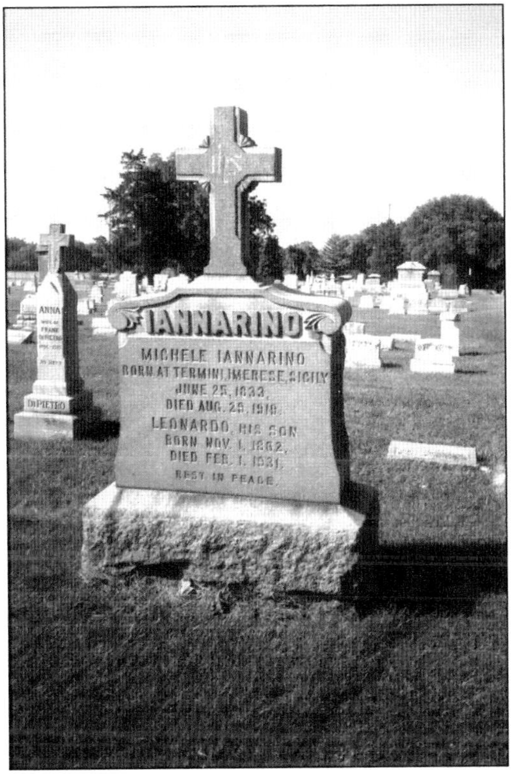

The epitaph reads, "Rest In Peace." Michele Iannarion was born at Termini, Imerese, Sicily, on June 25, 1833, and died August 19, 1919, at his residence on McCoy Street. Also interred on this lot is his son, Leonardo, who was born November 1, 1862, and died February 1, 1931, at the home of his sister in Indianapolis.

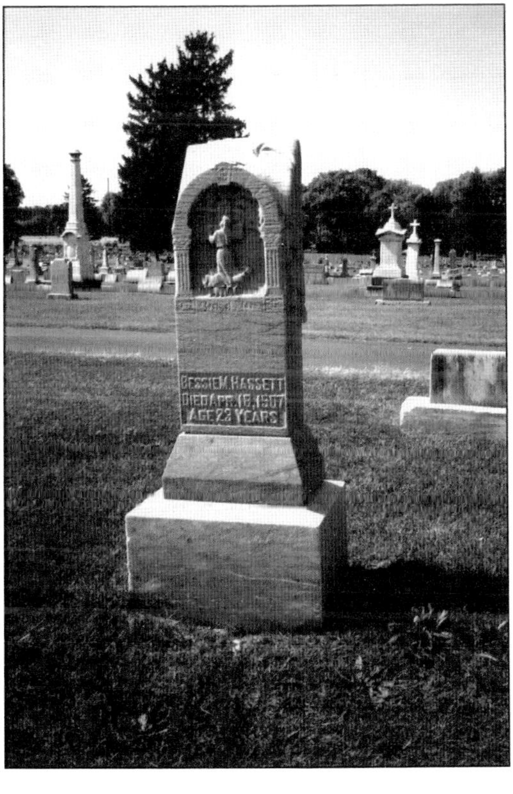

A month after she fell at a masquerade party at a skating rink, 23-year-old Bessie Hassett died on April 18, 1907. She was the daughter of Margaret Hassett. Her marker reads, "In Loving Remembrance."

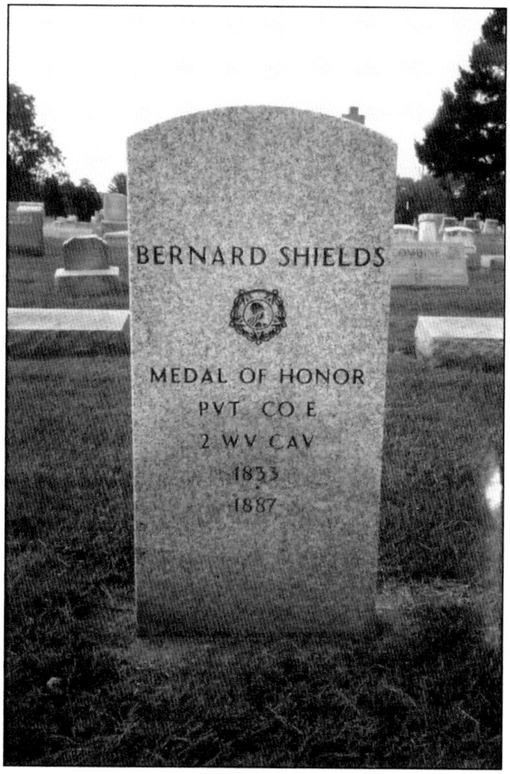

Civil War Congressional Medal of Honor recipient Pvt. Bernard Shields (2nd West Virginia Cavalry) captured the battle flag of the Washington Artillery at Appomattox Station, Virginia, on April 8, 1865. He entered service at Ironton, Ohio. Shields was born in Ireland in 1833 and died April 20, 1887. His wife was Anna Shields (1837–1910). In Mount Calvary Cemetery, 165 Civil War soldiers have been recorded as interred.

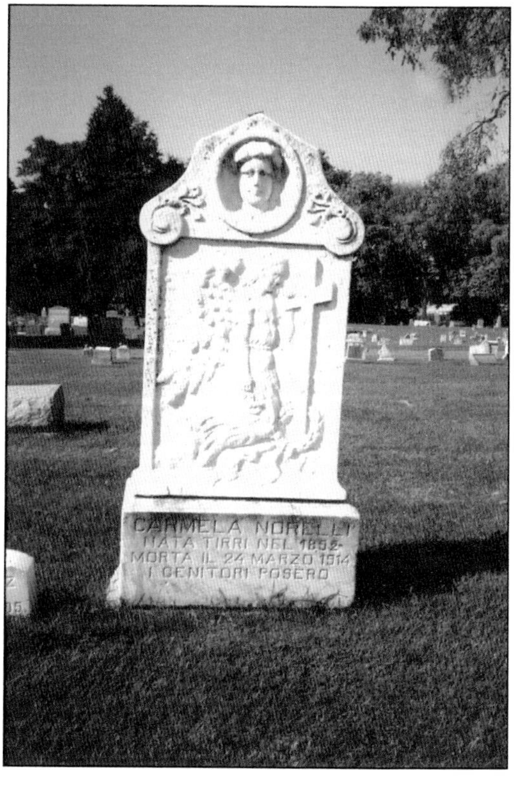

"Weep not, father and mother, for me, For I am waiting in glory for thee," is the epitaph for Carmela Norelli "Morrell." She was born in 1892 and died March 24, 1914. Carmela was the wife of Frank Morrell. Her husband, a four-day-old child, her parents, brothers, and sisters survived her.

A military funeral was held at St. John the Baptist Church for James Baldassaro, private first corporal in 113th Infantry 29 Division. Born July 15, 1896, he died December 26, 1932. During World War I, Baldassaro was gassed during the Argonne engagement. He was a member of the American Legion and was survived by his wife and six children.

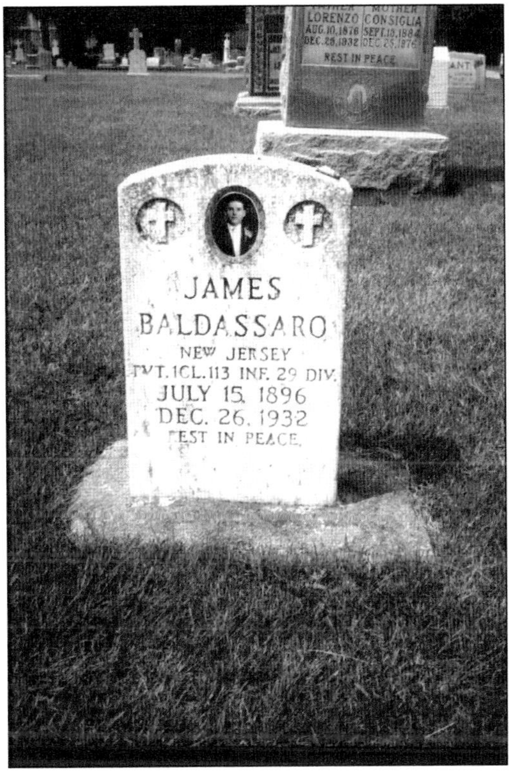

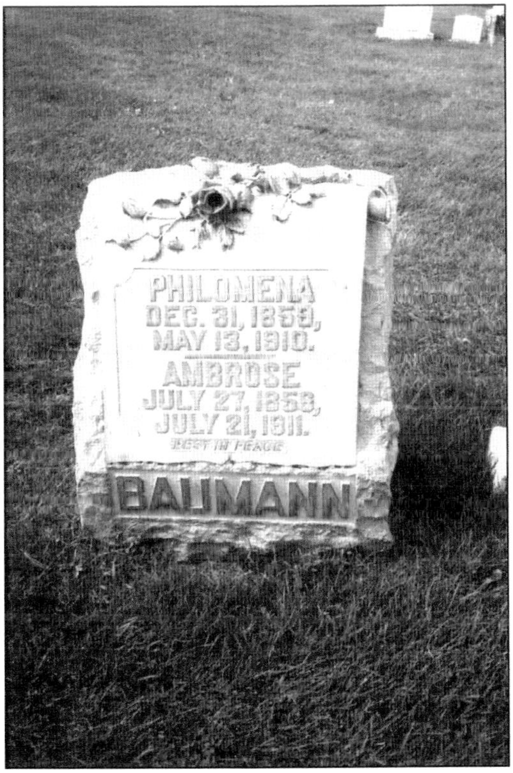

Ambrose Baumann was a Columbus jeweler located at 1200 North High Street. Baumann was born July 27, 1858, and died July 21, 1910. His wife, Philomena Baumann, was born December 31, 1858, and died May 13, 1910.

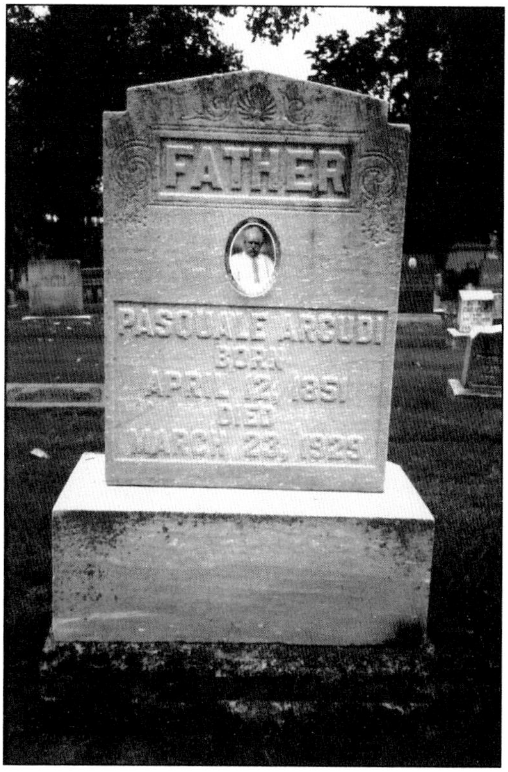

A porcelain portrait is inserted into the monument of Pasquale Arcudi. Arcudi was born April 12, 1851, and he died March 23, 1929. Arcudi was a laborer. His funeral took place at St. John the Baptist Church. His wife, Concetta Arcudi, died in 1941.

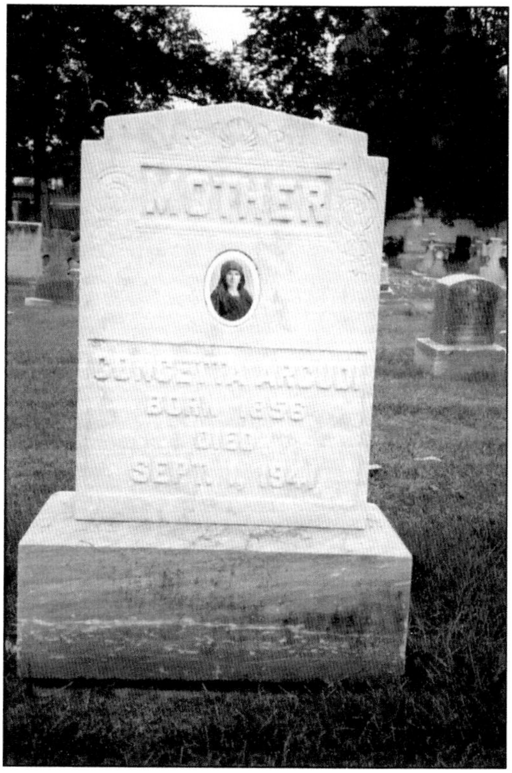

Concetta's porcelain portrait is inserted into her monument. Concetta was born in Italy in 1856 and died September 1, 1941. She was a resident of Columbus for 35 years and a member of Holy Rosary congregation at St. John's Church and the mother of Antoinetta Giamarco, a grocer on Curtis Avenue.

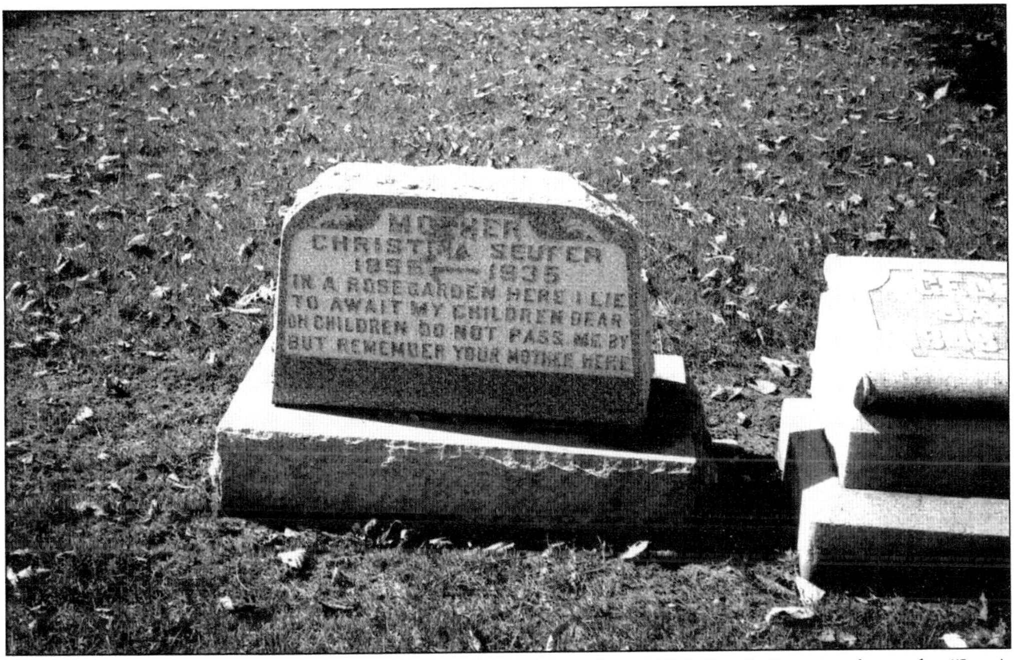

Christian Seufer was born in 1856 and died in December 1935. Seufer's epitaph reads, "In A Rose Garden Here I Lie To Await My Children Dear. Oh Children Do Not Pass Me By But Remember Your Mother Here." Seufer died at the home of her daughter near New Albany. Her funeral was held at St. Paul's Monastery in Westerville.

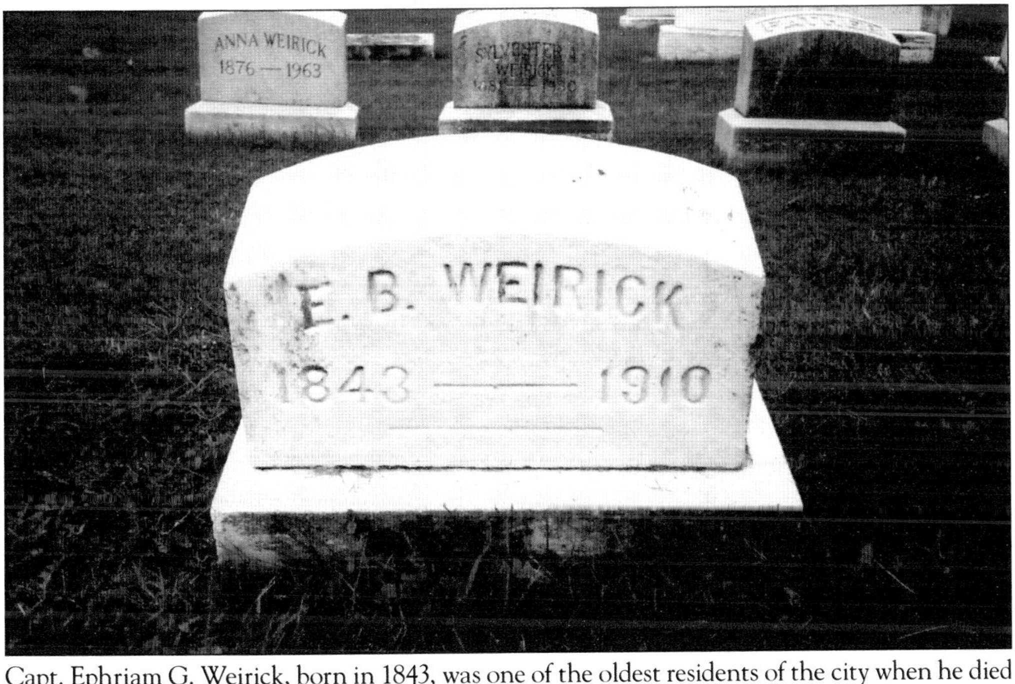

Capt. Ephriam G. Weirick, born in 1843, was one of the oldest residents of the city when he died December 12, 1910. Captain Weirick, for a number of years, was commander of the Knights of St. George and a pioneer of St. Mary's Parish, where his funeral took place. Captain Weirick's son Sylvester was connected with the Union Clothing Company.

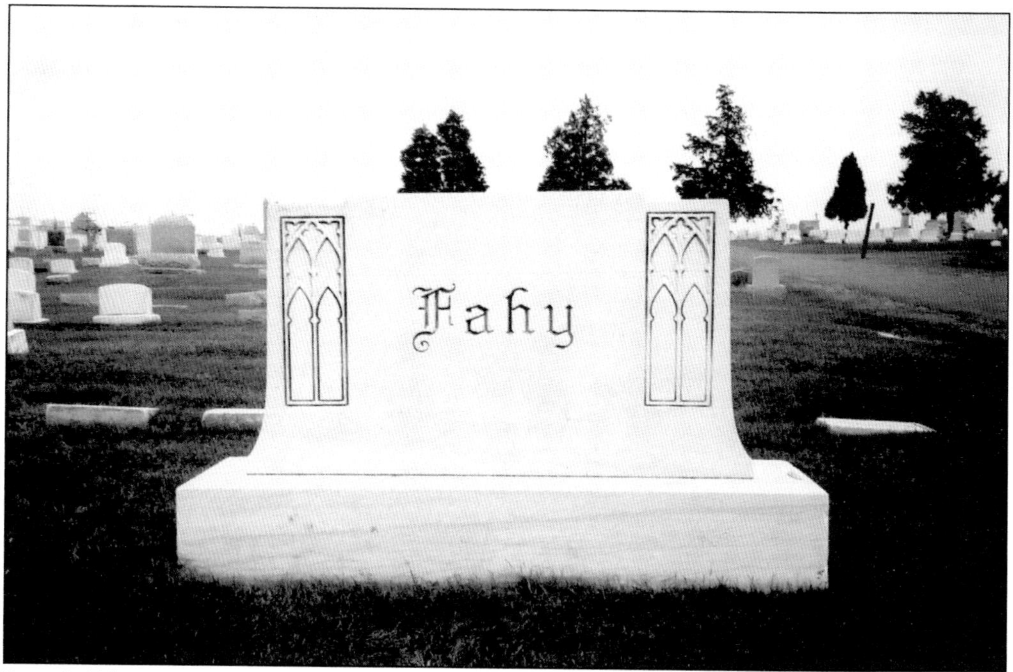

Patrick Fahy was a former postmaster at New Straitsville, Ohio, and a resident of Columbus for 20 years. He died at his Dennison Avenue home, May 25, 1917. A native of Ireland, he was familiar with the Irish language and was able to translate and write it. In a 1910–1911 city directory, Fahy is listed as a baggage man. His wife, Margaret, died June 2, 1922.

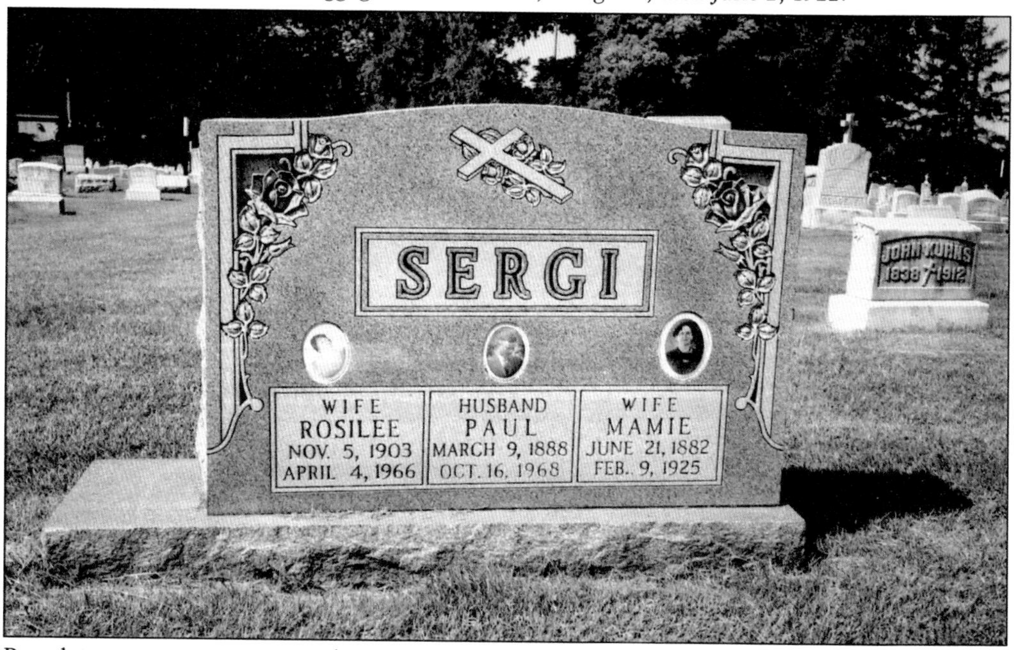

Porcelain portraits are inserted into the monument of Paul Sergi, who was born March 9, 1888, and died October 16, 1968, and his two wives. Mamie Sergi was born June 21, 1882, and accidentally strangled to death in her kitchen February 9, 1925. His second wife, Rosilee Sergi, was born November 5, 1903, and died April 4, 1966.

Leo Hall, son of Catherine Hall, was born in 1890 and died May 4, 1912, from injuries he received April 24, when his motorcycle collided with a streetcar at the corner of Oak and Eighteenth Streets. He was employed as a stereotyper for the *Columbus Citizen* and a member of the Catholic Order of Foresters, the Buckeye Athletic club, and the Stereotypes' Union.

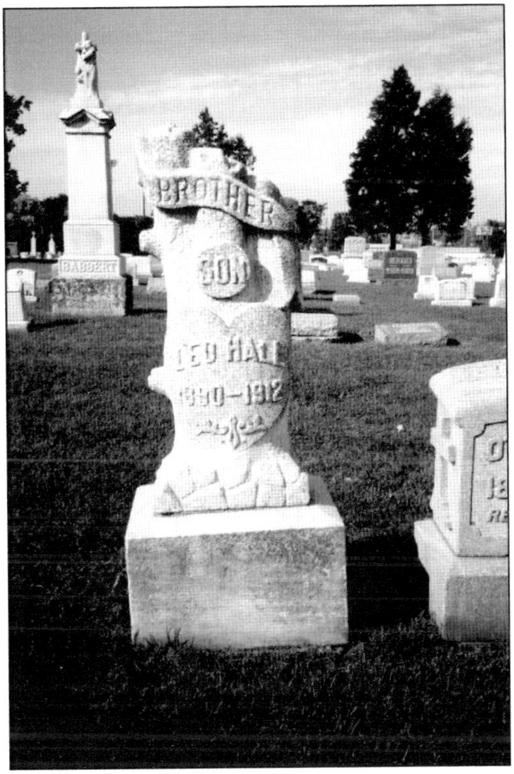

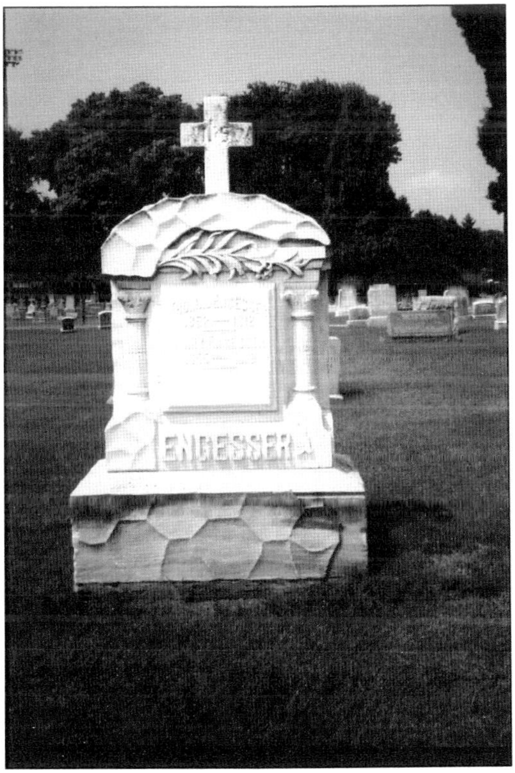

Mary Engesser, a 57-year-old invalid for 22 years, died at her City Park home on February 15, 1913. Engesser was born in Germany in 1855, and came to America in 1883. Her husband, Thomas E. Engesser, was born in 1852 and died in April 18, 1912.

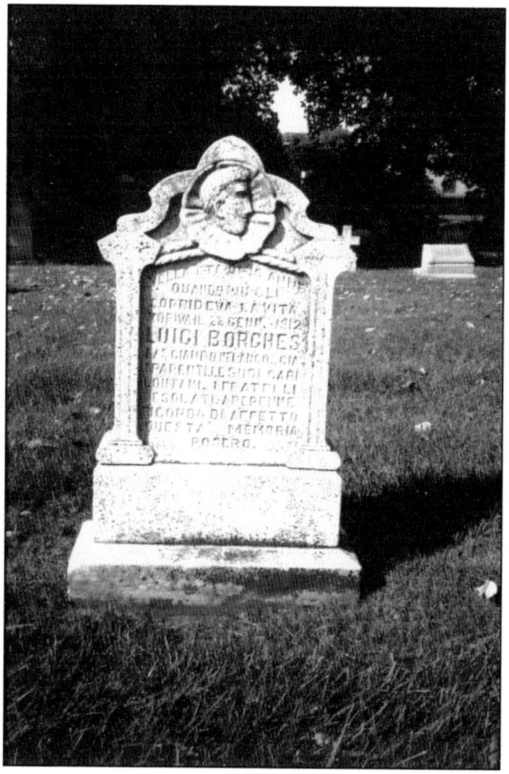

This unusual monument is the final resting place of Louis Borghes, who died at the age of 19, January 25, 1912. His funeral mass was from Sacred Heart Church.

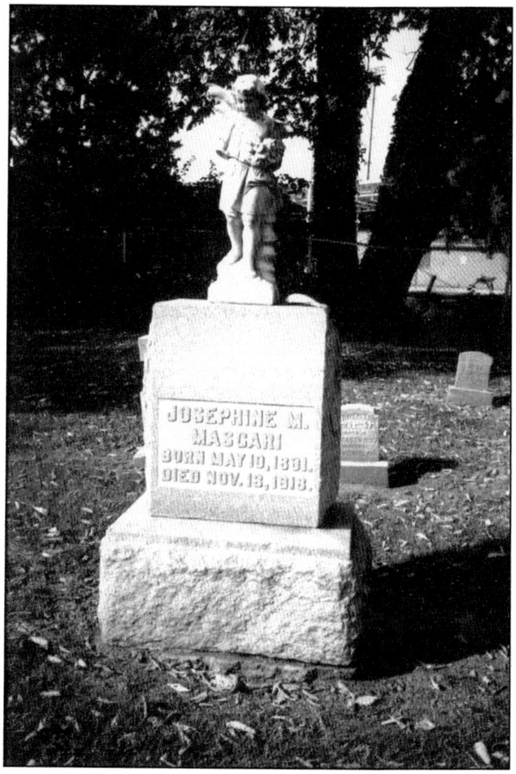

Josephine M. Mascari, the 27-year-old wife of Benjamin Mascari, died of pneumonia November 18, 1918. Josephine was born May 10, 1881. Her funeral was held at the residence.

Antonio "Jack" Toney Pallott was 26 years old when he died May 16, 1923. Born March 1, 1887, Pallott died of tuberculosis. His picture is inserted into his monument. His widow, Rosie Pallott, a son, and two daughters survived him.

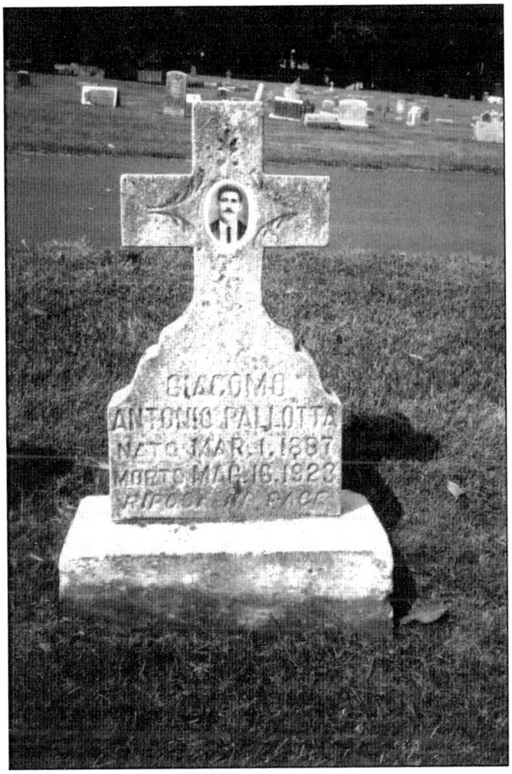

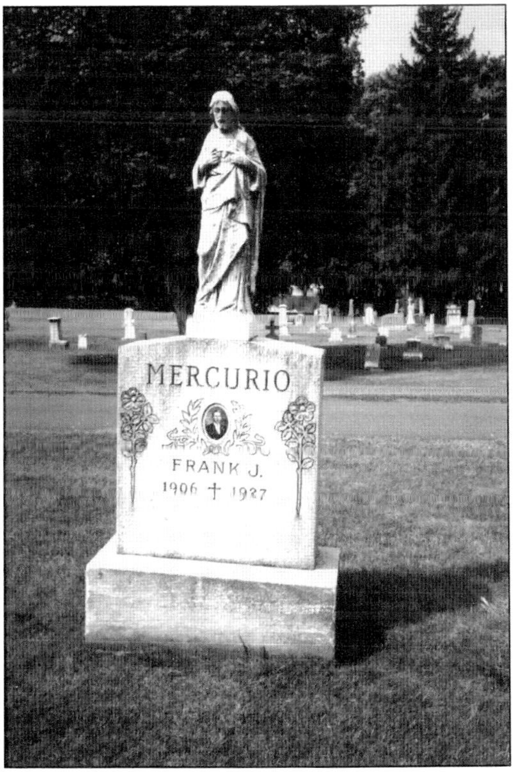

Frank J. Mercurio was born in 1906 and died September 4, 1927, after an illness of four months. The 21-year old fruit dealer was the son of Mrs. and Mrs. John Mercurio. Mercurio was a member of the Knights of Columbus and the Holy Name Society.

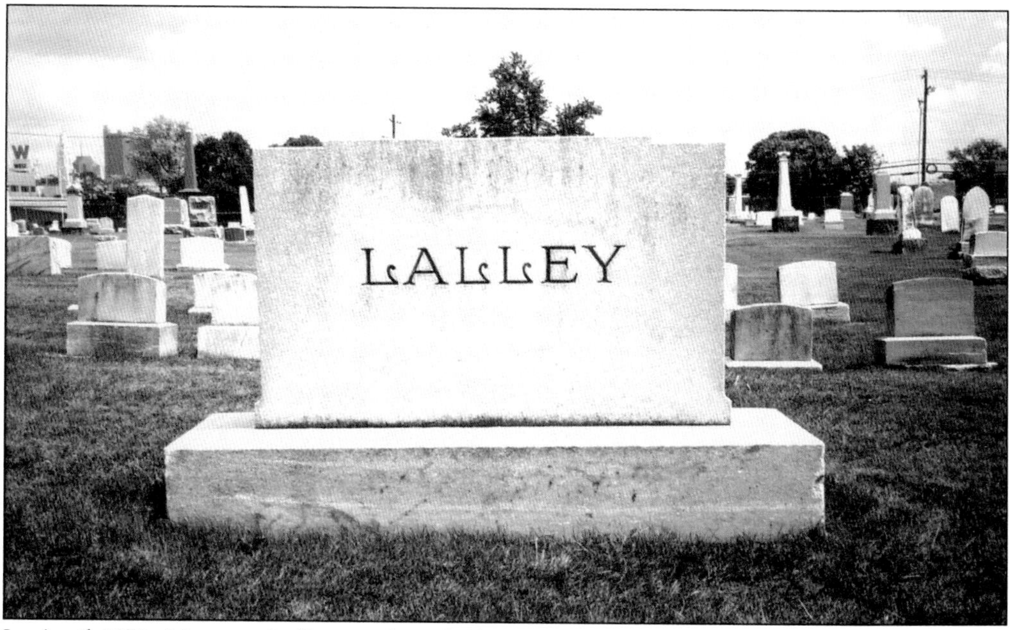

In April 1872, Margaret Lalley purchased 12 grave spaces at the cost of $35 in Cathedral B section, lot number 104. Margaret died January 25, 1917. Also interred are Alfred Lalley, Joseph Lalley, Clara Lalley Schumaker, and Isabella Wittmann and two-year-old son Charles, who died October 17, 1876. Her husband, Bartholomew W. Lalley, died July 5, 1897. In 1895, Bartholomew was listed in the city directory as a blacksmith.

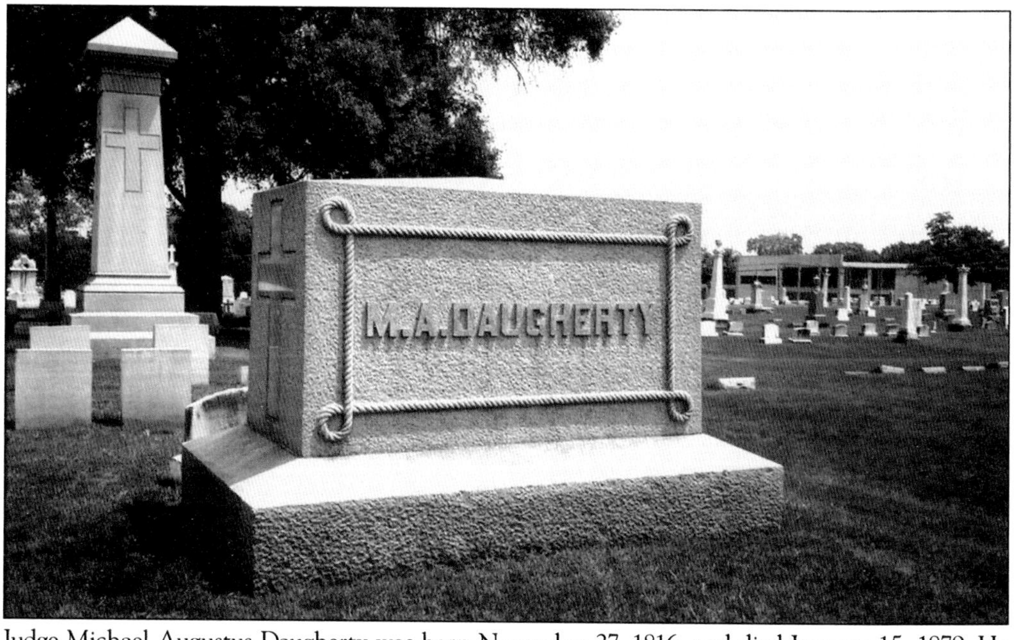

Judge Michael Augustus Daugherty was born November 27, 1816, and died January 15, 1879. He practiced law in Lancaster and later formed a partnership with Hunter Hocking II. In 1870, he was elected to the state senate, served on the Ohio Judiciary Committee, and ran for attorney general in 1873. Gov. Willam Allen appointed him a member of the Codifying Commission in April 1875. He married Phebe M. McCalum, who died January 2, 1899. They never had children.

Carmine J. Lombardi was born October 24, 1872, and died April 16, 1920. Lombardi was employed with the Jeffrey Manufacturing Company, manufacturing mining equipment, elevating devices, and power transmission machinery. The top of his monument serves as a birdbath. His monument is engraved with the Woodmen of the World memorial, a fraternal insurance society for persons over the age of 16 founded in 1890.

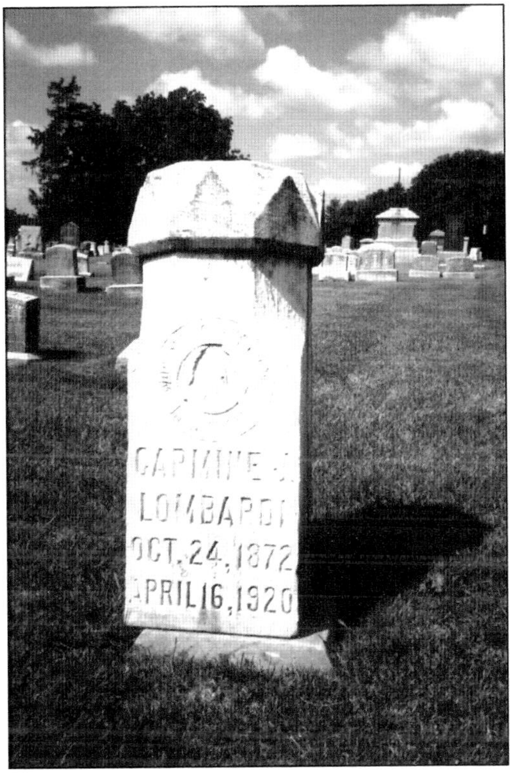

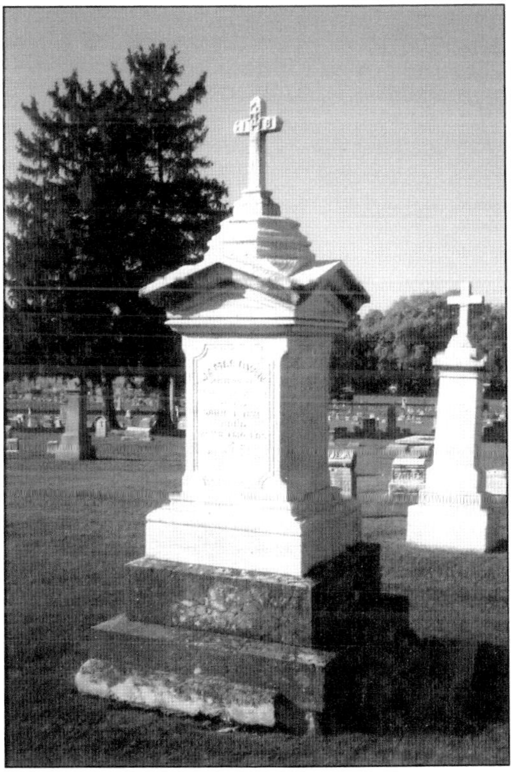

James Ryan a native of Ireland died June 1, 1875, at the age of 39. His wife, Susan Zettler Ryan, was born in 1838 and died July 7, 1908. Susan was an inmate of the county infirmary and died from the effects of senile exhaustion.

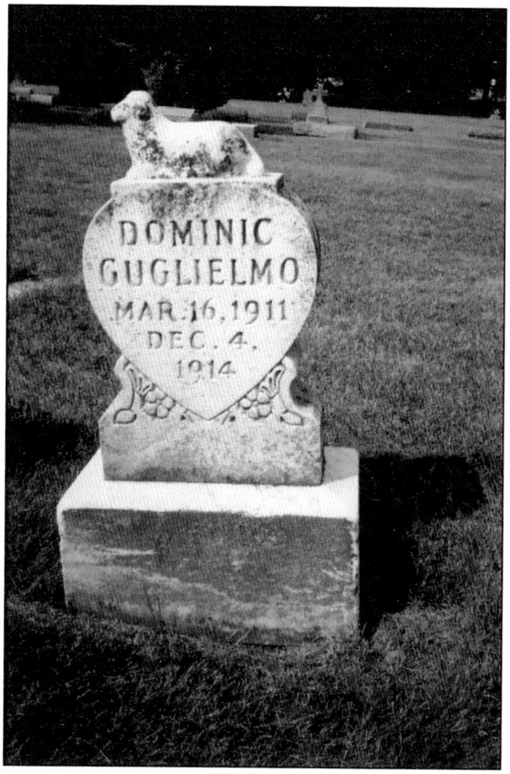

The figure of a lamb often appears on a child's grave and is a symbol of innocence. Dominic Guglielmo Williams was born March 16, 1911, and died December 4, 1914 of meningitis. He was the three-year-old son of Mr. and Mrs. Angelo Williams.

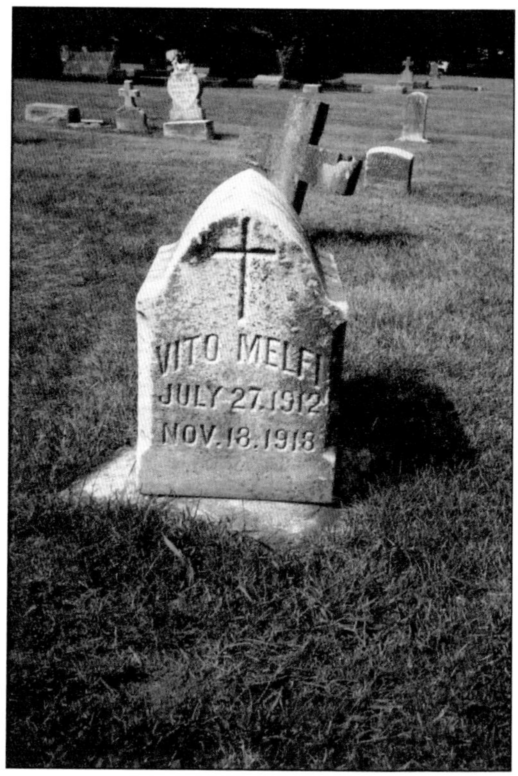

This very simple monument is the final resting place of six-year old Vito Melfie, who was born July 27, 1912, and died November 18, 1918.

Stephen Miller died December 30, 1909. The 23 year old is memorialized with this guarding angel that carries a bouquet of flowers. The inscription is almost illegible. Miller was struck on the head during a fight at a dance hall after he assaulted a man on Christmas Eve. He died from this wound.

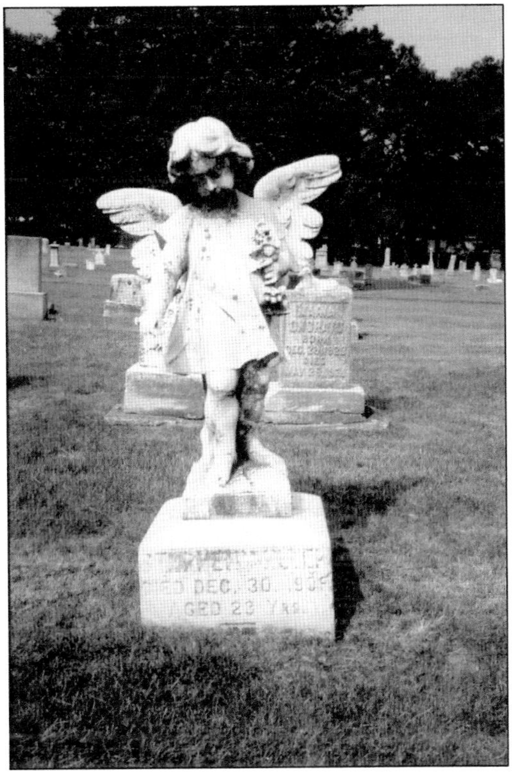

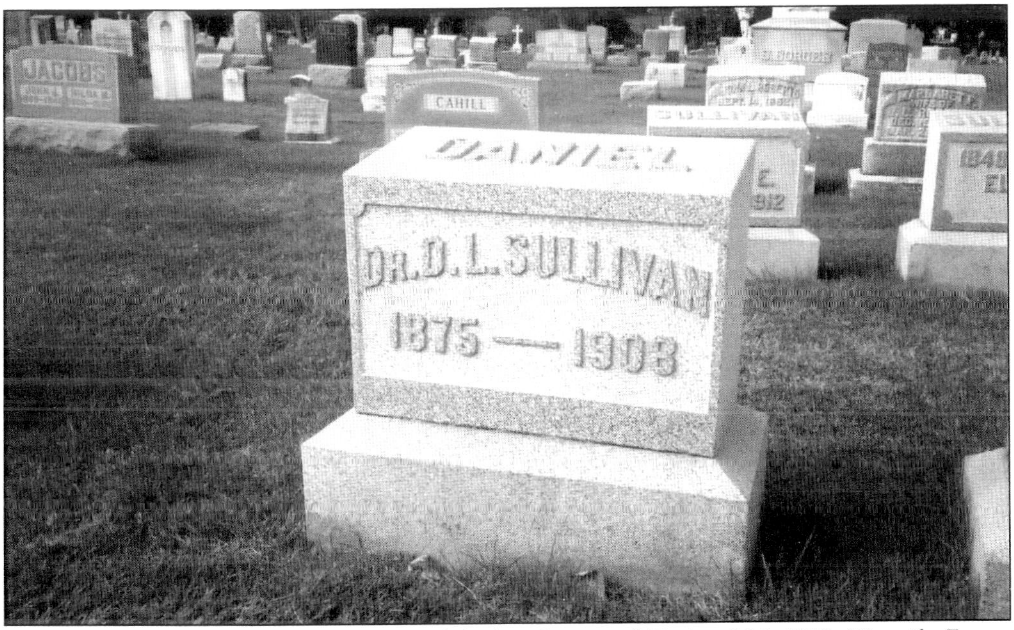

Dr. Daniel Sullivan was born in 1875 and died at the age of 33, April 24, 1908. His wife, Emma Sullivan, was born in 1871 and died at age 38, one year after Daniel, in 1909. Daniel graduated from Ohio Medical College in 1898 and maintained an office at the corner of Washington and Long Streets. Interred in the Sullivan plot are James A., Jane, George, Ella, and Dan Sullivan, who died in 1912.

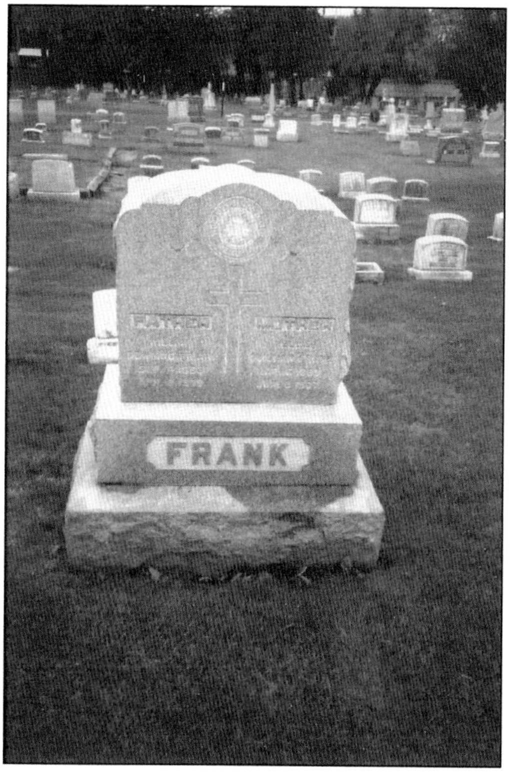

William D. Frank, born September 4, 1893, and his brother John were killed while defending their father's grocery store at 1221 Parsons Avenue, April 1908. William joined the Catholic church when he married and is interred in Mount Calvary Cemetery. His wife, Helen Quillian Frank, died June 3, 1907. John was buried in Union Cemetery.

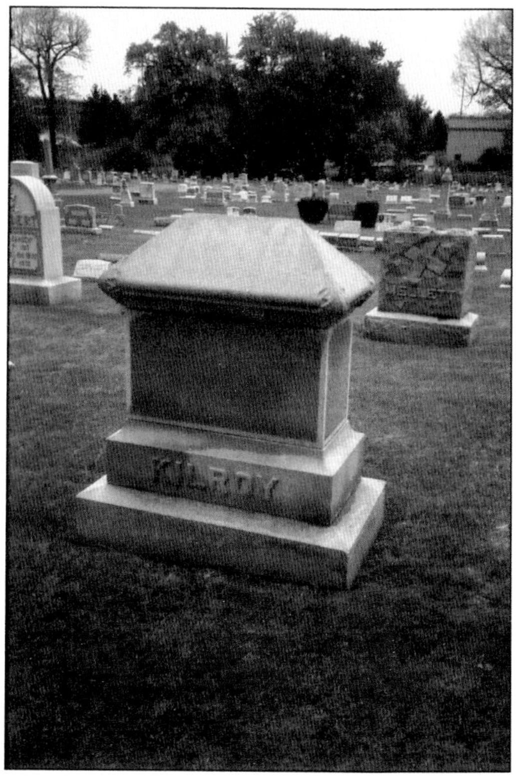

John Kilroy was for 30 years chief engineer at the Columbus Waterworks. Catherine Redman Kilroy was a member of a prominent Zanesville, Ohio, family. In 1863, when Gen. John Morgan made his famous raid through southern Ohio, her brother, John Redman, was an engineer on a railroad train carrying almost 1,000 Union solders that Morgan and his men attacked. Catharine died April 15, 1909.

Martin Meagher died November 14, 1925, from injuries he received in an automobile accident. His son, Rev. Fr. Victor Meagher of Winanoc, Indiana, conducted the Meagher Requiem High Mass. Mary Meagher died November 8, 1946, and was one of the original members of St. Catherine's Church. She was a native of Nenagh, County Tipperary, Ireland, and came to this country as a child.

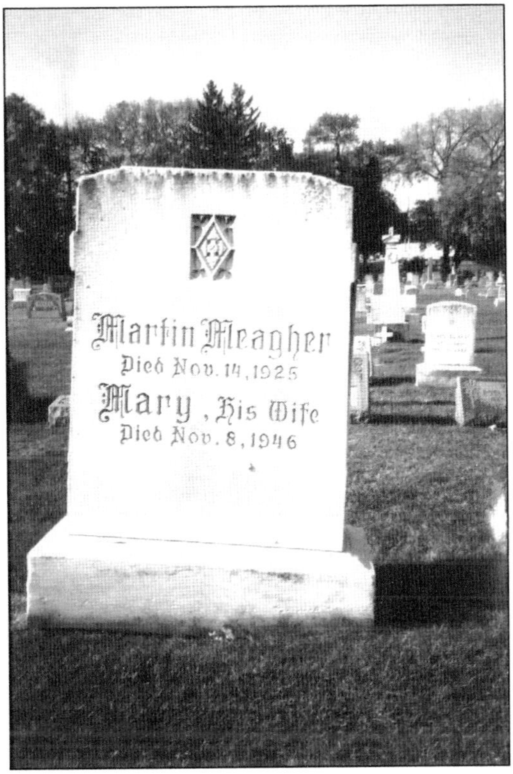

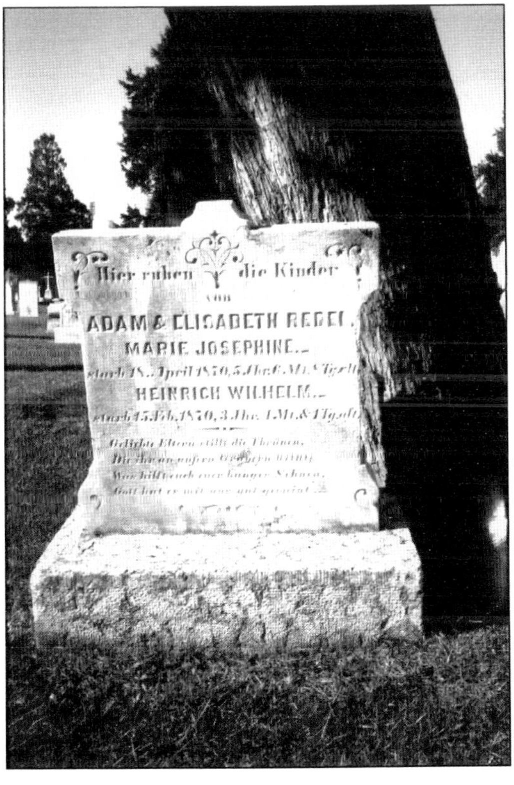

On February 25, 1876, Adam Redel purchased six graves space in Holycross section 6, lot 140. His wife, Elizabeth Redel, died October 31, 1904. A son Heinrich, age three years four months, died February 17, 1870, and a daughter Sophia, age five years seven months, died April 21, 1870. Adam is believed to have died March 11, 1901.

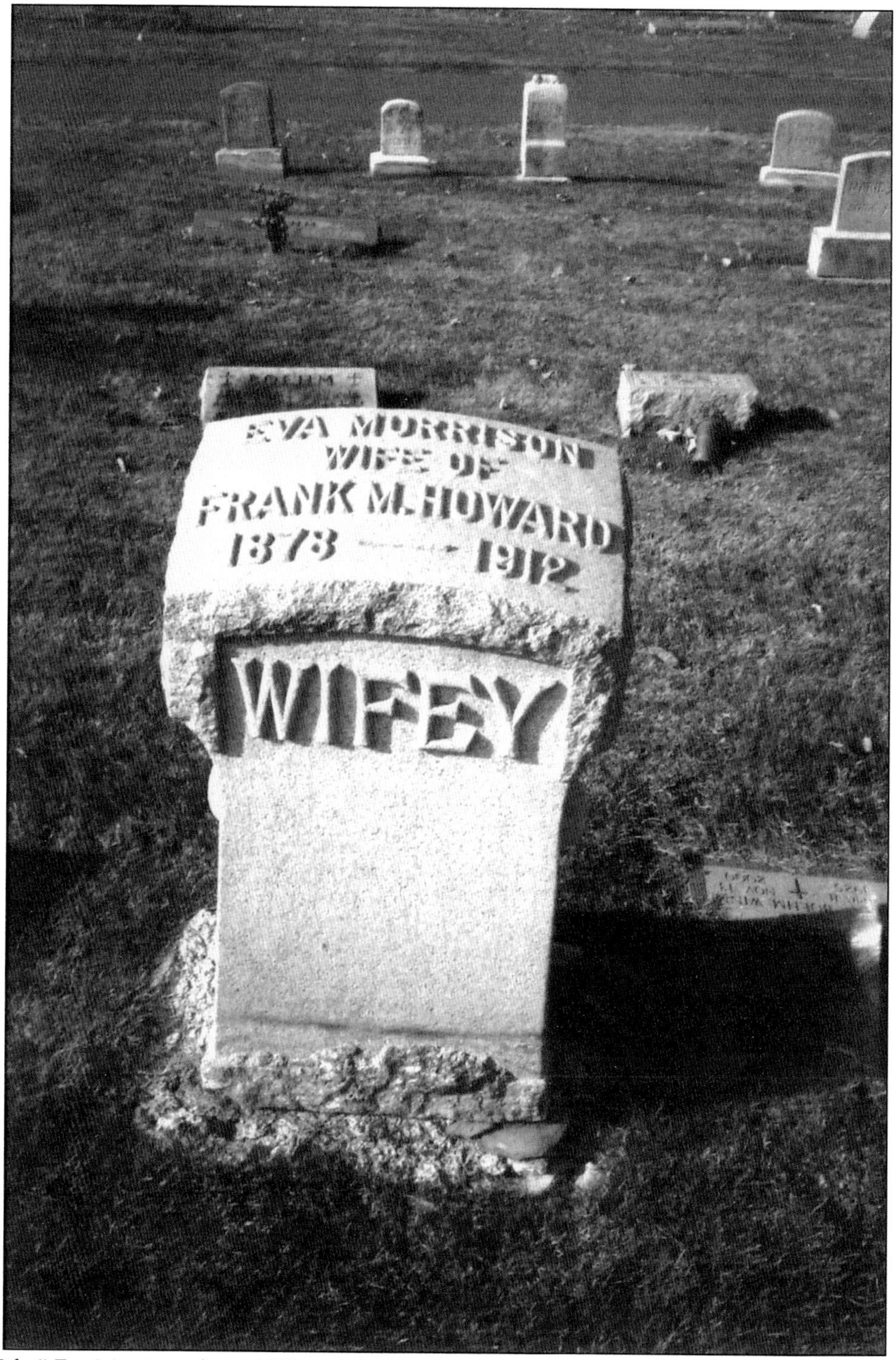

"Wifey" Eva Morrison, born 1873 and died 1912, was the wife of Frank M. Howard. Frank died March 10, 1939. He was a former employee of the old Columbus Buggy Company and was secretary for the Howard Dye Works on Lockbourne Avenue. In 1911, Frank resided at 39 West Maynard Avenue.

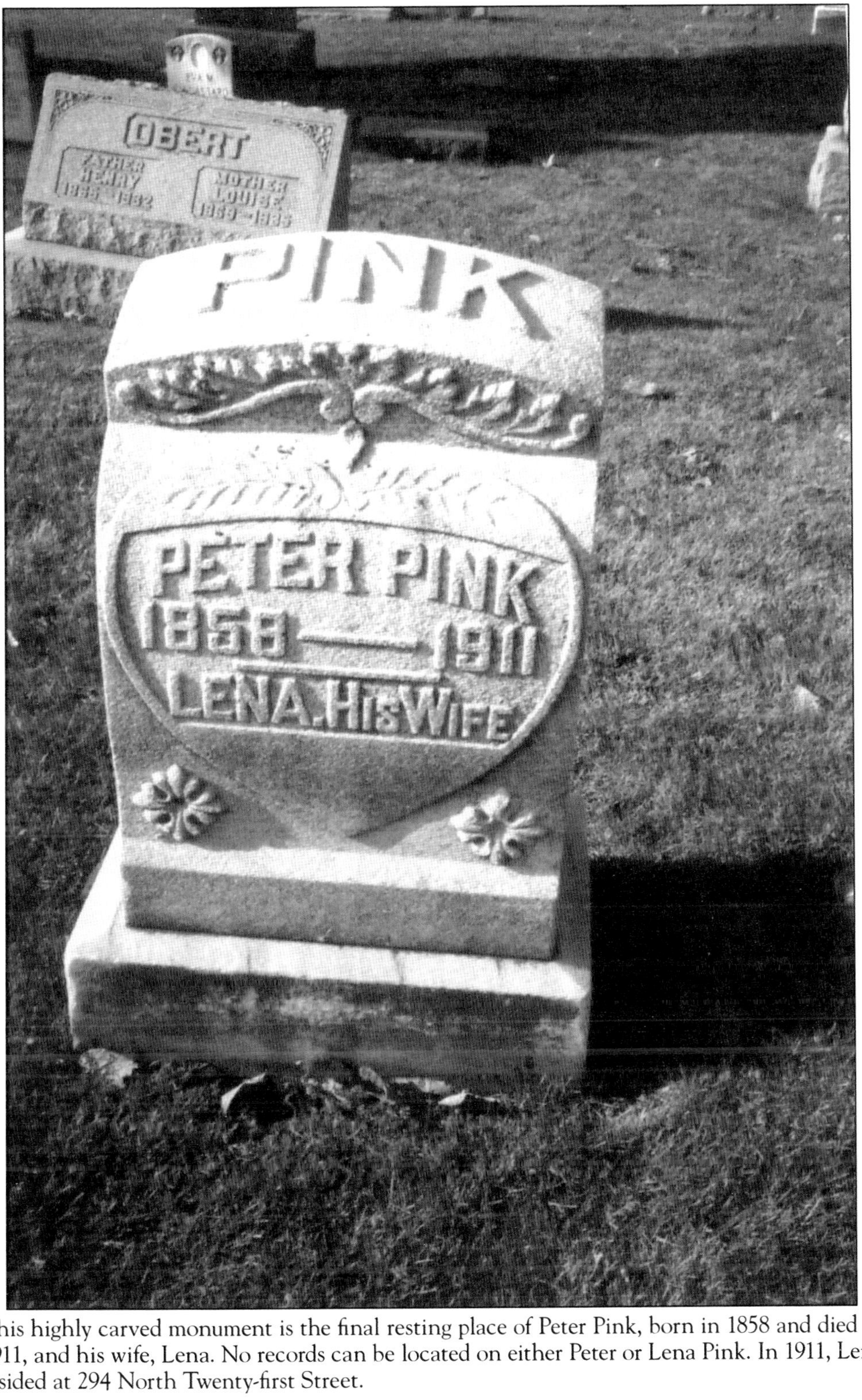

This highly carved monument is the final resting place of Peter Pink, born in 1858 and died in 1911, and his wife, Lena. No records can be located on either Peter or Lena Pink. In 1911, Lena resided at 294 North Twenty-first Street.

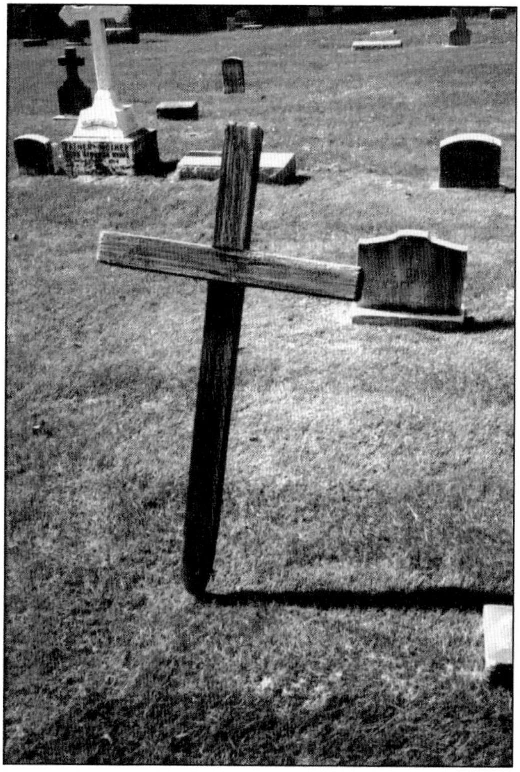

They all have a story to tell and this is the story of a cemetery and those interned. This crudely handmade cross marks the final resting place of an unknown person, known only to God. This grave is located in the single section of this historical cemetery. No name or dates indicates the deceased, they are still remembered with this crude cross, constructed by a loved one.

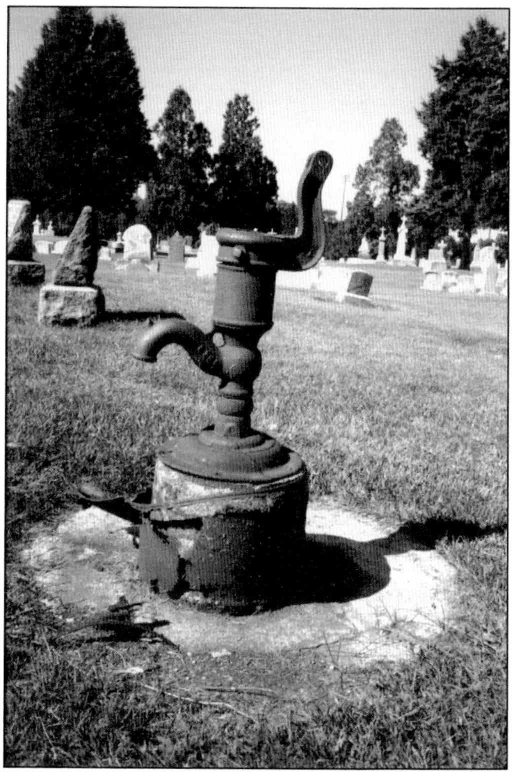

Years of erosion have worn away this old water pump. Part of this cemetery's historical past, it stands as a testimonial of service that is no longer in operation. This old pump supplied water to mourners who would bring flowers to those interred within the grounds. No artificial flowers are allowed between March 1 and November 1. No vigil candles are permitted, and no pets are allowed in cemetery sections.

Four

Infamous and the Famous

Throughout this historical cemetery are located various burial sections and within these areas are interred the infamous and the famous. In a section located at the western edge of this cemetery is an area referred to as Potter's Field, which was set aside for the burial of paupers or unknown persons. Here is the final resting place of those infamous souls that were convicted of outrageous acts of crimes committed against society or the less fortunate. It is not known just how many of those souls are interred in this section of this historical cemetery. Crude monuments mark the graves of some of the infamous. Others interred are unknown and lost to time as no monument indicates their final resting place, only a grassed over area. Many of those infamous that are interred here were executed at the Ohio Penitentiary.

Within burial grounds, the land is termed either consecrated or unconsecrated. The term consecrated means dedicated to the service of God according to the rites of the Roman Catholic Church. All burials took place in either consecrated or unconsecrated ground. In a section to the south, the soil is unconsecrated and interred within this area would have been Christians of other denominations, those of other faiths, or those of no faith. Cemetery burial registers do not indicate a complete listing of those interred in this unconsecrated section. Many graves are not marked or the timeworn monuments are not legible. This is evident throughout other sections of this cemetery.

Burial of a loved one is seen as their final resting place where they will find peace and tranquility. One of the most famous interred in consecrated soil is Graham McNamee, a radio broadcasting pioneer, whose voice was one of the most recognized in national radio.

Whether they were infamous or the famous, someone, someplace at one time, did not forget them. Whether it is the construction of a homemade monument that marks their final resting place, a magnificent monument of granite that towers above, or a grass covered area that is mowed yearly or covered with autumn-colored leaves or winter snow, they are resting somewhere in this historical cemetery.

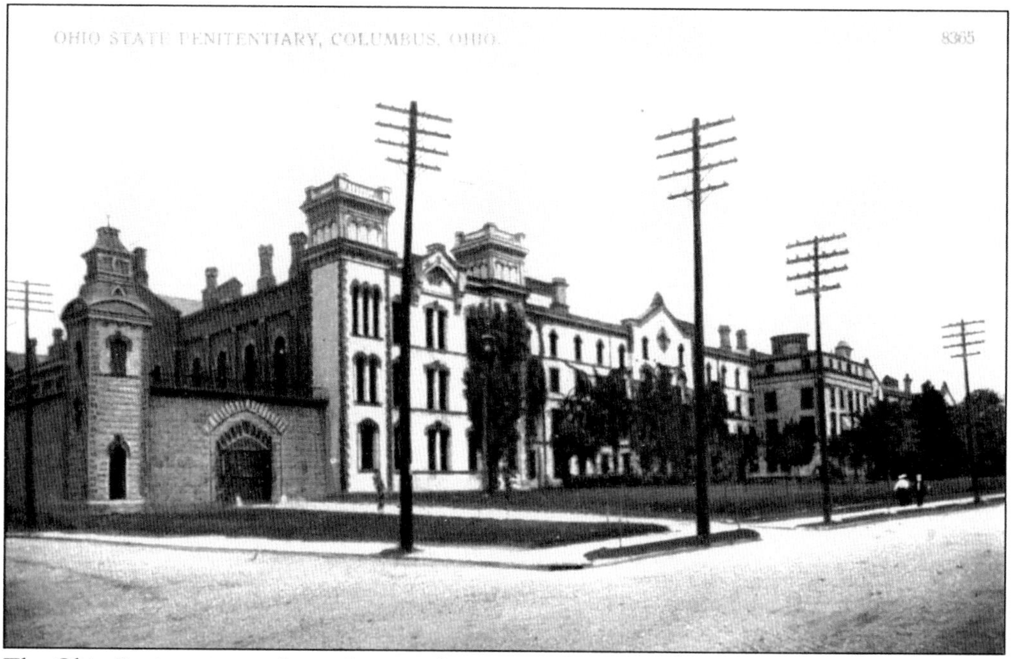

The Ohio Penitentiary is shown here in this 1908 postcard. Razed in 1998 to make way for the Arena District, this major prison once housed novelist O. Henry and, during the Civil War, members of John Hunt Morgan's Confederate cavalry. Along with several of his men, Morgan escaped captivity and returned to the South. (Dean Collection.)

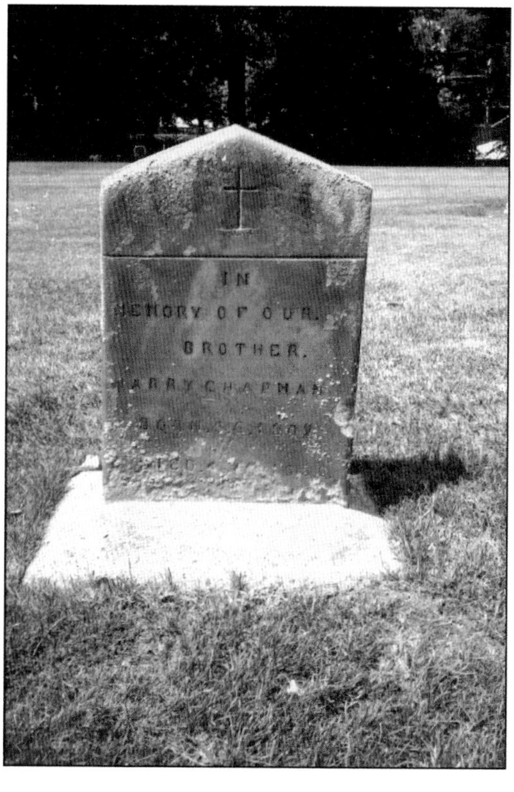

Harry Chapman was executed April 9, 1939, in Ohio Penitentiary for the slaying of a patrolman with two accomplices, Harry Dingledine and his son Henry Dingledine, in a gun battle near Springfield in September 1937. He was buried in potter's field, a section set aside for the burial of paupers or unknown persons. Chapman's picture was the 220th to hang in the gallery in the execution chamber. Prisoners made his monument.

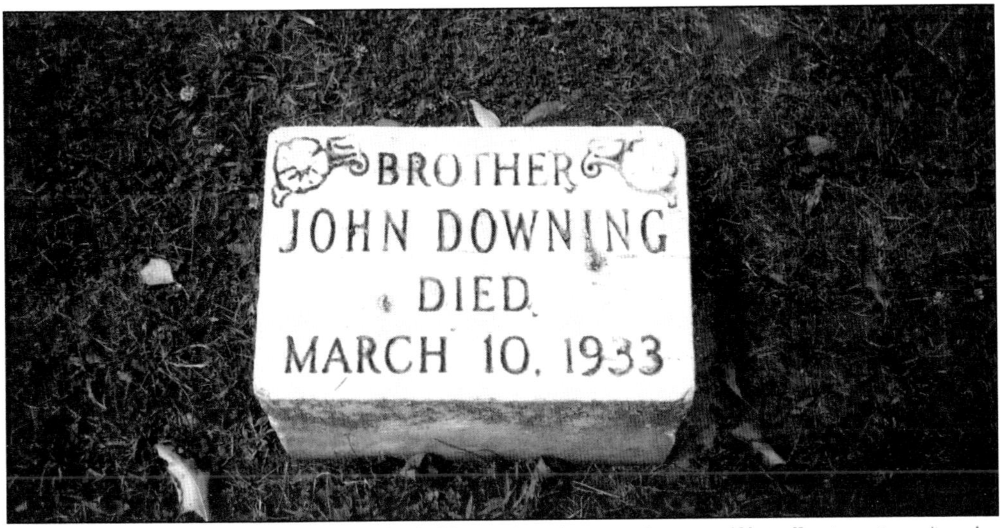

John "Red" Downing died March 10, 1933, in the electric chair in Ohio Penitentiary for the slaying of Mrs. Daniel J. Bonzo, wife of the chief parole and record clerk at Ohio Penitentiary. Prisoners made his monument and referred to him as a "brother."

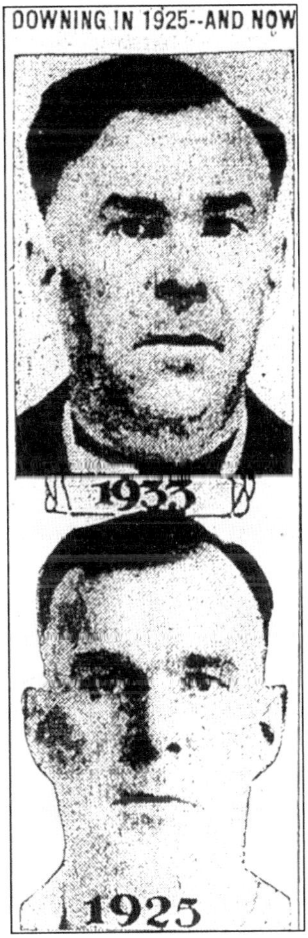

These two pictures of Downing appeared in a local Columbus paper, showing him as he appeared in 1925 and later in 1933. (Columbus Metropolitan Library.)

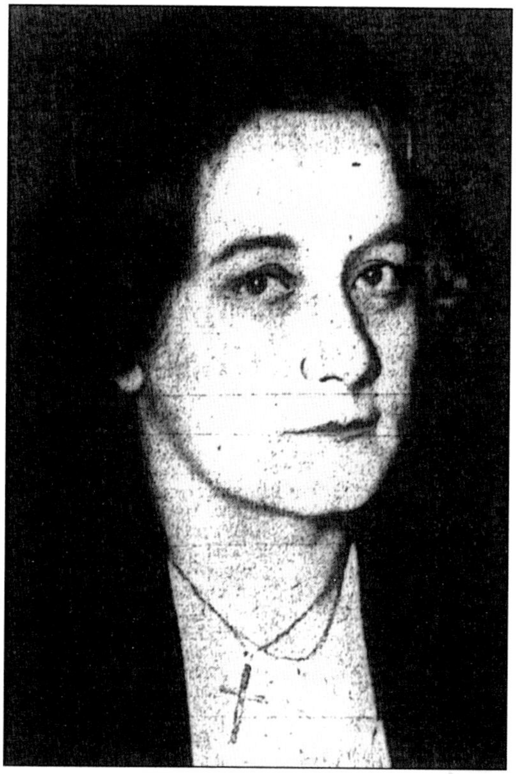

Anna Marie Hahn, born July 7, 1906, and executed December 7, 1938, was convicted after a sensational four-week trial in 1937 and sentenced to death in Ohio's electric chair. Hahn is interred in Potter's Field and flanked by unmarked graves of men and women. Prisoners made her modest monument. (Columbus Metropolitan Library.)

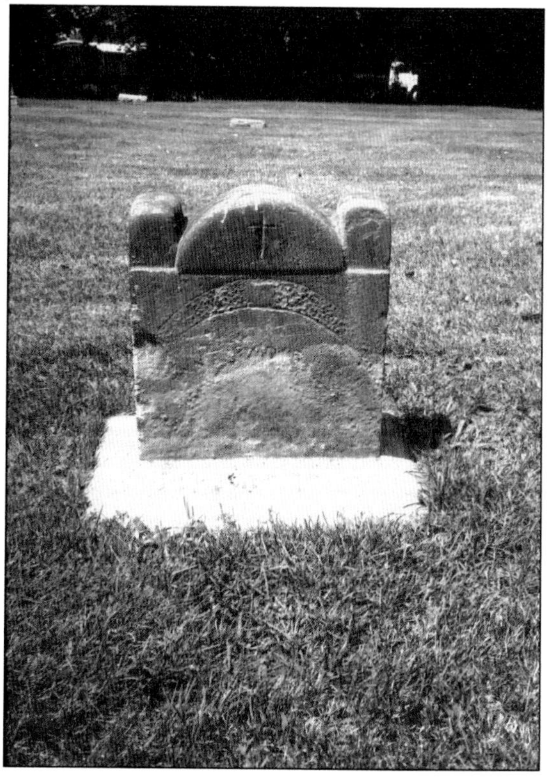

Hahn was the first female serial killer to die in the electric chair in the state of Ohio. She was referred to as "Ohio's Borgia," the "Black Widow," and the "Beautiful Blonde Killer." She was suspected in numerous poisoning deaths when she began poisoning in the Cincinnati German community for monetary gain. After giving birth to an illegitimate son, her family shipped her off to America in 1929. In Cincinnati, she married Philip Hahn.

Mount Calvary Cemetery suffered heavy flooding during the flood of 1913, destroying records and property. In an unmarked grave in the single grave, or the unconsecrated section, is interred the remains of Dayton, Ohio, physician Dr. Oliver C. Haugh. His records and the site of his final resting place are lost. On November 4, 1905, he killed his father, mother, and brother by injecting hyoscine into them and then set fire to the house. Hyoscine is also known as scopolamine and is a tropane alkaloid drug, obtained from the solanacease (nightshades) plant, and can be highly toxic. An overdose can cause death. Haugh was put to death in the Ohio Penitentiary annex April 20, 1907. His last words were, "I think that it is the Spirit of God that makes me so indifferent". Mrs. Haugh accompanied her husband's body to Mount Calvary Cemetery. There were no flowers, no chant, and no requiem. His obituary stated, "the felon was buried as he had lived and died, alone and unwept save by his wife."

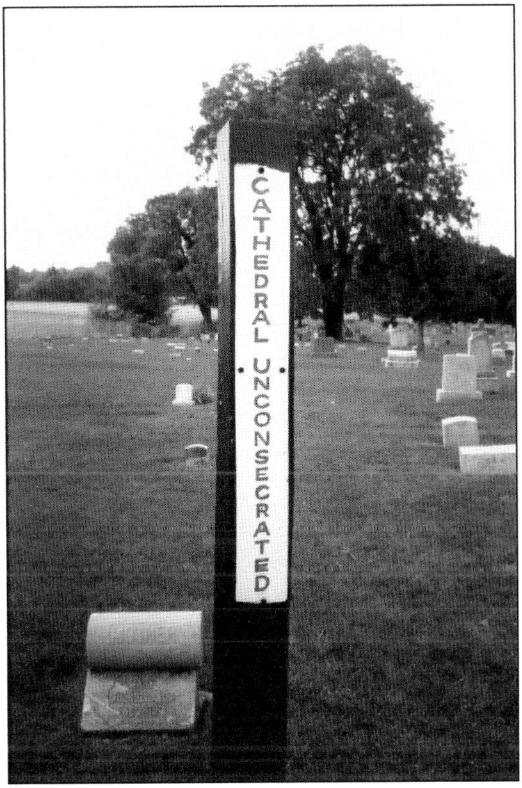

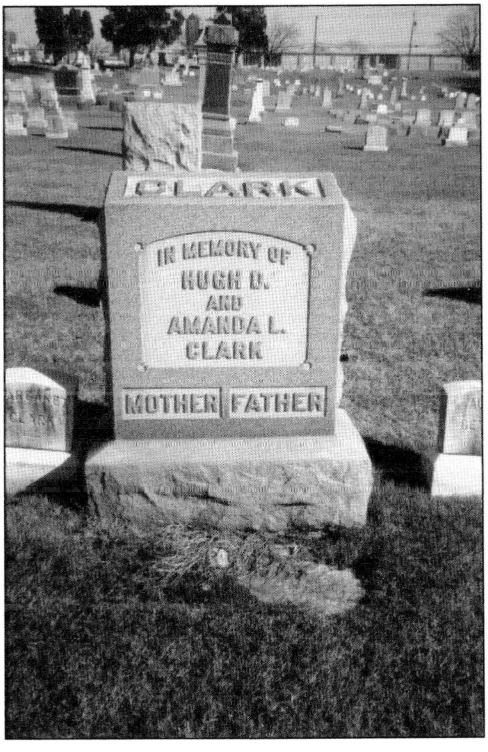

Hugh D. Clark invented the first air seal, diving belt, and burglarproof vault in 1898 in Columbus. He was the founder and president of the Clark Grave Vault Company. Clark died September 3, 1915. In 1917, Allen F. Beck purchased the company from the Clark estate. Beck died in 1955 and was interred in Green Lawn Cemetery.

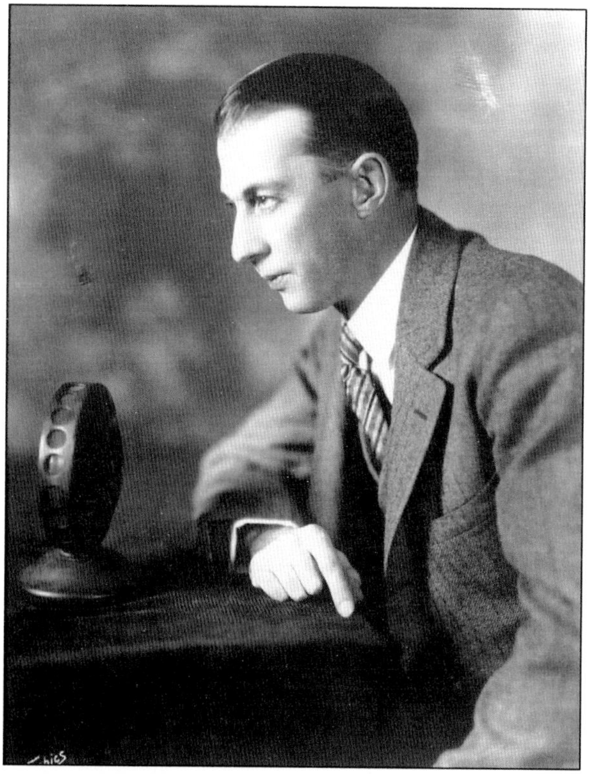

Graham McNamee was born July 10, 1888, and died May 9, 1942. He was the most recognized national radio personality in its first commercial decade. His voice was heard conveying national political conventions, presidential inaugurations, and Charles Lindbergh's historic transatlantic flight to France in 1927. In 1921 he married Josephine Garrett, a concert and church soprano, who later sued for separation. During the 1930s his stature declined. McNamee ended every broadcast with a distinctive phrase. "This is Graham McNamee speaking. Goodnight, all."

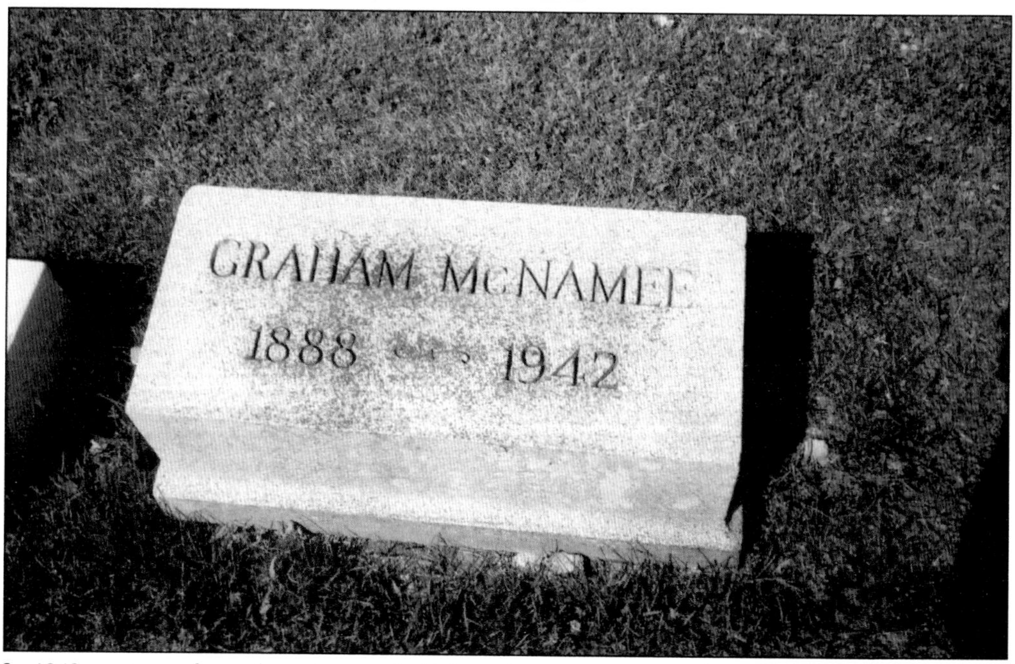

In 1942, a private funeral service was held for radio announcer Graham McNamee in New York City. Honorary pallbearers were those that had been associated with McNamee during his long career in radio. McNamee died in St. Luke's Hospital in New York City. His body was sent to Columbus, Ohio, for burial in Mount Calvary Cemetery.

BIBLIOGRAPHY

Barquílla de la Santa Maria (Catholic Record Society-Dicoese of Columbus). Vol. III No. 12. December 1977.

Barquílla de la Santa Maria (Catholic Record Society-Dicoese of Columbus). Vol. XVI, No. 3, June 1991.

Barquílla de la Santa Maria (Catholic Record Society-Dicoese of Columbus). Vol. XVI, No. 4, April 2005.

Barquílla de la Santa Maria (Catholic Record Society-Dicoese of Columbus). Vol. XXX, No. 3, March 2005.

Columbus City Directory 1888–1889. Columbus: 1889.

Columbus Dispatch. *Dust of the Bones of Algonquins in State House Brick*. November 13, 1910.

Columbus Trades and Labor Assembly of Columbus, Ohio. *Twentieth Century Official Illustrated History of the Columbus Trades and Labor Assembly and its Affiliated Organizations*. Columbus: The Berlin Printing Company, 1901.

Cooney, Rev. msgr. Roger P., ed., and Rev. Robert A. Gonzales. *The Spirit of John Joseph Jessing: Priest, Orphans' Friend, Visionary*. Columbus: The Pontifical College Josephinum, 1999.

Edwards, Richard. *Industries of Ohio*. Columbus: Historical Publishing Company, 1878.

Fitzpatrick, Stephen A. and U. S. Morris. *History of Columbus Celebration, Franklinton Centennial*. Columbus: The New Franklin Printing Company, 1897.

Miller, C. L. *Postmortem Collectibles / C. L. Miller*. Atglen, Pennsylvania: Schiffer Publishing, 2001.

Ohio Genealogical Society, Franklin County Chapter. *Columbus, Ohio: Its History, Resources, and Progress, by Jacob Studer published 1873*. Columbus: the Chapter, 1979.

Pinta, Emil R., M.D. *A History and Chronology of Ohio's Medical Schools, Colleges, and Universities*. September 1989.

Raphael, Marc Lee. *Jews and Judaism in the Midwestern Community: Columbus, Ohio, 1840–1975*. Columbus: Ohio Historical Society, 1979.

Taylor, William Alexander. *Centennial History of Columbus and Franklin County, Ohio*. Vol. I. Chicago-Columbus: S. J. Clarke Publishing Company, 1909.

———. *Centennial History of Columbus and Franklin County Ohio*. Volume II. Chicago, Columbus: S.J. Clarke Publishing Company, 1909.